Connecting with Others

Connecting with Others

Lessons for Teaching Social and Emotional Competence

GRADES 6-8

Rita C. Richardson & Elizabeth T. Evans

Research Press   2612 North Mattis Avenue   Champaign Illinois   61822
(800) 519-2707   www.researchpress.com

To all the teenagers of the world:
May their road to adulthood be paved with peace, love, and hope.

CONTENTS

FIGURES

FOREWORD

The antisocial behaviors of adolescents in schools, homes, and communities have caused grave concern throughout the general population. The numerous problems facing today's youths have accentuated the need for corrective actions. Stricter, more punitive measures are often proposed as an immediate solution. The irresponsible actions of many adolescents are often attributed to perceived permissive policies in public schools; moreover, the media occasionally encourage this perception. Others disagree and believe that the majority of public schools generally endorse strict control over students. While punishment suppresses inappropriate behaviors, it does not teach appropriate behaviors. Recent reports indicate that boys and girls who are consistently punished develop social difficulties.

With the onset of adolescence, the social life of students changes radically and stressors are increased. Adolescents are in a state of transition from childhood into adulthood. In their search for identity they feel they must separate from their parents or other adults and seek the support of their peers. The group becomes all important. Unfortunately, many group members participate in antisocial or illegal activities, such as drinking alcohol, taking drugs, and engaging in illicit sexual behavior. Their reasoning is often distorted by egocentrism; consequently, their communication patterns are usually self-centered. They lack the skills of socially appropriate communication and peaceful conflict resolution. Adolescents need to learn to internalize control, to appreciate responsible independent actions and cooperative decision making. Respect for self and others and the ability to empathize are important skills. In addition, teaching the significance of a strong sense of self-esteem can give adolescents clear direction as they enter adult life.

Students must be prepared to become productive democratic citizens by learning to be self-disciplined, responsible, and compassionate. This cannot be achieved through punishment and coercion, but rather through teaching social and emotional competencies. Punitive discipline is counterproductive and models negative practices to resolve problems.

Parents and teachers must collaborate and teach adolescents the value of social skills and help them become productive and compassionate citizens. Social and emotional skills can be taught and nurtured. The authors of *Connecting with Others* have succeeded in presenting a comprehensive program that can enable students to function as responsible and sensitive human beings.

JOHN BRADSHAW

AUTHOR AND EDUCATOR

ACKNOWLEDGMENTS

In bringing forth the *Connecting with Others* program for young adolescents, I owe a great deal to my coauthor, Dr. Elizabeth T. Evans. I wish to thank Beth for her enthusiasm, creativity, and contributions throughout the process. I also wish to thank my two teenage granddaughters, Laura, who recently turned "sweet 16," and Samantha, 14 years old. They allowed their grandmother to step into their wonderful world of excitement and confusion. They introduced her to their music, their vocabulary, and their quite developmentally appropriate egocentrism.

I owe my basic humanitarian beliefs to my parents, who nurtured me with a sense of fairness, responsibility, love, and justice. My first psychology professor, John Bradshaw, reinforced these values. I thank him for being my mentor and for expressing his belief in me in the foreword to this book.

RITA C. RICHARDSON

INTRODUCTION

INTRODUCTION

In the past 12 years, violence, drug use, and teen pregnancy have accelerated in our society and have infiltrated a younger group of students. The middle school years have become more stressful and troublesome, with the highest school dropout rate during the eighth and ninth grades (Sautter, 1995). In addition, young adolescents frequently cease to be compliant to authority figures and begin experimenting to discover their own identity. This is the age of rebellion and the time of questing for independence. It is also the age of insecurity and longing to belong to a social circle.

Traditionally, schools have emphasized academics, giving little attention to students' social and emotional needs. However, the need for social and emotional education has become increasingly apparent. Lack of social and emotional competence can prevent meaningful relationships and can contribute to negative self-concept, depression, and aggressiveness. Recently, attention has been drawn to the importance of emotional intelligence by such notable advocates as Howard Gardner (1993) and Daniel Goleman (1995). They propose that, beyond cognitive intelligence, emotional intelligence is critical to leading a healthy and well-adjusted life.

The *Connecting with Others* program for grades 6–8 continues the work begun with two earlier volumes in the series, focusing on grades K–2 and grades 3–5, respectively (Richardson, 1996a, 1996b). Based on Evans and Richardson's friendship model (1989), the program described in this book addresses the basic social and emotional needs of young adolescents. Specifically, it deals with relationships, awareness, empathy, decision making, and social codes and standards. Some of the skill areas and lessons reprise and reinforce those included in the first two volumes. Two skill areas of particular importance to this age group have been added: "Self-Advocacy and Assertiveness" and "Time Management and Organization." The lessons in these two areas help young adolescents acquire the skills they need to express responsible assertive behavior and to succeed in school and the community.

Ultimately, parents and educators are responsible for teaching children and youth the skills that can enable them to better understand themselves and others. We hope the *Connecting with Others* program will help students in their journey toward a self-actualized adulthood.

THEORETICAL FRAMEWORK

The lessons in the *Connecting with Others* program are based on three main theories: cognitive behavior modification, Transactional Analysis, and responsible assertion. Combined, these theories serve as a foundation for teaching responsibility, self-discipline, empathy, respect for self and others, and interpersonal skills. A Preliminary Lesson gives students an overview of these three theories. The skill area lessons refer to and reinforce these theoretical concepts; therefore, the Preliminary Lesson should be taught before any skill area instruction takes place.

The following discussion and the Preliminary Lesson itself provide a general overview of these theoretical viewpoints. Teachers may wish to seek further information on these topics to develop their understanding. The list of references and suggested readings at the end of this introduction is a place to start.

COGNITIVE BEHAVIOR MODIFICATION

Pioneered by Donald Meichenbaum (Meichenbaum, 1977), cognitive behavior modification (CBM) procedures are intended to teach people to modify their own thoughts, and thus their behavior. In CBM activities, teachers model self-management strategies, then encourage students to practice and learn to regulate their own thinking and behaviors by themselves. Self-regulation skills involve verbal mediation (self-talk), self-recording, and self-evaluation. These procedures are based on an internal reward system as opposed to an external reward system. In other words, teachers encourage students rather than use continual praise and other forms of external reinforcement. Students learn to control their own impulses and delay gratification.

In the *Connecting with Others* program, CBM concepts are expressed as four Thinking Steps, explained in the Preliminary Lesson and then referenced in the various skill area lessons:

- **STOP:** Use a technique to keep yourself from acting impulsively—for example, taking a few deep breaths, counting to 10, or taking a walk around the block.

- **THINK:** Examine the situation and think about the consequences of certain behaviors. Ask, "What am I doing? What will happen if I continue?"

- **PLAN:** Think about possibilities, brainstorm alternatives, choose the best plan, and put it into effect.

- **CHECK:** After you have tried one plan, check to see if it is working. If so, give yourself credit. Enjoy a sense of satisfaction—you've earned it. If not, start over and use another plan.

TRANSACTIONAL ANALYSIS

The basic concepts of Transactional Analysis (TA), as described by Eric Berne (1964) are central to the *Connecting with Others* program. Specifically, TA recognizes three ego states: Parent, Adult, and Child. In the *Connecting with Others* program, students are taught to recognize multiple modes of behavior, referred to as attitudes people assume across different situations and interactions. The Preliminary Lesson and skill area lessons refer to two aspects of the Child attitude: the Enthusiastic Me and the Impulsive Me. The Parent also assumes two aspects: the Caring Me and the Bossy Me. The Adult is referred to as the Thinking Me. Students are led to examine their behavior in relation to these three ego states and to discriminate when and where each of the attitudes is appropriate.

ASSERTION TRAINING

In assertion training, students learn to discriminate between aggression, nonassertion, and assertion. Aggression is certainly a direct expression; however, aggressive behavior is characterized by dishonesty, inappropriateness, and violation of the rights of others. Nonassertion involves an outright failure to express one's feelings, thoughts, and beliefs, or an expression so self-effacing that the message is lost or misunderstood. Finally, assertion involves expressing thoughts, feelings, and beliefs in a direct and appropriate way. Assertive behavior shows respect for both one's own and others' rights (Lange & Jakubowski, 1976).

Assertion training gives students cognitive and affective strategies to advocate for themselves. These strategies combine cognitive restructuring, acknowledgment of emotions, and behavioral rehearsal to empower students and give them control. To sensitize students to the feelings and rights of others, the *Connecting with Others* program teaches both direct assertion and empathetic assertion, or acknowledgment of another's viewpoint plus a directly assertive statement of one's own. By acting assertively, students develop self-respect and respect for others.

SKILL AREAS

Skill lessons are grouped into eight skill areas:

Skill Area 1: Awareness of Self and Others

Skill Area 2: Communication

Skill Area 3: Responsibility

Skill Area 4: Self-Advocacy and Assertiveness

Skill Area 5: Conflict Resolution

Skill Area 6: Cooperation and Collaboration

Skill Area 7: Love and Caring

Skill Area 8: Time Management and Organization

These areas are not sequential, and, after students have mastered the content of the Preliminary Lesson, lessons may be conducted in any order. The content is intended to be flexible; teachers are encouraged to be creative and devise additional activities relevant to students' specific environments and situations.

Each skill area includes five lessons, for a total of 40 lessons. Each lesson presents a major goal and four specific learning objectives. The table on pages 6–8 lists the lessons and their main goals. In addition, each skill area concludes with an activity designed to reflect the lessons' main goals and draw together the main teachings of that area. This activity is in the form of a role-play situation, with established characters, dialogue, and questions for evaluation and feedback. The use of this role-play is also intended to be flexible: Teachers may choose to have students read the role-play aloud and discuss, act it out in small groups or in the larger class, or use it as a springboard for writing and acting out their own scenarios.

LESSONS & THEIR GOALS (GRADES 6–8)

SKILL AREA 1: AWARENESS OF SELF AND OTHERS

Lesson	*Goal*
1 Who Am I?	To develop personal awareness and understanding
2 I Feel, Therefore I Am	To recognize feelings
3 Friendship Is Golden	To appreciate true friendships
4 Many Thanks	To show gratitude and accept appreciation
5 Mutual Admiration Society	To accept and give compliments

SKILL AREA 2: COMMUNICATION

Lesson	*Goal*
1 I Hear You	To demonstrate effective listening
2 Let's Talk	To communicate positively with others
3 Communicating without Talking	To recognize the importance of nonverbal communication and cultural differences in nonverbal expression
4 Social Needs, Social Deeds	To recognize social aspects of communication
5 Unpolluted Language	To recognize language taboos and learn the importance of using more acceptable words and expressions

SKILL AREA 3: RESPONSIBILITY

Lesson	Goal
1 Where Am I Going?	To plan long-term and short-term goals
2 I Did It Myself	To complete assigned tasks independently
3 Understanding Directions	To follow and give directions
4 Let Me Check	To identify and apply self-management skills
5 Taking Responsibility	To assume responsibility for personal actions

SKILL AREA 4: SELF-ADVOCACY AND ASSERTIVENESS

Lesson	Goal
1 Help! I Need Somebody	To ask assertively for assistance
2 Take the First Step	To offer and give assistance
3 Why Should I?	To analyze and discuss fair and unfair rules and practices
4 Yes Sir, Yes Ma'am, but . . .	To respond positively and assertively to authority figures
5 I Can Say No to You	To respond logically to peer pressure

SKILL AREA 5: CONFLICT RESOLUTION

Lesson	Goal
1 I Can Say No to Me	To practice self-control
2 Try and Try Again	To find alternative solutions in conflict situations
3 Give and Take and Mediate	To demonstrate understanding of the processes of negotiation, mediation, and compromise
4 Words Can Sometimes Hurt	To respond appropriately to teasing
5 Room for Improvement	To accept and give constructive feedback

SKILL AREA 6: COOPERATION AND COLLABORATION

Lesson	*Goal*
1 Together We Will Overcome	To develop the concept of cooperative teamwork
2 Patience Is a Virtue	To learn to delay gratification and practice patience
3 We're in This Together	To learn how to interact successfully with others
4 A Balancing Act	To become aware of the importance of equality
5 What's Your Type?	To understand how one's own and other people's personality types influence group interactions

SKILL AREA 7: LOVE AND CARING

Lesson	*Goal*
1 Understanding Our Differences	To show tolerance, respect, and understanding for differences
2 A Walk in Your Shoes	To show empathy
3 Many Faces of Love	To recognize that love can be felt and expressed in many ways
4 Love and Responsibility	To identify behaviors and responsibilities associated with intimate relationships
5 With or without Conditions	To distinguish between expressions of unconditional versus conditional love

SKILL AREA 8: TIME MANAGEMENT AND ORGANIZATION

Lesson	*Goal*
1 What Time Is It?	To be punctual
2 Time Flies	To develop a system of time management
3 Time to Relax	To develop strategies to relax and reduce stress
4 At Your Best	To understand personal energy cycles
5 Time for Fun	To choose appropriate leisure activities

LESSON PROCEDURE

The lessons in this third volume of *Connecting with Others* generally follow the same format as for the two volumes for the elementary grades, with the omission of an initial focusing story (which we felt was too juvenile for young adolescents) and the addition of the concluding role-play activity. Each lesson presents the main goal, specific learning objectives, and a list of materials needed. The teaching sequence is then as follows:

OPENING

- Review: After the first lesson, a review of the preceding lesson's content.

- Stating Objectives: A statement of what the learner does to demonstrate learning and why the learning is important.

INSTRUCTION

- Teaching and Guided Discussion: Presented in the form of "script," discussion and guided questions designed to elicit information from students and encourage active participation.

- Monitoring Knowledge and Comprehension: An activity designed to permit the learner to demonstrate understanding of the information presented.

- Guided Practice: A teacher-directed activity that causes the learner to apply the information presented.

- Assessing Mastery: An activity to determine whether a learner requires reteaching or independent practice.

RETEACHING

- Independent Practice: The application of information presented without the assistance of the teacher.

- Evaluation and Feedback: An activity to determine the degree to which the learner has met objectives and to convey that degree of progress to the learner.

CLOSING

- Summary: A review of main ideas and objectives.

- Generalization: An activity that relates the lesson's objectives to real-life experiences or future learning.

ENRICHMENT

- Optional activities that expand on basic learning.

It is important to stress that the teaching scripts are given only as guidelines. Teachers are encouraged to use their own language while adhering to the lesson's goal and objectives. Examples typical of the specific setting can encourage student interactions.

TEACHING STRATEGIES

Several strategies are consistently used throughout the program to teach the intended skills. These include the following:

- Behavioral rehearsal: Practicing appropriate behaviors

- Cooperative learning: Participating in group activities to promote cooperation rather than competition

- Expressive media: Engaging in art, music, and creative writing

- Creative visualization: Visualizing projected experiences

- Hypothetical dilemmas: Considering situations to clarify attitudes and to encourage critical thinking and choices

- Role-playing: Acting out situations, dramatic writing

- Self-management strategies: Self-recording, self-evaluation, and self-reinforcement

- Verbal mediation: Thinking overtly and covertly (positive self-talk)

- Community involvement: Working in the community or school (for example, peer tutoring in lower grades)

- Journaling: Documenting daily events to promote reflection on past experiences and help students prepare for the future

PROGRAM IMPLEMENTATION

PLACEMENT IN THE CURRICULUM

The *Connecting with Others* lessons may be presented as a separate curriculum, or they may be incorporated in academic subjects such as social studies, language arts, or health education. Advisory groups or homeroom periods are also logical placements for the program. However the program is integrated into the school setting, it is best to conduct social skill instruction at least three times a week. This schedule offers continuity yet gives students ample time to practice the skills outside the teaching setting. Teachers may use their professional judgment in allocating time for each lesson, giving consideration to students' levels and needs.

GENERAL GUIDELINES

Some general guidelines to help ensure program success are as follows:

1. Be flexible. Modify or adapt activities to meet the needs of the students, the classroom, and the school.

2. Model prosocial behaviors throughout the day.

3. Use a variety of methods. Incorporate a balance of large- and small-group discussions, hands-on activities, and individual projects.

4. Keep records on activities that have been successful—and not so successful.

5. Refrain from preaching or imposing your own beliefs and values.

6. Avoid embarrassing students during group discussion and respect students' right to privacy.

7. Substitute names suggested in the lessons when students in the class bear the same names.

8. Provide opportunities for generalization and transfer of skills taught in the classroom.

9. Encourage students to make connections between what they have learned in the lessons and their real lives.

10. Keep your program current by correlating lesson goals and objectives to activities students feel are important.

11. Organize a card catalog by skill area and expand the program by adding your own activities for future use.

CREATING A SUPPORTIVE LEARNING ENVIRONMENT

Many factors contribute to a supportive program environment. Ground rules for participation are particularly important to everyone's sense of safety. Early on, develop group rules for discussion. Be sure to include student input. Some sample ground rules follow:

1. Listen without interrupting.

2. Respect the rights and feelings of others (no insulting remarks, profanity, put-downs, or sarcasm).

3. Each student has the right to participate.

4. Each student has the right to "pass" if he or she does not want to respond or share opinions.

INVOLVING PARENTS AND COMMUNITY

The Parent Newsletters in Appendix A have been included to encourage parents to continue practicing program skills in the home. Appendix B offers a bibliography listing materials for professionals and for students. Many of these titles can be shared with parents. (This list is by no means comprehensive, and teachers are encouraged to incorporate additional resources as appropriate.)

Other suggestions for promoting parent and community involvement are as follows:

1. Involve and communicate with parents: Explain that the program teaches good citizenship skills and discuss the importance of character education.

2. Encourage parents to reinforce at home the objectives being taught.

3. Whenever possible, invite parents to class sessions.

4. Establish a channel of communication to keep parents informed. Use the Parent Newsletters and encourage parents to suggest strategies.

5. Share ideas with other school personnel: librarian, office staff, cafeteria workers, administrators, and so forth.

6. Involve university students in field experience activities. Pair a university student with an adolescent in need of a role model.

7. Involve students in community work whenever possible—for example, helping with Special Olympics, organizing a party for younger children, raising funds for special projects, collecting toys for tots, and tutoring younger students or students with special needs.

8. Increase multicultural awareness through correspondence and other exchanges with adolescents from different cultures. Draw on the cultures already present in your school and involve members of the community if necessary.

REFERENCES AND SUGGESTED READING

Alberti, P., & Emmons, M. (1982). *Your perfect right: A guide to assertive behavior* (4th ed.). San Luis Obispo, CA: Impact.

Bash, M.A.S., & Camp, B.W. (1985). *Think aloud: Increasing social and cognitive skills— A problem-solving program for children (Grades 5-6).* Champaign, IL: Research Press.

Berne, E. (1964). *Games people play.* New York: Grove.

Combs, A.W. (1991). *The schools we need: New assumptions for educational reform.* Lanham, MD: University Press of America.

Curran, D. (1992). *Working with parents.* Circle Pines, MN: American Guidance Service.

Evans, E.T., & Richardson, R.C. (1989). Teaching friendship skills: Key to positive mainstreaming. *Journal of Humanistic Education and Development, 27,* 138–151.

Freed, A.M. (1991). *TA for teens.* Rolling Hills, CA: Jalmar.

Gardner, H. (1993) *Multiple intelligences: The theory in practice.* New York: Basic.

Gawain, S. (1982). *Creative visualization.* San Rafael, CA: New World.

Ginott, H. (1969). *Between parent and teenager.* New York: Avon.

Ginott, H. (1972). *Teacher and child.* New York: Macmillan.

Glasser, W. (1990). *The quality school: Managing students without coercion.* New York: HarperPerennial.

Glenn, H., & Nelsen, J. (1987). *Raising self-reliant children in a self-indulgent world.* Rocklin, CA: Prima.

Goleman, D. (1995). *Emotional intelligence: Why it can matter more than IQ.* New York: Bantam.

Gordon, T. (1974). *Teacher effectiveness training.* New York: Peter H. Wyden.

Gordon, T. (1991). *Discipline that works: Promoting self-discipline in children.* New York: Plume.

Harris, T.A. (1969). *I'm OK—You're OK: A practical guide to Transactional Analysis.* New York: Harper & Row.

Helmstetter, S. (1987). *The self-talk solution.* New York: Pocket Books.

Lange, A.J., & Jakubowski, P. (1976). *Responsible assertive behavior: Cognitive/behavioral procedures for trainers.* Champaign, IL: Research Press.

Meichenbaum, D.H. (1977). *Cognitive behavior modification: An integrative approach.* New York: Plenum.

Missildine, W.H. (1963). *Your inner child of the past.* New York: Pocket Books.

Montgomery, M., Bitney, J., & Redpath, A. (1993). *Critical issues: Readings for thinking and writing.* Circle Pines, MN: American Guidance Service.

Myers, I.B. (1995). *Gifts differing: Understanding personality types.* Palo Alto, CA: Davies-Black.

Post, J. (1989). *Into adolescence: Living in a family.* Menlo Park, CA: Walter S. Johnson Foundation.

Richardson, R.C. (1996a). *Connecting with others: Lessons for teaching social and emotional competence (Grades K–2).* Champaign, IL: Research Press.

Richardson, R.C. (1996b). *Connecting with others: Lessons for teaching social and emotional competence (Grades 3–5).* Champaign, IL: Research Press.

Sautter, R.C. (1995). Standing up to violence. *Phi Delta Kappan, 76,* K1–K12.

Taylor, C. (1990). *Dangerous society.* East Lansing: Michigan State University Press.

Williams, P. (1990). *Good kids, bad behavior.* New York: Fireside.

Wirths, C. (1987). *I hate school: How to hang in and when to drop out.* New York: HarperTrophy.

Workman, E., & Katz, A. (1995). *Teaching behavioral self-control to students.* Austin, TX: PRO-ED.

PRELIMINARY LESSON

COGNITIVE BEHAVIOR MODIFICATION

Before beginning, you will need to copy Figures 1–3 to share with the group.

TO THE TEACHER

Adolescents frequently exhibit deficits in metacognition. As a result, they may behave impulsively rather than reflectively or may respond to peer pressure rather than reach independent decisions. Metacognition is simply the ability to reflect upon one's thoughts. It is thinking about thinking. The principles of cognitive behavior modification promote critical, independent thinking and help students delay gratification.

Activities based on this concept are designed to promote awareness and problem solving. These activities encourage reflective decisions and reduce impulsivity. Students can be taught to examine all important facts relating to decision making and planning prior to taking any action. In addition, they can be directed to evaluate the outcomes of their actions.

GUIDED DISCUSSION

Young children rely on adults to give them direction and help them make decisions. As children grow older, they begin to make their own decisions and depend on themselves. Taking charge of your life involves understanding yourself and controlling your own behaviors.

SELF-MANAGEMENT

Self-management means being aware of your own thoughts and behavior and taking steps to change your behavior so you can do better at home, at school, and in the community. It involves self-talk, self-recording, and self-evaluation.

Self-talk

Self-talk is thinking aloud or silently to yourself. It helps to identify problems and solutions. Statements like "I can do it" and "I can think for myself" are examples of *positive self-talk*. They encourage independence and self-esteem. Statements like "I'm such a loser" or "I'll never be able to do that" are examples of *negative self-talk*. They discourage people from taking chances and learning new things.

Distribute copies of Figure 1 (Self-Management) and have students complete Part I.

When are some times you might be able to use self-talk to help you get control?

Elicit responses. Model self-talk in an audible tone and then in a whispered tone. Guide students in practicing self-talk.

Self-recording

We are often unaware of what we say or do. We can increase understanding by keeping track of our behavior; this is called *self-recording*. Self-recording is a way of monitoring our behaviors by recording them each time they occur.

For example, my friend wanted to give up smoking, so she recorded in a journal each cigarette she smoked. She dealt with her urge to smoke by making up a schedule. She planned to smoke one less cigarette per day until she gave up smoking altogether.

You can also increase behavior through self-recording. *(Personalize the following example.)* I don't drink enough water, so I count every glass of water I drink. Do you have a behavior you wish you could increase or decrease?

Elicit responses and discuss—for example, increasing time spent on homework or decreasing the number of arguments with siblings. Have students write down their chosen behavior on Part II of Figure 1. Discuss various ways to record frequency (golf counters, beads, tally marks) or duration (clock, sand timer, kitchen timer), then direct students to write down their recording method as well.

Self-evaluation

Self-evaluation means deciding whether or not your plan has worked. For example, if you want to increase the time you spend doing homework, you could keep track of the time you spend every day for a week. At the end of the week, you could look at the times to see whether you are actually spending more time and, if so, how much.

Refer students to Part III of Figure 1 and have them specify a date to review their data. Help students identify whether a duration or frequency graph would better help them evaluate outcomes. (Sample duration and frequency graphs are shown in Figure 2.) Follow up this activity on the specified date(s); help students graph their data and discuss outcomes as a group.

THE THINKING STEPS

The Thinking Steps are a way you can get control of your behavior every single day, rather than having your behavior control you. There are four Thinking Steps: STOP, THINK, PLAN, and CHECK.

Distribute copies of Figure 3 (The Thinking Steps) and discuss each step. Have students refer to this page as you discuss the following example.

Let's see how one student used the Thinking Steps to help her change a problem behavior. Lila had a problem with cursing. She wasn't aware of how frequently she cursed, but she constantly got into trouble. She decided to use the Thinking Steps.

- **STOP:** One day in the middle of a curse word, she bit her lip and stopped herself.

- **THINK:** She thought to herself, "I've got to change—even the boys are making fun of my garbage mouth."

- **PLAN:** She made a PLAN to make a tally mark on a sheet of paper every time she cursed. She continued recording the number of times she cursed every day for a week.

- **CHECK:** At the end of each day, she counted her tallies and recorded the total. At the end of the week, she recorded each day's total on a graph. She noticed that she didn't curse as much as before and said to herself, "I did it. I'm awesome!"

Discuss the following questions.

1. What did Lila do to help her STOP her impulsive behavior?

2. What are some other ways to stop and get control? *(You could count to 10, sing a song, talk to your own reflection in the mirror.)*

3. What did Lila do in the THINK step? *(She realized her problem and anticipated consequences.)*

4. During the PLAN step, Lila decided on a solution to her problem. What could Lila have used as a back-up plan in case her first plan didn't work? *(She could get help from a friend or teacher or substitute an acceptable word or phrase whenever she had the urge to curse.)*

5. In the last step, CHECK, Lila thought about whether or not her plan had worked. When she discovered that it had, she congratulated herself by saying, "I did it. I'm awesome!" What kind of talk was she using? *(She was using positive self-talk.)*

6. Lila was successful, so she felt proud of herself. What could she have done if her plan did not work? *(She could have tried her back-up plan.)*

Self-Management

Name: _____ Date:_____

Part I: Self-Talk

Change the statements from negative self-talk to positive self-talk.

1. I'm impossible. I'll never understand how this works.

   _____

2. Face it—this is just too hard for a girl.

   _____

3. I get blamed for everything. What's the use?

   _____

4. I wish I looked different. I'd be more popular.

   _____

5. I might as well accept it. I mess everything up.

   _____

Part II: Self-Recording

I want to increase/decrease the following behavior (circle one):

_____

_____

I can record my behavior by:

_____

_____

Part III: Self-Evaluation

I will evaluate my behavior on the following date: _____

Figure 1

Sample Duration
& Frequency Graphs

Duration Graph: Increasing Time Doing Homework

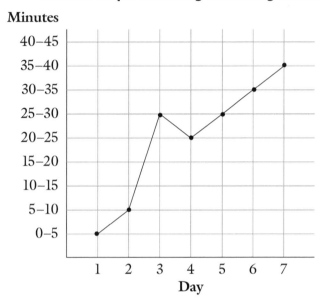

Frequency Graph: Decreasing Items of Clothing Left on the Floor

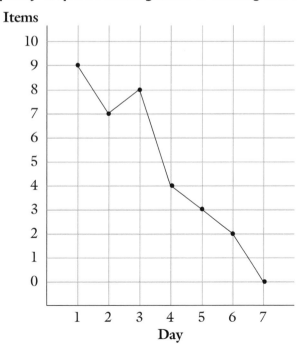

Figure 2

21

The Thinking Steps

STOP

Use a technique to keep yourself from acting impulsively—for example, taking a few deep breaths, counting to 10, or taking a walk around the block.

THINK

Examine the situation and think about the consequences of certain behaviors. Ask, "What am I doing? What will happen if I continue?"

PLAN

Think about possibilities, brainstorm alternatives, choose the best plan, and put it into effect.

CHECK

After you have tried one plan, check to see if it is working. If so, give yourself credit. Enjoy a sense of satisfaction—you've earned it. If not, start over and use another plan.

Figure 3

TRANSACTIONAL ANALYSIS

Before beginning, you will need to copy Figure 4 to share with the group.

TO THE TEACHER

Many teen problems result from a lack of positive interactions and understanding between adolescents and adults. Adolescents can change their behavior with both adults and peers by examining their attitudes and interactions in various situations. Transactional Analysis offers a helpful framework to examine different attitudes and the behaviors that derive from them.

GUIDED DISCUSSION

THE ME'S

We all demonstrate different attitudes at different times and with different people. We call these attitudes the "Me's." It is fine to have these different attitudes; however, it is important to consider the time and place before deciding which attitude is the best one.

Enthusiastic Me and Impulsive Me

Sometimes your attitude is like a child's. The child has two attitudes: the Enthusiastic Me and the Impulsive Me. When you behave in a fun-loving way, you show an Enthusiastic Me attitude. Everyone needs to release this attitude occasionally. When was the last time you showed an Enthusiastic Me attitude?

Discuss.

Our childlike attitude can also be mean and impulsive, and that's not OK. An Impulsive Me attitude can be malicious, difficult, and impatient. When was the last time you showed your Impulsive Me attitude?

Discuss.

Caring Me and Bossy Me

We often use an attitude like that of a teacher or parent—someone who acts with authority. This is the parent attitude. The parent attitude can be either nurturing or critical. We call these attitudes the Caring Me and the Bossy Me.

When you assume a Caring Me attitude you are consoling and good to yourself. You may say something like "I am so tired. I've got to get some rest." The Bossy Me is more likely to be scolding and say something like "I'm so lazy. I should stop fooling around and get to work." The Bossy Me sends very critical messages and also uses domineering body language. Can you give me some examples?

Elicit responses—shake a finger, hands on hips, clench teeth, fold arms, and so on.

Thinking Me

The third attitude we assume is the adult, or the Thinking Me. This attitude is our referee and keeps us in balance. This part of us is like a data-processing computer. It examines the behavior of the other Me's and decides whether to accept the behavior or reject it. Being fun-loving and carefree at a ball game is OK. However, it is not OK during a serious classroom discussion. The Thinking Me suppresses impulsive and authoritarian attitudes and allows a person to reach logical, mature decisions.

Distribute copies of Figure 4 (Who, Me?) and have students complete. Discuss answers as a group.

FEELINGS

Everyone has feelings. Feelings serve us by providing important information about what is happening around us and how we are dealing with it. Sometimes these feelings are positive, and sometimes they are negative. All feelings are OK, even so-called negative feelings. It's OK to feel angry, jealous, or sad. However, it's not OK to show these feelings by behaving in ways that can hurt ourselves or others.

Some people feel that they are not OK but pretend to be OK. They'll do anything to get attention from other people, even if it means getting into trouble. Being OK means having a positive self-concept. When we get feelings that are not OK we may despair, panic, or act belligerent. The Thinking Me helps us STOP, THINK, PLAN, and CHECK before feelings lead to trouble.

POSITIVE AND NEGATIVE TRANSACTIONS

A *transaction* is an exchange between two people. When the transaction is positive, we feel OK. Negative transactions make us feel not-OK. Negative transactions happen when people misunderstand each other. For example, if you ask me, "Did I leave my books on your desk?" my Impulsive Me might answer, "How should I know—I'm not your personal slave." Our transaction is not OK. Who can tell why this transaction is not OK?

Elicit responses and discuss.

Positive transactions lead to OK relationships. Negative attitudes like prejudice keep us from having positive transactions. Attitudes coming from the Impulsive Me and the Bossy Me can also cause people to fight or withdraw. For example, what if I used an Impulsive Me attitude and said, "I'm so tired of cleaning up. You pig, get up off your chair and help"? What if I used a Bossy Me attitude and said, "You ought to be ashamed for being so lazy and sloppy"? How would you be likely to feel?

Elicit responses. Next have students generate examples of situations when they were Enthusiastic, Impulsive, Caring, Bossy, and Thinking. Discuss how the different Me's relate to OK and not-OK interactions with others. Sample situations follow.

- Enthusiastic Me: Show me how you looked when your favorite team won or when your grades on your report card improved 100 percent.

- Impulsive Me: Think of a time you felt angry. Did you act out your anger? Did your Impulsive Me take over?

- Caring Me: How can you express a Caring Me attitude toward someone who is in pain?

- Bossy Me: Were you ever bossy to a younger brother or sister? How?

- Thinking Me: Your Impulsive Me says, "Come on, let's have a drink." Your Bossy Me says, "You're impossible. Won't you ever learn drinking isn't good for you?" What does your Thinking Me say?

Who, Me?

Name: _____ Date:_____

In the space to the left, identify the different Me's: Enthusiastic Me, Impulsive Me, Bossy Me, Caring Me, Thinking Me.

_____ 1. You no-good *%#! I'm going to tell on you.

_____ 2. Punching him is not going to solve my problem.

_____ 3. I ought to be ashamed of myself. I must watch my cursing.

_____ 4. I'm glad I was able to tell Ken no. Good for me!

_____ 5. Now let me tell you how to do it.

_____ 6. Mrs. Brown, Jeff is copying Mary's answers.

_____ 7. Jeff, it's not fair to copy answers.

_____ 8. Awesome! I like the new science experiment.

_____ 9. I'm sorry you have a bad cold. You should take care of yourself.

_____ 10. If she gives you a hard time, just sock her in the nose.

Write your own sentence to illustrate each of the following Me's.

1. Enthusiastic Me

_____

2. Impulsive Me

_____

3. Caring Me

_____

4. Bossy Me

_____

5. Thinking Me

_____

Figure 4

ASSERTION TRAINING

Before beginning, you will need to copy Figure 5 to share with the group.

TO THE TEACHER

Adolescent development is characterized by a search for personal identity. Identity formation is a time of detachment from adults and a time for personal assertion. Frequently, the need for assertion manifests itself as rebellion. Many parents and teachers misinterpret adolescents' expression of independent thought as rude and challenging. Although some youth do reject the values of society, most seek traditional goals and emulate the standards of their parents.

Assertion training can help adolescents express themselves without violating the rights of others or alienating their teachers, parents, or peers. Assertion involves both cognitive and affective behaviors. There are two types of assertive behaviors, direct assertion and empathetic assertion. This program refers to both types.

GUIDED DISCUSSION

There are three different kinds of behavior: aggressive, nonassertive, and assertive.

AGGRESSIVE

People who are aggressive try to control and humiliate others. They seek to win at any cost. Their self-centeredness and "me-ness" turns into meanness. They may behave violently or dishonestly to get what they want. They do not consider the rights of others, nor do they respect authority. Some aggressive people really feel inferior, anxious, and afraid, but they attempt to cover up these feelings by bullying others and by acting tough.

NONASSERTIVE

Nonassertive people generally lack self-esteem and feel at the mercy of others. They have a great need for attention and recognition, but they won't stand up for themselves. Instead, they try to win approval by doing what others want them to do. They may also try to gain power indirectly, by making other people feel guilty or by using sneaky ways to get even. Their nonassertive behavior frequently results in their helplessness or failure. They lack self-confidence, often feel self-pity, and are sometimes victimized by others, who tend to view their self-defeating attitude as weakness. Nonassertive people often build a wall around themselves because they feel it is just too painful to be around people. A nonassertive person would have difficulty saying no to drugs, alcohol, and other problem behaviors.

ASSERTIVE

Assertive people communicate their feelings and needs in a straightforward way without violating the rights of others. They are able to establish healthy relationships and have positive interactions. Assertive people are self-confident and reflective. They think of consequences and consider how others will feel before they act or speak. Learning to say no assertively is one important way to express opinions. Remaining silent in some situations shows assertion because it may take courage not to respond in an aggressive manner. People can learn to be assertive by believing in themselves and by using their Thinking Me.

Sometimes assertive behavior can get you into trouble. If so, being nonassertive is OK. For example, it might not be a good idea to be assertive with someone you strongly suspect will react by hitting you. Aggressive behaviors are never acceptable, however. They destroy positive relationships and are often self-destructive, too.

Let's suppose a group of students were unjustly punished in school and decided to get even by writing graffiti on the school walls. Writing the graffiti is an aggressive response. How could they respond assertively instead?

Elicit responses and discuss. For example, the students might appoint a spokesperson to approach the principal and tell their side of the story.

Direct assertion

Direct assertion is an honest, straightforward statement of your feelings and desires. For example, if your friend keeps pressuring you to smoke a cigarette or take a drink, you could simply say, "I'm not into that. Please don't ask me again."

Empathetic assertion

In certain situations direct assertion is required. However, many situations call for empathetic assertion instead of direct assertion. In empathetic assertion, you address the other person's feelings, motives, and desires before you give an assertive response. This type of assertion works well with adults, who may feel that direct assertion from a young person is disrespectful. For example, if your dad keeps telling you how to do your science project and you wish he would stop, you could say, "I understand you would like to help me and I appreciate it, but I would rather do it myself."

Distribute copies of Figure 5 and have students complete. Discuss their answers as well as situations in which they feel empathetic assertion would be better than direct assertion, and vice versa.

Direct versus Empathetic Assertion

Name: _____ Date:_____

Place a check mark in the box to indicate whether the following statements are examples of direct or empathetic assertion.

	Direct	Empathetic
1. I can't make it at 4 o'clock. How about 5 o'clock instead?	☐	☐
2. I'm really too busy to take on another responsibility right now.	☐	☐
3. I know you'd like me to attend the meeting, but I have another appointment I can't change.	☐	☐
4. No, thank you. I don't want to go out tonight.	☐	☐
5. I realize you want me to feel like part of the crowd, but I don't want to get started smoking. It's too hard to quit.	☐	☐
6. Thank you so much for thinking of me, but I cannot accept your gift.	☐	☐
7. Not for me—I can live without drugs.	☐	☐
8. You feel confident you won't get caught if you skip school, but I just don't want to take the chance.	☐	☐
9. I'm going to need another 10 minutes to finish this report.	☐	☐
10. I appreciate your offering me a ride, Dad, but I don't mind walking home.	☐	☐

Figure 5

29

General Review

Figure 6 (Role-Play Review) and Figure 7 (General Review) reinforce the concepts underlying all three theories. Students may complete these activities after all the theories have been taught.

- For the Role-Play Review, pair students and assign one of the situations listed to each pair. Allow a brief period for students to create a dialogue, then instruct each pair to role-play the situation. Encourage discussion following each role-play.

- For the General Review, have students complete as instructed and then discuss answers as a group.

Role-Play Review

Situation 1

Explain to the assistant principal why you were late for class. Use a Thinking Me attitude.

Situation 2

Convince your mother that you are responsible enough to stay at a friend's house overnight. Use the Thinking Steps to develop a plan.

Situation 3

You are at a football game, and your team made a touchdown. Talk to a friend about your feelings. Use your Enthusiastic Me attitude.

Situation 4

You are baby-sitting for a 3-year-old child, and the child keeps slapping you. Describe how you can be assertive, not aggressive, in stopping the child's behavior.

Figure 6

General Review

Name: _____ Date:_____

Place a check mark beside the best answer.

1. Which Me is responding in the following example?

    Sue: Let's go to my house and listen to records.

    Pam: Sounds like fun, let's go!

    _____ a. Enthusiastic Me

    _____ b. Impulsive Me

    _____ c. Caring Me

    _____ d. Bossy Me

    _____ e. Thinking Me

2. In which of the following situations would the response "Get off my back" be appropriate?

    _____ a. Student responding to a teacher.

    _____ b. Student responding to a teasing friend.

    _____ c. Student responding to a crawling tarantula.

3. Which is an assertive response?

    _____ a. So I'm late—want to make something of it?

    _____ b. Why am I late? I don't know.

    _____ c. I'm sorry I'm late—I overslept. I'll try to do better.

4. Which of the following are examples of empathetic assertion? (There may be more than one.)

    _____ a. Please, Mother, I'd rather do it myself.

    _____ b. Mother, I know you want to help, but I'd rather do it myself.

    _____ c. No, John, I do not want to start smoking.

    _____ d. John, you're my friend, but I don't need to start smoking.

Figure 7

33

5. Which is the Bossy Me response?

_____ a. You better straighten up and stop smoking.

_____ b. I worry about your health. Please stop smoking.

_____ c. Smoking is hazardous to your health.

6. Which of the following is an assertive response?

_____ a. Me, take your money? I, I, I . . .

_____ b. No, I did not take your money. Please stop accusing me.

_____ c. I didn't take your crummy money, take this (throws a punch)!

7. Your friends in school won't accept a new girl who has just arrived from a different country. You like her. To be assertive you can:

_____ a. befriend her and be honest with your friends.

_____ b. befriend her and ignore your friends.

_____ c. ignore her and keep your friends.

8. Gossipy Gail corners you and starts badmouthing your friend Cindy. Which is the assertive, Thinking Me response?

_____ a. You think so, ahem, I see.

_____ b. Gail, you've got a big mouth and a dirty mind. Get out of my face.

_____ c. Gail, Cindy is my friend. I'd rather not listen to gossip.

Answer the following questions.

1. John was assertive and truthful, but his teacher misinterpreted his behavior as "sassy." What can John do?

_____

2. Donna cannot say no. Her friends are always taking advantage and giving her the dirty work. Donna does not want to lose her friends. What can she do?

_____

3. Ron has a reading disability. He tries to hide it by withdrawing. What can Ron do to make more friends?

_____

4. Tess is friendly to students in special education classes, but her peers make fun of her. What can Tess do to help them understand?

_____

Figure 7 continued

AWARENESS OF SELF & OTHERS

Who Am I?

GOAL

- To develop personal awareness and understanding

OBJECTIVES

- Identifying changes in the adolescent years
- Recognizing personal strengths
- Recognizing personal weaknesses
- Developing plans for self-improvement

MATERIALS

- Multiple Intelligences Worksheet (Figure 8)
- Paper and pencils
- Student portfolio materials (academic work, photographs, videotapes, art, journal entries, creative writing, and so on)

PROCEDURE

OPENING

Review

None needed.

Stating Objectives

In this lesson we will learn that it is important to recognize and appreciate our personal strengths. It is equally important to recognize our weaknesses and be willing and able to improve.

INSTRUCTION

Teaching and Guided Discussion

●————— **Identifying changes in the adolescent years**

The middle school years are often very confusing and difficult for students. Can you tell me why?

Elicit responses and discuss.

Adolescence is a critical time because you are growing physically and emotionally. Your bodies change as well as your feelings. But most important, the way you feel about yourself will determine your attitudes and behavior. Will you adopt a positive and healthy attitude, behave with confidence, and develop a healthy self-concept? It is not unusual for teens to question past values or to become unsure of themselves: Am I pretty or handsome enough? Am I smart enough? Will I be accepted by the group?

Many teenagers give in to peer pressure because they lack self-confidence. Yet other teenagers value being their own person and "march to their own tune." What does that expression mean?

Elicit responses and discuss.

●————— **Recognizing personal strengths**

You have different strengths and talents. *(Personalize the following examples.)* I think one of my special talents is cooking. My nephew is good at playing baseball, and my niece makes straight A's in math. Most people think intelligence is being smart in academic subjects like English, math, history, and so on. What do you think it means to be intelligent?

Elicit responses. Stress the idea that intelligence means being able and willing to excel at something and that excellence involves personal strengths.

Actually, there are many kinds of intelligences. A psychologist named Howard Gardner has identified seven kinds of intelligences.

Distribute copies of Figure 8 (Multiple Intelligences Worksheet) and have students complete the first part. Discuss students' responses.

Some people may be very intelligent in math and science (logical/mathematical) but cannot get along with other people (interpersonal). Some people have problems reading but are great musicians or artists. An IQ score does not measure everything about a person. Our attitudes affect how we use our personal intelligences. An Enthusiastic Me attitude and a Thinking Me attitude can help us develop the many intelligences within us.

Note: The concepts in Figure 8 are derived from *Multiple Intelligences: The Theory in Practice* by Howard Gardner, 1993, New York: Basic.

When we recognize our strengths we feel good about ourselves. However, we sometimes use an Impulsive Me attitude or a Bossy Me attitude to put ourselves down, and then we feel sorry for ourselves. Before we allow self-pity to get the best of us, we must use the Thinking Steps—STOP, THINK, PLAN, and CHECK—to stop feeling sorry for ourselves and to discover our strengths.

Recognizing personal weaknesses

Nobody is perfect, and we all have certain weaknesses. *(Personalize the following example.)* I like to sing, but I don't have a good singing voice. I also have difficulty getting to places on time. My first weakness does not interfere with my life, but my second weakness often gets me in trouble because when I am late it upsets other people in my work and personal relationships. Other people have difficulty controlling their tempers. How can that cause trouble?

Elicit responses and discuss.

It is difficult to admit that we have weaknesses because of pride or because it may be painful. To avoid pain we get on the defensive. We refuse to acknowledge our weaknesses and make excuses. Before making excuses we need to STOP, THINK, PLAN, and CHECK. Are we being honest with ourselves?

Developing plans for self-improvement

The first step to improving is recognizing our strengths and weaknesses. You may be able to tell what your strengths and weaknesses generally are by looking at your ratings on the top part of the Multiple Intelligences Worksheet.

We can improve on our weaknesses through careful planning and checking. For example, if we have difficulty getting along with others, then we need to work on our interpersonal intelligence. We can't all be great athletes, singers, artists, or mathematicians, but we can improve on getting along—that's a very important intelligence to nurture because it affects the rest of our lives. We can also improve the other intelligences through work and practice.

Refer students to the second part of the Multiple Intelligences Worksheet. Help students identify an area to work on, then develop and record a specific plan to improve.

By improving ourselves we develop confidence and better self-esteem. Self-esteem means the way you think and feel about yourself. Do you like the way you look? Do you perceive yourself to be awkward or graceful? Do you wish you looked different? A positive self-esteem is important no matter your age, gender, or ethnicity. It affects every aspect of your life.

People with poor self-esteem often experience failure because they may not be motivated or willing to try. They are easily influenced by others because they lack self-confidence. They feel devalued, defensive, and easily frustrated.

Do you remember assertive, nonassertive, and aggressive behaviors? Which person is likely to have the healthiest self-esteem?

Elicit responses and discuss. Review these concepts as necessary from the Preliminary Lesson.

Monitoring Knowledge and Comprehension

Ask the following questions.

1. Why are the teenage years a time for discovery?

2. Paul is not very good at math, but he can write poetry and play the piano. Kenisha loves to study the stars and planets and enjoys being with people. What are their intelligences (strengths)?

3. Refugio is good at math but has difficulty understanding the English language. He is also poor at playing tennis. Which of his weaknesses should he try to improve first?

4. How would you help Refugio deal with his most important weakness?

Guided Practice

Choose from the following activities.

1. Direct students to write their names vertically on a sheet of paper and then compose an acrostic describing a strength or reflecting a self-affirmation. For example:

   Me, I am a precious gift,
   I like the way I am.
   Never will I put myself down.
   Deep in my heart, I can
   Yearn to grow in self-esteem.

2. Guide each student in assembling a personal portfolio to reflect his or her unique abilities and personality. Decide as a group what should be included in the portfolio: academic work, photographs, videotapes, artwork, journal entries, creative writing, and so forth.

Assessing Mastery

Ask students to take out paper and pencils. Read the following statements aloud, then have students identify which Me attitude is expressed.

1. If I study, I know I can pass the test. *(Thinking Me)*

2. I should be ashamed of myself for _____. *(Bossy Me)*

3. This is fun! I'm great at shooting baskets! *(Enthusiastic Me)*

4. I may not be good at sports, but I'm an OK person. *(Caring Me)*

5. I'm a real loser. Everyone is better than I am. *(Impulsive Me or Bossy Me)*

6. I'll ask Jake to tutor me in math. I know I can do it. *(Thinking Me)*

7. I am so lazy. I really should stop fooling around. *(Bossy Me)*

8. I may not be an A student, but I get along with people. *(Thinking Me)*

9. Why can't I do anything right? *(Bossy Me)*

10. I'll help the new kid in school to get around. *(Thinking Me)*

RETEACHING

Independent Practice

Direct students to write an essay (or make an audiotape recording) in which they evaluate their strengths, their weaknesses, and their plans for improvement.

Evaluation and Feedback

Evaluate the essays and give individual feedback in writing or in a personal conference. You can also ask each student to make a positive "I-can" statement concerning plans for improvement.

CLOSING

Summary

> In this lesson we learned that the early teen years are difficult years because young people are looking for an identity. We all have special strengths. Nobody is perfect—we all have our weaknesses. We can improve on our weaknesses through careful planning and work.

Generalization

Choose from the following activities.

1. Have students put the plan they identified on the Multiple Intelligences Worksheet into effect. Afterwards, discuss outcomes as a group.

2. Direct students to write an autobiography. Encourage them to revise and type their finished products on a computer, if possible. They may illustrate moments in their lives by scanning photographs of themselves and their family and friends. If a scanner is not available, students may illustrate their autobiographies with snapshots or drawings.

ENRICHMENT

1. Discuss the following quotations:

   > To thine own self be true,
   > And it must follow as the night the day,
   > Thou canst not then be false to any man.
   >
   > —*William Shakespeare*

   > Every person has the right to feel that "because of me was the world created."
   >
   > —*The Talmud*

   > I am somebody! I may be poor—but I am somebody!
   > I may be in prison—but I am somebody!
   > I may be uneducated—but I am somebody!
   >
   > —*Jesse Jackson*

As you love yourself, so shall you love others. Strange but true, but with no exceptions.

—*Harry Stack Sullivan*

No one can make you feel inferior without your consent.

—*Eleanor Roosevelt*

I own me, and therefore I can engineer me. I am me and I am okay.

—*Virginia Satir*

Believe in yourself and what others think won't matter.

—*Ralph Waldo Emerson*

You are surrounded by hundreds of people more timid than you are.

—*Edward S. Martin*

2. Have students create a topical bulletin board including sayings or mottos like the ones in the previous activity. They may quote those they have heard or compose their own.

3. Direct students to sit in a circle. Ask each student to make a positive statement about the neighbor to his or her right. (If necessary, model a positive statement or two to break the ice.) Follow this activity with an art project. Direct students to make a sticker or button stating their neighbor's good quality. For example: "Ruth Is A-OK," "Fred Is Fabulous," "Hilda Is a Computer Whiz."

Multiple Intelligences Worksheet

Name: _____ Date:_____

Give yourself a numerical rating to show how strong you think you are in each of the following areas.

3 = Very strong

2 = Moderately strong

1 = Weak

Part I

_____ Logical/mathematical (scientific thinking, mathematical abilities)

_____ Visual/spatial (artistic abilities, finding your way in space)

_____ Body/kinesthetic (athletic abilities, dancing abilities)

_____ Musical/rhythmic (musical abilities)

_____ Interpersonal (person-to-person relationships)

_____ Intrapersonal (self-reflection, self-awareness)

_____ Verbal/linguistic (making up stories, speaking, debating)

Part II

What area do you most need to work on?

_____

What is your plan to improve?

_____

_____

_____

_____

_____

_____

Figure 8

43

I Feel, Therefore I Am

GOAL

- To recognize feelings

OBJECTIVES

- Identifying various feelings
- Expressing feelings
- Demonstrating understanding of others' feelings
- Dealing with disturbing feelings

MATERIALS

- Feelings and Behaviors (Figure 9)
- What Else Could I Do? (Figure 10)
- Chalkboard or easel pad

PROCEDURE

OPENING

Review

In our last lesson we learned that adolescence is a time of physical and emotional growth. Everyone has special strengths and is unique in his or her own way. Nobody is perfect—some weaknesses interfere with our lives and may cause us difficulty. We can improve and develop better self-esteem if we are willing to plan and work.

Follow up on any generalization activities assigned during the last lesson.

Stating Objectives

In this lesson we will learn that there are many different types of feelings. All feelings are OK, but it is not OK to express feelings in a way that may be harmful to us or to others. We will examine how to recognize and consider the feelings of others. We will also learn how to deal with disturbing feelings.

INSTRUCTION

Teaching and Guided Discussion

● ———— Identifying various feelings

What do the words *angry, sad, happy, frustrated, loving,* and *excited* have in common? *(Students respond.)* Yes, they are all feelings. Even though you can't see feelings, you can tell if someone is angry, sad, happy, loving, frustrated, or excited. How is this possible?

Elicit responses and discuss.

You can tell by the way the person looks, acts, or talks. Let's discuss a feeling we have all had: anger. Now help me list the behaviors and other indicators that show when someone is angry.

Elicit responses and list on the chalkboard or easel pad. Responses may include yelling, being silent, withdrawing, flushing of the face, perspiring, staring, clenching fists or teeth, cursing, and fighting. Repeat the activity using different feelings.

All of these responses are good indicators of feelings. However, your behavior does not always indicate how you feel. Sometimes you may appear to be happy but really feel very sad. It is difficult to disguise your feelings for a long period of time.

● ———— Expressing feelings

It is OK to feel angry, but what we do with our angry feelings will determine how others will react. It is not OK to hurt others. Nobody *makes* us angry. We are responsible for our own feelings. We choose to be angry, sad, or happy. Situations may trigger certain feelings, but our feelings belong to us.

(Adapt the following example as appropriate.) I read in the newspaper about a young driver who became angry at a motorcyclist who cut in front of his car. The driver went after the motorcyclist and shot him. How do you think the driver felt, and how else could he have handled his feelings?

Discuss.

What makes you angry, and how do you handle your anger?

Elicit responses and discuss.

Following the Thinking Steps is important in handling anger constructively. The STOP step gives us a chance to chill out. We also need to THINK of the consequences of an angry behavior. The PLAN step allows us to consider our alternatives. Finally, we can CHECK our plan to see if it is working.

Another constructive way of expressing anger is to use an "I" message instead of a "you" message. For example, instead of saying, "You make me so angry" you say, "I feel angry because I feel hurt."

Have students change the following statements from "you" messages to "I" messages.

1. You always let me down. *(I feel disappointed when you don't do what you have promised to do.)*

2. You never help out around here with the dishes. *(I feel I am the only one responsible for doing the dishes, and that isn't fair.)*

3. You're such a nerd. You make me look bad when you kiss up to Mom. *(I feel upset because I don't get the chance to show Mom I'm responsible, too.)*

Some feelings are uncomfortable, but many are pleasant. Affection is a good feeling. We express affection in many ways with different people. When expressing affection we first must find out whether the person wants to receive our affection. We must also consider the time, the place, and the way we express affection.

●——— Demonstrating understanding of others' feelings

It is important to understand our feelings and how to express them, but it is also important to understand the feelings of others. There are times when we may be insensitive to what our friends, family members, or other adults are feeling. To understand someone else's feelings, we need to listen to what the person is saying and to what the person is not saying. What do you suppose I mean by that?

Elicit responses and discuss.

That means we listen to the person's words and tone of voice and watch the person's body language and facial expressions. Expressions like "Oh, forget it," "It's nothing," " I don't like _____," or "I hate _____" may indicate that the person is not expressing his or her true feelings. *(Personalize as appropriate.)* For example, I had a student who couldn't afford to go to ball games or to the movies, so she kept saying she hated ball games and movies. She felt very sad and lonely because she was left out. Have you ever had an experience where you kept your true feelings inside?

Discuss.

●——— Dealing with disturbing feelings

A number of feelings are disturbing. Grief is one of them. Grief is a human reaction to an unhappy event such as the death of a family member, a divorce, an illness, a move to a new home, or a break-up with a boyfriend or girlfriend. Like anger, grief is an OK feeling. Grieving helps us accept our losses. However, if someone is grieving for a very long time, the person needs to find help. When an unhappy event takes place, such as losing a friend, people may go through a period of shock and denial. They don't want to believe it is happening to them. Once they realize the event has happened, the shock and denial may turn to anger. They become resentful that this is happening to them. The next feeling they experience may be guilt. Why?

Elicit responses and discuss.

They may begin to question themselves and believe that the event was somehow their fault or that they could have prevented it. Guilt sometimes turns into depression, and then people may feel lonely and afraid to face each new day. This is the stage when people either get a handle on their feelings or become more depressed. Once they are able to accept the situation, they can find new hope, recover, and make new friends.

Where might a person seek help in times of grief or when having another disturbing feeling?

Elicit responses and discuss. Examples may include a school counselor, a family member, a teacher, a camp leader, or another trusted adult.

Monitoring Knowledge and Comprehension

Ask the following questions.

1. What feelings do you experience before a final exam?

2. How can you properly express anger and affection?

3. Can you always tell how people feel? Why or why not?

4. Why is grief such a disturbing feeling, and how do people cope with grief?

Guided Practice

Distribute copies of Figure 9 (Feelings and Behaviors) and have students complete.

Assessing Mastery

Discuss students' responses as a group. Accept all reasonable answers.

RETEACHING

Independent Practice

Distribute copies of Figure 10 (What Else Could I Do?) and have students complete.

Evaluation and Feedback

Review students' answers. Evaluate for understanding of positive alternative behaviors and give feedback as appropriate.

CLOSING

Summary

In this lesson we learned that there are many different types of feelings. All feelings are OK, but it is not OK to express feelings in a way that is hurtful to us or others. Our behaviors usually reflect our true feelings, but there are times when our behaviors do not reflect our feelings. We discussed how to recognize and consider the feelings of others. In addition, we learned some ways to deal with disturbing feelings.

Generalization

Direct students to keep a journal for a week to record their feelings and how they handled those feelings. Entries may be shared or kept private at the students' discretion.

ENRICHMENT

1. Have students use a thesaurus (either book or computer) to find synonyms for the following feeling words.

bored	grateful
determined	guilty
jealous	suspicious
shocked	heartbroken
disappointed	anxious
satisfied	loving
frustrated	happy
confused	confident

2. Divide the class into two groups. Write feeling words on separate index cards. A member of one group picks a card and acts out the feeling, as in charades. The other group guesses the feeling.

3. Discuss the following statements:

   I'm laughing on the outside, crying on the inside.

   Feeling fine, feeling cool, even feeling like a fool—man, it's great just to be feeling.

   They're your feelings. Let them show.

   Boys should never cry.

   I'm feeling blue.

Feelings & Behaviors

Name: _____ Date:_____

List a behavior that would show the following feelings. Use your dictionary to look up any words you do not know.

Feeling   **Behavior**

excited   _____

                _____

frustrated   _____

                _____

happy   _____

                _____

sad   _____

                _____

jealous   _____

                _____

scared   _____

                _____

angry   _____

                _____

loving   _____

                _____

confident   _____

                _____

Figure 9

hateful

_____

_____

anxious

_____

_____

depressed

_____

_____

relieved

_____

_____

rejected

_____

_____

pleased

_____

_____

proud

_____

_____

used

_____

_____

appreciated

_____

_____

indifferent

_____

_____

Figure 9 continued

What Else Could I Do?

Name: _____ Date:_____

Suggest alternative behaviors in response to the following feelings.

Example:

My mother yells at me. I feel *angry* and yell back.

Alternative behaviors: I listen quietly and leave the room.

1. A classmate copies my homework. I feel *cheated* and tear up his homework.

Alternative behaviors: _____

_____

2. I waited too long to write my book report. I feel *frustrated* and throw the book on the floor.

Alternative behaviors: _____

_____

3. I have no friends. I feel *sad* and withdraw to my own space.

Alternative behaviors: _____

_____

4. All the boys like Linda. I feel *jealous* and call her names.

Alternative behaviors: _____

_____

Figure 10

FRIENDSHIP IS GOLDEN

GOAL

- To appreciate true friendships

OBJECTIVES

- Identifying qualities of a true friendship
- Identifying different levels of friendship
- Learning how to maintain friendships
- Accepting oneself as one's own best friend

MATERIALS

- Chalkboard or easel pad
- Index cards (optional)
- Paper and pencils
- Art supplies (markers, poster paper, old magazines, glue)

PROCEDURE

OPENING

Review

In our last lesson we learned that all feelings are OK, but it is not OK to express feelings in a way that is harmful to ourselves or to others. Behaviors usually reflect feelings, but there are times when we do not show our true feelings. We discussed how to recognize and consider the feelings of others. We also learned how to deal with disturbing feelings such as grief.

Follow up on any generalization activities assigned during the last lesson.

Stating Objectives

In this lesson we will identify the qualities of a true friendship. There are different levels of friendship. Some friends are closer to us than others. We must work at keeping friends and at accepting ourselves as our own best friend.

INSTRUCTION

Teaching and Guided Discussion

●————— **Identifying qualities of a true friendship**

Abraham Lincoln once said, "The better part of one's life consists of friendships." Friendships are special at every age, but they are especially so during the teenage years, when being part of the group is very important. What qualities and characteristics do you want in a friend?

Elicit responses, list on the chalkboard or easel pad, and discuss. Possible responses: Someone who is loyal, who shares, who cares, who is honest with you, who likes you, who won't hurt you, who enjoys the same things you do, whom you can trust and depend on, and who is there for you.

All of these qualities are important in a friend. A true friend will not be influenced by your race, gender, ethnicity, or disabilities. A true friend accepts your strengths and weaknesses and does not like you just because of your money, fame, or intelligence. A true friend will accept you for what you are and will not expect anything in return but your friendship.

●————— **Identifying different levels of friendship**

There are different levels of friendship:

- *Acquaintanceship* means we know someone and that person knows us. We are friendly with acquaintances, but we do not spend time with them outside of the situation where we know them. Someone who is in one of your classes at school is an acquaintance.

- Next we have *casual friendships.* We spend time with these people and like them, but our friendship is superficial—on the surface—and we do not expect a deep bond. Someone you just enjoy playing tennis with would be a casual friend.

- We also have *deep friendships.* In a deep friendship, we exchange secrets or confidences as well as enjoy the person's company in many different situations. We expect these friends to be loyal and trustworthy, and they expect the same of us.

- Deep friendships are very special, but they are not intimate. We have *intimate friendships* with boyfriends or girlfriends—someone we love in a romantic way. These relationships involve a deep emotional bond. They may or may not include physical expressions of affection.

If appropriate, expand the discussion to include adolescent dating and sexual behavior. Lesson 4 in Skill Area 7 (Love and Caring) includes material on this subject.

●————— **Learning how to maintain friendships**

A lasting friendship takes work. We cannot take a good friend for granted. Just like a fire, a friendship needs to be kindled. How can you kindle a friendship?

Elicit responses and discuss.

What if someone said that your best friend had spread mean rumors about you? What would be your first reaction?

Elicit responses.

Before you react to the situation, you need to STOP and take time to THINK. If you react when you are angry, you may damage the friendship beyond repair. What is a good PLAN to find out what really happened and to maintain the friendship?

Accept any answers.

Next you choose the best plan and follow through. Afterwards, you CHECK your plan and ask yourself, "Did I find out what really happened?" and "Is the friendship worth maintaining?" Casual friends come and go, but deep friendships built on care, loyalty, and trust can last a lifetime. By using our Thinking Me we are able to maintain true and lasting friendships.

●———— Accepting oneself as one's own best friend

Who is your best friend? What about your best friend makes you happy?

Elicit responses and discuss.

You are your own best friend. Only you can make you really happy. Happiness is within you. Your other friends can help bring out the happiness within you. When you are your own best friend, you are able to resist pressure from others to do things that are against your beliefs. It is important to feel proud of yourself, to give yourself compliments, and to say, "I'm an OK person. I can be a good friend to you and to me."

Monitoring Knowledge and Comprehension

Ask the following questions.

1. What qualities are needed for a true friendship to develop?

2. What are the different levels of friendship?

3. What are some things you can do to maintain a good friendship?

4. Name some ways to be good to yourself—after all, you are your own best friend.

Guided Practice

Have students form small groups. Ask each group to discuss how they could maintain the friendship described in one of the following situations. (If desired, you can write the situations on individual index cards.) One group member may record the group's ideas to share with the larger group.

- *Situation 1:* You have made friends with an elderly couple in your neighborhood. Your peers think you are a nerd and make fun of you.

- *Situation 2:* You find out that your best friend has told your secret to another person. You feel betrayed.

- *Situation 3:* A group of exchange students from another country are now attending your school. You have become their friend. Your other friends don't like the idea.

- *Situation 4:* Your friend has an emotional problem and sometimes acts silly. He wants to go to the game with you. All your other school friends will be there.

Assessing Mastery

Have students write a brief essay entitled "My Special Friendship" or a letter addressed to themselves as "Dear Best Friend."

RETEACHING

Independent Practice

Have students develop a bulletin board with the theme of friendship. Ask each student to contribute a motto or compose an original one.

Evaluation and Feedback

Discuss the following sayings.

A friend in need is a friend indeed.

Make new friends, but keep the old
The new are silver, but the old are gold.

Do unto others as you would want others to do unto you.

No person is an island in and of itself. Every person is a piece of the continent, a part of the main.

—*John Donne*

Love of one's neighbor is the only door out of the dungeon of self.

—*G.K. Chesterton*

We cherish our friends not for their ability to amuse us, but for ours to amuse them.

—*Evelyn Waugh*

Do not use a hatchet to remove a fly from your friend's forehead.

—*Chinese proverb*

CLOSING

Summary

Friends are important to everyone. We want our friends to be loyal, honest, trustworthy, dependable, and caring. There are different levels of friendship, ranging from acquaintances to intimate friends. You must work hard to maintain a true friendship. Remember, you are your own best friend.

Generalization

Have each student make a "Friendship Chart" listing and illustrating interests, conversation topics, and activities to be shared with a friend.

ENRICHMENT

1. Instruct students to write a poem with friends and enemies as opposites. On the first line write one word, second line two words, third line three words, fourth line six words, fifth line three words (change feeling), sixth line two words, last line one word (opposite of first line). For example:

Friends
Loyal, trustworthy
Caring, sharing, honest
Working together to form lasting friendships
Making people sad
Hateful, treacherous
Enemies

2. Ask students to bring in and share recordings of songs with friendship as the theme (for example, "Bridge over Troubled Water," by Paul Simon).

3. Discuss the following sayings:

   Wherever there is a human being there is a chance for kindness.

   —*Seneca*

   The best way to destroy an enemy is to change him into a friend. Perhaps any of us could get along with perfect people. But our task is to get along with imperfect people.

   —*Richard L. Evans*

MANY THANKS

GOAL

- To show gratitude and accept appreciation

OBJECTIVES

- Understanding the importance of being grateful
- Demonstrating gratitude to others
- Accepting being appreciated
- Dealing with reactions when unappreciated

MATERIALS

- Thank-You Questions (Figure 11)
- Art supplies (markers, card stock, poster paper)

PROCEDURE

OPENING

Review

In our last lesson we learned that friends are important to everyone. We want our friends to be loyal, honest, trustworthy, dependable, and caring. There are different levels of friendship, ranging from acquaintances to intimate friends. You must work hard to maintain a true friendship. Remember, you are your own best friend.

Follow up on any generalization activities assigned during the last lesson.

Stating Objectives

In this lesson we will learn that it is important to be grateful and to express our gratitude. We will discuss our feelings and reactions when we are appreciated and when we are not appreciated.

INSTRUCTION

Teaching and Guided Discussion

●————— **Understanding the importance of being grateful**

When someone does something nice for you, are you grateful? *(Students respond.)* What does gratitude mean?

Elicit responses and discuss.

Gratitude means that you acknowledge the act of receiving. Many people are givers, and many people are takers. Parents are traditionally givers to their children. Sometimes children fail to show gratitude. Why?

Elicit responses.

Some children might take their parents for granted and expect their parents to give simply because they are the parents. Are you grateful for your family and friends? What about education? In some places, education is not available to all people. Look around you—what are you grateful for?

Accept any answers.

●————— **Demonstrating gratitude to others**

We need to be grateful for services, assistance, or gifts that we receive. What are some different ways to show our gratitude?

Elicit responses.

The easiest way to acknowledge a gift or a service is to say thank you. There are many ways to say thank you. You could say, "I appreciate that," "I'm glad you thought of me," or "That was really nice." You can also do something nice in return, smile, write a thank-you note, give a hug, or share a friendly moment. The main thing is that the other person knows you are grateful.

What if you receive a gift that you do not like? Can you still be thankful?

Elicit responses and discuss.

We may not like the gift, but we can appreciate the giving and the fact that someone thought about us. How often do you STOP and THINK about all the times your parents, your friends, or your teachers have made you feel OK? How often have you thanked them? How can you PLAN to express your gratitude in the future? Will you CHECK your plan to see if it works?

Elicit responses and discuss.

You can show gratitude for a friendship by saying, "I'm so glad you're my friend." You can show gratitude at home by commenting on something you usually take for granted. You could say, "Mom, that was a delicious meal" or "Dad, thanks for helping me with my homework." Don't forget that teachers feel appreciated when their students express gratitude. An Enthusiastic Me and a Thinking Me attitude are necessary to show appreciation.

Accepting being appreciated

I'd like you to close your eyes and think of a time when someone appreciated your gift or service. How did you feel? Did you get a nice feeling, or were you embarrassed?

Elicit responses.

We all like to be shown appreciation, and it is just as important to accept that appreciation as it is to give it. Receiving helps us realize our strengths and reinforces our self-esteem. By accepting people's appreciation, we make them feel good. Whenever we feel appreciated for our efforts, we have a tendency to repeat that performance. We work harder and put forth more effort.

Dealing with reactions when unappreciated

True appreciation comes from the heart and is sincere. When we are not appreciated, we feel used and taken for granted. We may feel angry and want to react in a negative way. Before we act out our anger, we need to STOP and THINK. Maybe the receiving people do not know how to give thanks, or maybe they are just insensitive to our feelings. We need to PLAN to be assertive and describe our feelings without getting angry. We can then CHECK our plan. If it worked, we can pat ourselves on the back for having good self-control.

(Personalize the following example.) Last year I went to a lot of trouble choosing the right gift for my friend's birthday. I waited, but she never acknowledged the gift. I was very disappointed and hurt, and I felt like never doing anything for her again. My Impulsive Me attitude was ruining our friendship. Did you ever feel that you were not appreciated at home, with your friends, or at school? What did you do?

Elicit responses and discuss.

If you feel unappreciated, you can clear up any misunderstandings by being assertive and by talking out the problem. When you are your own best friend, you can appreciate yourself even when others do not appreciate you.

Monitoring Knowledge and Comprehension

Ask the following questions.

1. Why is it important to be grateful?

2. Your neighbor helps you with your science project. How many ways can you show that you are thankful?

3. Reflect on the past week. How many times were you appreciated and how did you react?

4. You bought your friend a small bag of popcorn at the movies. Her reply was "Why didn't you get me a large bag?" How would you feel? What could you do?

Guided Practice

Distribute art supplies and have students make thank-you cards. Direct students to illustrate their cards and send them to people they wish to thank in school (for example, librarians, bus drivers, cafeteria workers, secretaries, teachers, principals), at home (family members), or in the community (friends, neighbors, community helpers).

Assessing Mastery

After students have given their cards, ask the following questions.

1. How did you feel when you gave your thank-you cards to people at school? At home? In the community?

2. How did they show appreciation for your efforts?

RETEACHING

Independent Practice

Have each student make up a thank-you poem or rap song for someone special. An example follows.

> Thank you, Mom, for being there for me,
> For helping me to grow and see
> That life can be so nice and sweet,
> To help me stand on my two feet.

Evaluation and Feedback

Have students complete Figure 11 (Thank-You Questions). Evaluate for understanding of the need to show appreciation and gratitude. Give feedback as appropriate.

CLOSING

Summary

In this lesson we learned that it is important to be grateful. We learned how to show gratitude to people in many different ways. We can say or write our thanks, or we can do something special in return. It is important to accept the appreciation shown to us. Whenever we feel unappreciated, we can be assertive and clear up misunderstandings, or we can appreciate ourselves even if others do not.

Generalization

Choose from the following activities.

1. Direct students to generate a list of the people in their lives who have helped them develop cognitively, physically, and emotionally. Guide them to express their gratitude (by spoken word, written word, or deed) and to extend help to someone else.

2. Direct students in a recycling or clean-up project to show appreciation for their community.

ENRICHMENT

1. Divide students into small groups and direct them to make a "thank-you poster." Posters might include thanks in different languages or symbolic illustrations of gratitude (smiling faces, handshakes, and so on).

2. Direct students to collect newspaper stories that deal with gratitude and appreciation (for example, heroic deeds, charitable donations).

3. Discuss President John F. Kennedy's quote "Ask not what your country can do for you, but what you can do for your country."

4. Obtain the lyrics to James Taylor's song "Thank You for Being a Friend" or Roberta Flack's "My Friend." Discuss.

Thank-You Questions

Name: _____ Date:_____

Complete the following sentences.

1. When someone thanks me I feel_____.

2. When I'm not thanked I feel _____.

3. I can show gratitude by _____.

4. When people take me for granted I feel_____.

5. I help someone across the street. I feel _____.

6. My neighbors are on vacation. I feel _____.

Answer the following questions.

1. Why do some children take their parents for granted?

2. How can you thank a friend for helping you with your homework?

3. How can you assertively tell someone who never shows gratitude that you do not appreciate his or her attitude?

4. How can we show appreciation for our community or country?

Figure 11

MUTUAL ADMIRATION SOCIETY

GOAL

- To accept and give compliments

OBJECTIVES

- Recognizing a true compliment
- Recognizing that giving compliments improves relationships
- Accepting compliments
- Giving self-compliments

MATERIALS

- Compliment, Flattery, or Back-Handed Compliment? (Figure 12)

PROCEDURE

OPENING

Review

In our last lesson we learned that it is important to be grateful. We need to show gratitude to people who are helpful, who give us gifts, or who appreciate us. There are many ways to show gratitude. We can say thank you or write a thank-you note, or we can do something special in return. It is important to accept and acknowledge appreciation. Whenever we feel unappreciated, we can be assertive and clear up the misunderstanding, or we can learn to appreciate ourselves.

Follow up on any generalization activities assigned during the last lesson.

Stating Objectives

In this lesson we will learn the difference between compliments, flattery, and back-handed compliments. We will recognize that giving compliments improves relationships. We will learn how to accept compliments and give ourselves compliments to acknowledge our own efforts.

INSTRUCTION

Teaching and Guided Discussion

●————— Recognizing a true compliment

What is a compliment?

Elicit responses and discuss. Answers may include praise, a pleasant remark, or an expression of respect, affection, or admiration.

Why do people give compliments?

Elicit responses and discuss.

We give compliments when we notice something positive about a person. It's telling a person, "I really like something about you." Compliments are frequently given to acknowledge a person's appearance, strengths, or actions. When they like each other, boys give compliments to girls, and girls give compliments to boys. A compliment is a sign of affection or kindness when it is honest. How do you feel when someone gives you a compliment?

Elicit responses and discuss.

A compliment makes us feel especially good when we are feeling bad about something. What is the difference between a compliment and flattery?

Elicit responses.

Flattery may sound like a compliment, but it is not sincere. People usually use flattery when they want something or want to be noticed. A "back-handed compliment" is something that sounds like a compliment but is really intended to be hurtful. It uses sarcasm and mockery. When people use flattery or back-handed compliments they are showing an Impulsive Me attitude.

Let's practice. Say I just bought a new jacket. Give me a sincere compliment, flattery, and a back-handed compliment.

Elicit responses. Point out that intent is often the difference between a compliment and flattery. Examples of the three types follow.

- *Compliment:* "That sure is a nice jacket." (Said sincerely and honestly.)

- *Flattery:* "That sure is a nice jacket. Oh, may I borrow your boom-box?" (Said to "butter you up.")

- *Back-handed compliment:* "I'm glad to see you finally got a new jacket." (Implies that there was something wrong with your old jacket.)

Recognizing that giving compliments improves relationships

Giving compliments helps our interactions with people. An interaction is an exchange of words and ideas. We interact with people in all walks of life—at home, at school, and in the community. When we give compliments sincerely, interactions become positive and we form friendly relationships. When should we give compliments?

Elicit responses and discuss.

Compliments are "ice breakers" and "fence menders." If you want to meet someone in particular, you might say, "Wow, I like that sweater—it's awesome." Your compliment may start a conversation and lead to a new friendship. If your mother is annoyed with you, STOP, THINK, and PLAN how to give her a compliment to show that you want to renew your relationship with her. Remember to avoid using flattery and CHECK your plan. What are some other ice-breaker and fence-mender situations?

Elicit responses and discuss.

Accepting compliments

How do you accept compliments? Do you feel embarrassed, or do you just shrug it off and ignore the compliment? *(Personalize the following example.)* Yesterday someone told me I looked really nice in my new sweater. I felt embarrassed because there were other teachers standing around, and I didn't know if it was flattery or a sincere compliment. My Impulsive Me response was "Oh! This old thing, I've had it for years." I didn't STOP or THINK of that person's feelings, did I? It is OK to be complimented. Compliments make us feel good, and they also make the person giving the compliment feel good. My PLAN is to acknowledge compliments from now on and to CHECK the reactions of the person giving the compliment to determine whether my plan is working.

Giving self-compliments

How often do you take the time to give yourself a compliment—to say to yourself, "Good for me!" or "I'm so proud of myself—I did it"? It is very important to send positive messages to yourself and to recognize your own accomplishments. You can do this without bragging or boasting. You need to recognize the difference between boasting and complimenting yourself. People who constantly talk about themselves are self-centered and typically will not have positive interactions with others. An honest self-compliment acknowledges achievement in a realistic manner. By giving yourself compliments, you build your self-esteem and develop an "I-can" attitude. If you've done something well, be sure to recognize your good work and give yourself a compliment.

Monitoring Knowledge and Comprehension

Ask the following questions.

1. Make a list of different ways to give compliments.

2. How would you respond to the following:

   Wow, your tennis shoes are awesome!

   Your haircut looks gross.

   I like your jacket, but it wouldn't look good on me.

3. How can giving compliments improve relationships?

4. How can you tell whether a person is giving you a sincere compliment, flattering you, or giving you a back-handed compliment?

5. Why is it important to compliment yourself?

Guided Practice

Form a circle. Direct students to give a sincere compliment to the student on the right. Tell the student receiving the compliment to acknowledge it. Repeat until everyone has received a compliment.

Assessing Mastery

Have students respond to the following compliments.

- You did a great job on your science report.

- You really know how to pick your clothes—you look great.

- It was nice of you to help Linda with her project.

- You are very kind to help with the toy drive.

RETEACHING

Independent Practice

Instruct students to give themselves compliments for their own accomplishments. Have them mention first what they have done and then give themselves the compliment. For example: "I've completed all my homework—I'm awesome." Students may write their compliments privately, if they wish.

Evaluation and Feedback

Direct students to complete Figure 12 (Compliment, Flattery, or Back-Handed Compliment?). Evaluate for understanding and give feedback as necessary.

CLOSING

Summary

In this lesson we learned the difference between a compliment, flattery, and a back-handed compliment. A sincere compliment can improve or strengthen a relationship. Flattery is dishonest, and back-handed compliments are insulting. People often use flattery for selfish reasons. Giving and accepting a compliment can make us feel good and lift our spirits. A self-compliment recognizes our achievement without boasting or bragging.

Generalization

Select from the following activities.

1. Direct students to design a compliment card for a friend, family member, teacher, or neighbor. They must first list the quality in the person that they admire the most and then write an appropriate compliment.

2. Direct the students to keep a journal recording the compliments they give to others and to themselves.

ENRICHMENT

1. Divide students in two groups and instruct each group to write a short skit. One group's topic will be flattery, and the other group's topic will be sincere compliments. Act out the skits.

2. Discuss the following expressions:

   Flattery will get you nowhere.

   They just want to butter you up.

   Imitation is the sincerest form of flattery.

Compliment, Flattery, or Back-Handed Compliment?

Name: _____ Date:_____

Identify each statement as a compliment (C), flattery (F), or a back-handed compliment (B). Be prepared to justify your answer.

_____ 1. I like the way you fixed your hair today.

_____ 2. I love your hair job—your roots don't show.

_____ 3. You must have the most beautiful hair in the whole world.

_____ 4. I bet you can play baseball better than the pros.

_____ 5. The cream is working—your acne hardly shows.

_____ 6. You play basketball better than Shaq.

_____ 7. You made 100 on your test—that's great.

_____ 8. What I like about you is your kindness and your sincerity.

_____ 9. Your dress looks like a Paris creation.

_____ 10. Those cheap jeans really hide your weight well.

Figure 12

ROLE-PLAY: AWARENESS OF SELF & OTHERS

CHARACTERS

Ben, Zena, Naushi, Mr. and Mrs. Rogers

SITUATION

Ben Rogers, an African American seventh grader, has moved with his family from a small town to a large city. Back home, African American students were the minority, but Ben had no problems being accepted by the other students. He excelled in academics as well as in sports. All this changed when he moved. His middle school was huge, and he felt like just a number. There were many minority students in school, including Asian Americans, Hispanic Americans, and Arab Americans. Some of them could hardly speak English, and he couldn't understand those who did. One day, at the end of school, he overheard a conversation between two Asian American students, Zena and Naushi.

Zena: Did you talk to the new student, Ben? I think he's cute.

Naushi: My parents told me not to talk to him—he may be dangerous.

Zena: Dangerous! He doesn't look dangerous. Why do you say that?

Naushi: Black people commit many crimes.

Zena: Well, so do white people and Asians, too.

Naushi: You always see it on television. Blacks are dangerous.

Zena: Well, I don't think he is dangerous. He has good manners. He picked up all the papers I dropped. I think we should talk to him.

They walk away. Ben is stunned at first and mumbles to himself.

Ben: Why don't these foreigners go back where they came from? I am a born American. I'll show them dangerous.

Ben storms into his house and yells at his surprised parents.

Ben: Why did we have to move to this crummy place full of foreigners? They think all blacks are criminals.

Mr. Rogers: *(In a calm voice)* Get a grip, Ben, and think. Why do you suppose they think African Americans are criminals?

Ben: I don't know—because they're stupid, I guess.

Mrs. Rogers:	Think again, son. Do they know many African American people?
Ben:	I guess not, but they didn't give me a chance.
Mr. Rogers:	It sounds like Zena was willing to give you a chance. She thought you were cute.
Mrs. Rogers:	How do you suppose Naushi got the idea that African American people are criminals?
Ben:	I guess the news doesn't show the positive actions of black people.
Mr. Rogers:	Son, the news seldom announces the daily good actions of anybody—it's too boring.
Ben:	Yeah, not sensational, but I still don't understand.
Mrs. Rogers:	Well, suppose I announced that we are moving to India or Egypt. What would be your first impression of the people and the living conditions?
Ben:	Oh, no! Please, this city is bad enough. Well, I think we would live in a very crowded area full of cows or camels, surrounded by people who couldn't speak English.
Mr. Rogers:	Ben, those are preconceived ideas, and Naushi also has preconceived ideas about African Americans.
Mrs. Rogers:	What could you do to change Naushi's ideas?
Ben:	I could continue to be friendly and show an interest in their culture and explain my culture to them.

Two weeks pass. Ben, Zena, and Naushi have become friends and are walking home.

Ben:	You have taught me a lot about your culture. I really thank you.
Naushi:	No, Ben, I need to thank you. I want to apologize for passing judgment without knowing you.
Zena:	No, no, I want to thank you. You're a great guy and very understanding.
Ben:	What is this? A mutual admiration society! I think you're both just awesome, and I'm glad we're friends.

EVALUATION AND FEEDBACK

1. How did Ben's parents help him reach self-understanding?

2. Which Me did Ben show when he overhead Naushi and Zena's conversation? Explain.

3. Describe Ben's feelings and Naushi's feelings at the beginning and at the end of the role-play.

4. Were Ben's feelings justified? Why or why not?

5. How did the students overcome their differences?

6. How did the students show their appreciation for one another's friendship?

7. How did the students compliment one another?

8. Was Ben's behavior assertive, nonassertive, or aggressive when he went home after overhearing the conversation?

9. Write a different ending for the story.

COMMUNICATION

I HEAR YOU

GOAL

- To demonstrate effective listening

OBJECTIVES

- Focusing attention when listening to a speaker
- Understanding when and when not to interrupt
- Using active and reflective listening
- Encouraging speakers to talk (door openers versus roadblocks)

MATERIALS

- Rules for Listening (Figure 13)
- Conversation Review (Figure 14)
- Roadblocks and Door Openers (Figure 15)
- Chalkboard or easel pad
- Poster board and markers (optional)
- Index cards (optional)

PROCEDURE

OPENING

Review

None needed.

Stating Objectives

In this lesson we will learn how to have positive conversations with others. Listening is an important part of having a conversation. Our body language and facial expressions often indicate interest and attention to a conversation. We will learn when not to interrupt and when it is OK to interrupt. When we listen actively, we listen to the feelings as well as to the words of the speaker. Door openers are statements to encourage conversations; roadblocks prevent conversations.

INSTRUCTION

Teaching and Guided Discussion

●———— Focusing attention when listening to a speaker

Communication is how we connect with each other. Good communication increases the chances of positive connections with others. What role does listening play in communication?

Elicit responses and discuss.

Listening is a major part of communication. When you listen, you must give your full attention to the speaker to understand the message. A good listener makes eye contact with the speaker and looks alert. Your body language tells the speaker that you are interested in what is being said. You face the speaker, and you may move a little closer. Occasional remarks such as "No fooling?" "Really?" "Awesome," "Oh, no," and "Tell me more" indicate that you want the speaker to continue and that you are following the conversation. A good listener has a clear focus on the conversation. A clear focus requires your full attention.

Distribute Figure 13 (Rules for Listening) and discuss. You may wish to give students poster boards and markers to make posters of these rules to display in the classroom.

Sometimes my attention wanders, especially when I have something important on my mind. When that happens, I use my Thinking Steps. I STOP and tell myself to make eye contact with the speaker. I THINK and redirect my full attention to the speaker. I PLAN to get rid of distracting thoughts by following and acknowledging what the speaker is saying. When the speaker stops talking, I CHECK my plan to see whether I understood the speaker's message. How do you redirect your attention when your mind wanders?

Elicit responses and discuss.

●———— **Understanding when and when not to interrupt**

Interrupting a conversation is not a sign of good listening. It is usually impolite to interrupt a conversation. It is best to wait for a pause in the conversation before we speak. Some people are self-centered and regularly interrupt conversations. I knew a person who constantly interrupted to describe a personal situation whenever someone talked about a problem or an event. Did that ever happen to you? How did you feel? What did you do?

Elicit responses and discuss.

Sometimes interrupting is necessary. It is always acceptable to interrupt in an emergency. In addition, it may be necessary to interrupt when someone talks and talks and does not give other people a chance to respond. In this case, it is permissible to interrupt politely and to assertively say something like "I understand where you are coming from. Give me a chance to speak. I think . . ." What are some other ways to interrupt politely?

Elicit responses and discuss.

Using active and reflective listening

When we use *active listening* we listen to the feelings as well as to the words of the speaker. For instance, if your friend asks, "Are we having a math test on Friday?" your first impulse may be to answer, "Dumb question. You know we always have a test on Friday." In this example you listened only to the words. If you were listening to the feelings you might think, "He knows we are having a test on Friday—he must be worried." Your answer could then be "Sounds like you are worried. Need any help?"

Whenever you use the Thinking Steps, you are being reflective. You STOP, THINK, PLAN, and CHECK your actions. When you use *reflective listening* you assume a Thinking Me attitude instead of jumping to conclusions in your responses. When engaged in a conversation with a friend, you can occasionally reflect or repeat your friend's message. For example, in answer to your friend's question about the Friday test, you can rephrase his question in this way: "You want to know whether we will have an exam on Friday." Your reflected message gives your friend a chance to talk out his feelings.

Active listening and reflective listening help you communicate. When was the last time you listened actively? Have you ever listened reflectively?

Elicit responses and discuss.

Encouraging speakers to talk (door openers versus roadblocks)

When we don't listen actively we put up *roadblocks* to communication. Just as roadblocks on a highway prevent the flow of traffic, roadblocks in a conversation prevent the flow of positive communication.

An Impulsive Me and a Bossy Me attitude often present roadblocks in a conversation. A Bossy Me attitude warns, judges, advises, and preaches. An Impulsive Me attitude ridicules, threatens, and uses sarcasm and fear. For instance, you may say to your friend, "What's the matter, scaredy cat? Are you afraid of the big, bad exam?" (Impulsive Me) or "If you study hard, you will do just fine" (Bossy Me). Your friend may get mad at you, or just turn away and disconnect.

The opposite of roadblocks are door openers. *Door openers* help conversation progress. When you use active and reflective listening you are using door openers. You are focusing your attention on what the speaker is saying, and you are encouraging the conversation to continue. Door openers let the speaker know you are interested. What door opener could you use if I said, "Should we decorate the room for the holidays tomorrow?" What would be a roadblock?

Elicit several responses. List on the chalkboard or easel pad and discuss.

Monitoring Knowledge and Comprehension

Ask the following questions.

1. What does it mean to focus your attention on a conversation?

2. When is interrupting a conversation appropriate? When is it inappropriate?

3. Respond to the following showing active listening and reflective listening: "I'm not feeling well."

What's the matter? *(active listening)*

I hear you say you aren't feeling well. *(reflective listening)*

4. Give an example of a door opener or a roadblock in conversation.

Guided Practice

Have students form small groups and direct each group to respond to one of the following situations. Reassemble in the larger group and discuss. If desired, you may write the situations on separate index cards.

- *Situation 1:* You are talking to your friend at school between classes, and you have only a few minutes. Your other friend barges in and interrupts your conversation.

- *Situation 2:* Your mother is sharing your family's plans for the summer vacation. You tell her you are listening. You are turned away from her, watching a show on television. You occasionally say, "Great, Mom."

- *Situation 3:* You are at the grocery store. The checkout clerk is explaining how she corrected an error on your receipt. She is speaking so fast you can barely understand her.

Assessing Mastery

Distribute copies of Figure 14 (Conversation Review) and have students complete.

RETEACHING

Independent Practice

Distribute copies of Figure 15 (Roadblocks and Door Openers) and have students revise the items as instructed. Sample door openers are as follows.

1. You don't like to . . .

2. Sounds like you need more information.

3. I hear you saying you want to be chosen for the basketball team.

4. Looks like you want to try.

Evaluation and Feedback

Discuss students' door openers and ask the following questions.

1. "If you don't finish your homework, you can't talk on the phone." What type of roadblock is this statement: judging, threatening, or preaching?

2. Change the previous statement to a door opener.

3. When is it appropriate to interrupt a conversation?

4. How are active and reflective listening statements door openers to a conversation?

CLOSING

Summary

In this lesson we learned that listening is an important part of communication. Our body language and facial expressions often indicate interest and attention to the conversation. Interrupting is impolite but is sometimes necessary. In active listening we listen to the feelings as well as to the words of the speaker. We use reflective listening by occasionally repeating or rephrasing what the speaker tells us. Roadblocks stop conversations, whereas door openers encourage conversations.

Generalization

Choose from the following activities.

1. Direct students to write scripts for appropriate interruptions at home or in any community setting. For example:

   Your parents are engaged in an important conversation with the neighbors. Interrupt them to tell them they have an emergency phone call.

   You wish to exchange a shirt for a smaller size. The sales clerk is chatting with another sales clerk.

   A police officer has wrongly identified you for writing graffiti on a wall and is threatening and scolding. Interrupt and state your defense.

   Your sister is listening to music through her headset and cannot hear your mother calling her. Interrupt her to give her the message.

2. Have students prepare a list of door openers, then practice active listening at home and with friends. Encourage students to avoid roadblocks.

ENRICHMENT

1. Have students interrupt appropriately in the following situations.

   The principal is having a serious talk with a student. You need to leave the campus immediately. Interrupt the principal.

   Your teacher is giving a history lecture. Interrupt to tell the teacher that your friend is feeling faint.

   You notice a small fire in a trash can in the gym. Interrupt the coach's conversation with a teacher.

2. Direct students to identify and name the feelings in the following statements.

   I hate Jessy. She said I dress weird. *(hurt, sad, offended)*

   Would you believe it! Mother liked my make-up. *(surprised, happy, appreciative)*

   I don't care if they won the game, they cheated. *(disappointed, spiteful, angry)*

   Ms. Jones, is our report due on Wednesday? *(worried, concerned, uptight)*

Rules for Listening

1. **Connect with the speaker.**
   Make eye contact and look at the speaker.

2. **Focus attention.**
   Clear your mind and listen to what is being said.

3. **Sustain attention.**
   Tune out distractions and keep paying attention.

4. **Don't interrupt.**
   If you get the urge to interrupt, gently bite your lip or pull on your ear. Allow the speaker to finish.

5. **Listen actively.**
   Listen to the speaker's feelings as well as to the words. Be aware of body language and facial expressions.

6. **Respond actively.**
   Without interrupting, use phrases such as "Oh, really?" "Great," and "That's unbelievable."

7. **Listen reflectively.**
   Occasionally let the person know that you understand. Say something like "I hear you say that *(summarize the person's message)*" or "I'll bet you felt *(suggest how the person might have been feeling)*."

Figure 13

Conversation Review

Name: _____ Date:_____

Fill in the blanks. Words to use: roadblock, actively, eye contact, door opener, reflective, communication.

1. _____ is an important part of communication.

2. When I listen to your feelings as well as to your words, I am listening

   _____.

3. You tell me, "I lost my new jacket. My mom will be furious."
   I tell you, "You lost your jacket—what can you do?" I am using

   _____ listening.

4. You tell me, "I lost my new jacket. My mom will be furious."
   I tell you, "You space cadet. Now you're going to get it." I am using a

   _____.

5. I tell you, "You look worried, what's the matter?" You tell me,
   "I lost my new jacket, my mom will be furious." I used a

   _____.

6. Looking at the speaker, or making _____,
   gives the message that you are interested in the conversation.

Figure 14

83

Roadblocks & Door Openers

Name: _____ Date: _____

Revise the following roadblock statements so they are door openers instead.

Roadblocks   **Door Openers**

1. Quit your complaining.   1. _____

                                              _____

2. You don't make sense.   2. _____

                                              _____

3. Well, if you want to get   3. _____
   on the basketball team,
   you'll have to practice   _____
   every day.

4. Are you crazy? That will   4. _____
   never work!

                                              _____

Figure 15

LET'S TALK

GOAL

- To communicate positively with others

OBJECTIVES

- Engaging in a conversation
- Using humor in a conversation
- Disagreeing appropriately in a conversation
- Using appropriate timing, tact, and tone in a conversation

MATERIALS

- Conversation Topics (Figure 16)
- Dialogue Topics (Figure 17)
- Paper cups and markers
- Paper and pencils

PROCEDURE

OPENING

Review

In our last lesson we learned how to listen effectively. Listening is an important part of communication. It involves focusing on the speaker and sustaining our attention. Interrupting is impolite but sometimes necessary. We examined appropriate ways to interrupt. In active listening we hear the feelings as well as the words of the speaker. We use reflective listening when we repeat some of what the speaker told us. Roadblocks are negative and door openers are positive points of communication.

Follow up on any generalization activities assigned during the last lesson.

Stating Objectives

In this lesson we will learn about the skills needed to engage in conversation. It takes knowledge to be a successful speaker. We will learn the importance of a sense of humor in conversation and that it is OK to disagree. The three "T's" of effective communication are timing, tact, and tone. It is important to choose the proper time and place to make a request. Be tactful and diplomatic, and avoid using a loud voice. The tone of your voice can convince or discourage your listener.

INSTRUCTION

Teaching and Guided Discussion

●——— Engaging in a conversation

Sometimes it is difficult to engage in a conversation. Why do you think so?

Elicit responses and discuss.

We may be afraid of rejection, we may feel shy or awkward, or we may be afraid of saying the wrong thing. How would you begin a conversation?

Elicit responses and discuss.

Greetings such as "Hi!" "Hello!" or "What's happening?" are examples of appropriate informal openings. "Good morning" or "Good evening" are examples of more formal ways to start conversations. Have you ever heard the phrase "small talk"? What do you think that means?

Elicit responses.

Small talk is light conversation. It is not serious conversation. It is chit-chat or casual talk among people.

In a conversation it is important to know something about whatever we are talking about. Sometimes we don't have the correct information and just repeat something we have heard "through the grapevine." What does that expression mean?

Elicit responses and discuss. Stress the importance of getting complete information from reliable sources.

In addition to getting information from people and sources we trust, we must also use a Thinking Me attitude. When we speak impulsively we often get into trouble. We need to STOP talking foolishly and THINK about what we are about to say. We PLAN to get the facts straight by going to reliable sources, then CHECK our plan. People are more likely to want to listen when we are well informed.

●——— Using humor in a conversation

Some people say or do things to make us laugh. What is the difference between a healthy sense of humor and a sick sense of humor?

Elicit responses and discuss.

A funny joke or action intended to make people happy is healthy humor. Sometimes people intentionally say or do things that hurt other people's feelings. Being different from the crowd is not funny. Yet some people make jokes about gender, race, religion, or disabilities. That's not healthy humor—it's sick humor. We laugh *with* people and not *at* people. We must respect, not attack, one another's differences.

A healthy sense of humor allows us to see the funny side of a situation. It is easier to join in the laughter when a funny thing happens to someone else. It is harder to have a sense of humor when we are the object of the joke. There are times when we misunderstand what is meant to be friendly laughter, and we may become very angry. Before we react angrily we need to STOP, THINK, PLAN, and CHECK. Are people laughing because whatever we did struck them as being funny, or are they really trying to hurt us? If they mean no harm, we laugh with them. We develop a sense of humor when we learn to laugh at ourselves. Sometimes we need to lighten up and not take ourselves so seriously. There are times to be serious and show our Thinking Me, and there are times to be funny and laugh and show our Enthusiastic Me.

Derogatory jokes, especially those with sexual content, put people down. We laugh at clean jokes that play on words, nonsense stories, riddles, puns, and silly comedies we watch on television. Remember, if the joke does not hurt you or somebody else, it is OK. Who can tell a funny joke that shows a healthy sense of humor?

Let students share jokes and enjoy. If you wish, have them share a limerick, a pun, and a knock,knock joke.

Limerick

There was a young man from Montana,
For lunch he ate one green banana.
I'm still hungry, he cried,
He yelled, growled, then sighed
Then found a sweet cake from Savannah.

Pun

Q: What is the difference between a boss and a grocery clerk?

A: A boss can give you the sack, but a clerk can sack your groceries.

Knock, Knock Joke

Q: Knock, knock.

A: Who's there?

Q: Sawyer

A: Sawyer who?

Q: Saw your teacher doing the macarena!

Disagreeing appropriately in a conversation

There are certain things that all people should agree about. We all agree children should not be abused. We all agree that hate crimes and acts of violence are wrong. We all agree that peace is better than war. What other topics do you think deserve universal agreement?

Elicit responses and discuss.

There are many things people do not agree on. It is fine to disagree, but how you disagree is important. When you choose to disagree, you should use a Thinking Me attitude and refrain from insults and put-downs. What are some put-downs you have heard?

Let students offer a few examples.

If you are expressing a personal opinion, not based on facts, remember to respect the other person's right to an opinion, too. Other people have different beliefs and values, and that's fine. Watch your attitude—are you coming from a Bossy Me or an Impulsive Me attitude? Are you using your Thinking Steps? Is your behavior aggressive, nonassertive, or assertive? How can you agree to disagree?

Elicit responses and discuss.

By agreeing to disagree you are giving others their right not to see things your way, and that's OK. They in turn should give you the same right.

Using appropriate timing, tact, and tone in a conversation

There are three "T's" in communication: timing, tact, and tone. It is wise to choose the right time and place to discuss certain topics. You must use the Thinking Steps and choose a time when you believe you will be successful. Suppose you want to convince your parents to raise your allowance. Would you discuss the subject when they are angry with you, or when they are tired after a hard day's work?

Discuss.

Many subjects require diplomacy and tact. Keep to your topic and back up your plan with reasonable facts. Just because all your friends are receiving larger allowances is usually not a good reason for you to get a raise.

Your tone of voice is also important. People usually resist messages given in a loud voice, while a message given in a hesitant, low voice may be ignored. Remember the Me's and use an Assertive Me attitude when you speak. Rehearse your plan and set it in motion. If you do not convince your parents this time, reevaluate your plan and make another.

Monitoring Knowledge and Comprehension

Ask the following questions.

1. You are trying to impress your friend, but you don't know much about her hobby of rock collecting. How can you carry on an informed conversation?

2. What is the difference between a healthy sense of humor and a sick sense of humor?

3. Why should you agree to disagree?

4. What are the "T's" in communication, and why are they important?

Guided Practice

Pair students or create two teams and have them take up opposing sides of the issues listed in Figure 16 (Conversation Topics).

Assessing Mastery

Direct students to take out paper and pencils and read aloud each of the following sentences pertaining to the previous activity. Have students fill in the missing portion. Discuss answers; validate different reactions and points of view.

1. When my friend disagreed with me, I felt _____.

2. I believe I was correct in my opinion because _____.

3. In responding, my tone of voice was _____.

4. I believe I (was/was not) tactful because I _____.

RETEACHING

Independent Practice

Choose from the following activities.

1. Pair students and direct them to briefly act out the following disagreements. Have students justify their positions.

   A student in your class insists that the Chicago Bulls did not win the NBA Championship in 1997.

   Your brother claims astronaut John Glenn was the first person to walk on the moon.

   Your friend insists that detergent Brand A removes grease stains better than detergent Brand B.

2. Plan a skit in which students can share jokes.

3. Have students illustrate paper cups with jokes and drawings. (For example: Draw a picture of a hot dog. Write, "What dog has no tail?")

4. Direct students to write sentences illustrating the meaning of the following statements. For example: "Gina really *put her foot in her mouth* when she gossiped about Trudy's alleged cheating."

   Put your foot in your mouth.

   Wake a sleeping dragon.

   Beat around the bush.

   Let the cat out of the bag.

Evaluation and Feedback

Direct students to write a short dialogue on one of the situations listed in Figure 11 (Dialogue Topics). Have them share with the larger group.

CLOSING

Summary

> In this lesson we learned how to engage in a conversation. We need to be knowledgeable before we can contribute to a conversation. A healthy sense of humor adds interest to a conversation. It is fine to disagree on personal opinions. Three "T's" for effective communication are timing, tact, and tone. Proper timing can provide success. Be tactful and diplomatic when engaging in a conversation. You usually should avoid shouting or very low voice tones. The tone of your voice can convince or discourage your listener.

Generalization

Have students keep a journal to describe conversations they overhear or are a part of in school and out. Direct them to look for how conversations are initiated, how humor is involved, and how disagreements are handled.

ENRICHMENT

1. Encourage students to think of a real or imaginary situation they feel is unfair and to make a plan to correct the situation through discussion. Have them rehearse their main points in front of a mirror. For example: "You received an F in physical education for the semester. You don't think it's fair because you failed to dress out only one time. You want to convince the teacher to change your grade."

2. Have students shut their eyes and visualize a situation in which they need to make a request. Have them imagine the right time and place, how to begin the conversation, what to say, and how to end the conversation. Discuss the experience.

3. Direct students to collect comic strips from newspapers. Have them select a favorite cartoon and share it with the class.

Conversation Topics

1. Girls (should/should not) be allowed to attend educational institutions that are traditionally for males only.

2. A curfew for teenagers (should/should not) be imposed in your city.

3. People who write graffiti (should/should not) be put in jail and given a large fine.

4. Cigarette smoking (should/should not) be banned from all public establishments (restaurants, airplanes, offices).

5. Year-round school is (better/worse) than the summer-off schedule.

6. All-boy or all-girl schools are (better/worse) than coeducational schools.

Figure 16

Dialogue Topics

Choose one of the following topics and write a short dialogue.

1. You and I are discussing the problem of hunger in our town. Convince me to donate a case of canned food to the local food bank.

2. You and your friend cannot agree on which is the coolest car, a Ferrari or a Jaguar. Include a beginning and an ending in your dialogue.

3. You want to start a conversation with the new teacher. Provide an opening and a topic of conversation.

4. You want to discuss your grades with your teacher. Be sure to say when would be a good time and where would be a good place for this dialogue.

5. I am trying to convince you that Chinese food is better than Italian food, but you disagree. Express your opinion.

6. Write a dialogue between you and your parents. Try to convince them to extend your weekend curfew.

7. Your friend wants to go bowling, but you want to go to the skating rink. Talk your friend into going skating.

8. Your friend feels depressed and sad. Tell your friend a joke to cheer him or her up.

Figure 17

Communicating Without Talking

GOAL

- To recognize the importance of nonverbal communication and cultural differences in nonverbal expression

OBJECTIVES

- Recognizing the importance of body language

- Recognizing the impact of facial expressions

- Recognizing different proximity zones

- Recognizing how the use of time sends a message

MATERIALS

- Nonverbal Messages (Figure 18)

- Get the Message? (Figure 19)

- Chalkboard or easel pad

- Paper and pencils

- Newspapers and magazines

PROCEDURE

OPENING

Review

In our last lesson we learned that it is important to know how to engage in a conversation. We discussed the need to be informed about a topic before we discuss it. Humor helps us talk to each other. It is also acceptable to disagree on personal opinions. Three "T's" for effective communication are timing, tact, and tone. Proper timing can help you get your message across. Tact is necessary in discussing some subjects. The tone of your voice can either convince or discourage your listener.

Follow up on any generalization activities assigned during the last lesson.

Stating Objectives

In this lesson we will learn how we communicate nonverbally and how the meaning of nonverbal signals is different in different cultures. We send messages through body language, facial expression, and proximity—how close we get to our listeners. We also communicate through the message of time.

INSTRUCTION

Teaching and Guided Discussion

●———— **Recognizing the importance of body language**

Communication does not necessarily involve talking. Can you name some nonverbal ways of communicating?

Elicit responses and list on the chalkboard or easel pad. Discuss.

Writing, smoke signals, sign language, lip reading, and Morse code are all ways of communicating without using the spoken word. Our bodies also talk. How does your body talk?

Elicit and record responses.

The way you stand, walk, or sit can send a message. Your body posture signals whether you are assertive, nonassertive, or aggressive. People often notice our body language before we begin to talk. Can you carry on a conversation for very long with your arms folded? *(Students respond.)* It's hard, isn't it? Our arms and hands add expression to what we are saying.

You can receive messages from other people's body language and predict what they are about to tell you. For example, if I fold my arms in front of my chest, what do you think I might say next?

Students respond. The general message is "I'm displeased."

●———— **Recognizing the impact of facial expressions**

Facial expressions often give you away. Your eyes, mouth, forehead, eyebrows—even your teeth—can convey your feelings and attitudes. When you make eye contact, you are saying that you are listening and interested. Angry people may twitch their mouths or clench their teeth. A surprised person often raises the eyebrows, and a sad person wrinkles the forehead.

Touch, gestures, facial expressions, and proximity can send positive or negative signals, depending on your background or culture. For example, in this country it is considered rude to stick your tongue out at someone—it signifies that you don't like the person. This expression is interpreted differently in New Zealand by the Maoris (Polynesian natives of New Zealand) and in other Polynesian islands. Sticking out the tongue means you like and appreciate a person! In many countries, making eye contact shows you are interested and involved. In some cultures, however, it is impolite to make eye contact with people in authority. Lowering the eyes when talking shows respect. Do you know of any other cultural differences?

Discuss.

●———— **Recognizing different proximity zones**

Proximity, how close or far you are from a person, can send a strong message. Imagine you are driving in traffic, and a police car pulls in behind you. What do you think would happen to your driving and to the rest of the traffic? What message does the proximity of the police car send to the drivers?

Elicit responses and discuss.

There are three proximity zones:

1. Intimate distance (shows very close relationship)

2. Personal distance (shows friendship)

3. Social distance (shows casual relationships in school or the community)

When I move away from you or get out of my chair and move toward the door, I am telling you that I want to end our conversation. If I move closer to you, the message is "I want to talk to you more or about something more personal."

Proximity changes in different cultures. For example, in the United States, Canada, England, and Australia, people are comfortable with about an arm's length for public interactions. In Arab and in Latin cultures, people tend to stand closer and touch each other more when communicating. A lack of awareness of someone's cultural preferences in proximity can interfere with communication.

●———— **Recognizing how the use of time sends a message**

We communicate different messages through the use of time. Students who are always late for school may be sending a message. They may be saying, "I don't want to be here" or "I have a problem getting to school." Being on time for a family event communicates respect. Being on time for a party or a game communicates happiness and willingness to be there. What we choose to do with our time also tells what we think is important.

Some cultures place greater emphasis on being on time than other cultures. People who regard time as very important may become upset with people who don't. They may perceive these people as uncaring and rude; however, that may not be the intended message. Before passing judgment, we need to STOP, THINK, PLAN, and CHECK. STOP your criticism and consider the person's individual circumstances. THINK: Is the person intentionally trying to aggravate you? PLAN to talk with the person and express your feelings. CHECK it out—did your plan work? It is important to be aware of cultural differences, or you may misunderstand the message and the messenger.

Monitoring Knowledge and Comprehension

Ask the following questions and discuss.

1. Shaking a fist is a nonverbal sign showing _____. *(anger)*

2. Name a sign that shows approval. *(thumbs up, "OK" sign, nod and wink)*

3. Why do you think people are less likely to believe you if your face has a blank expression? *(Answers will vary.)*

4. Which proximity zone am I using?

   I hold hands with my boyfriend or girlfriend. *(intimate distance)*

   I slap my friend on the back after a good play. *(personal distance)*

   I return my book to the librarian. *(social distance)*

5. I'm always the first one to arrive at the skating rink. My message is _____. *(I like skating.)*

Guided Practice

Select students to express feelings nonverbally, using body language and facial expressions. Direct the group to identify the message and the feeling.

1. Fold arms, tap foot. *(I'm waiting, I feel impatient.)*

2. Stamp feet, frown. *(I'm mad at you, I feel angry.)*

3. Shake a fist close to someone's face. *(I'll get even, I feel hostile.)*

4. Snap fingers, tighten lips. *(Hurry up, I feel frustrated.)*

5. Drop head, slouch, assume serious expression. *(I'm depressed, I don't feel so good.)*

Assessing Mastery

Divide the class into small groups and direct each group to play charades, using titles of movies or books. Direct each group to act out the title nonverbally for the class. Assess comprehension of the nonverbal communication.

RETEACHING

Independent Practice

Distribute copies of Figure 18 (Nonverbal Messages) and have students make a list of five such messages and their meanings. Some examples follow.

- Pat on the back. *(You're great.)*

- Hug. *(I love you.)*

- Wave. *(good-bye)*

- Wave with both arms. *(all clear)*

- Make a "V" with index and middle fingers. *(peace, victory)*

- Wink. *(special connection, friendship)*

Evaluation and Feedback

Distribute copies of Figure 19 (Get the Message?). Have students complete as instructed. Evaluate for understanding of nonverbal communication. Answers: 1–a, 2–a, 3–b, 4–b, 5–b, 6–b. Responses may vary; if so, have students offer rationales for their decisions.

CLOSING

Summary

In this lesson we learned that we can communicate without words. We send messages through our body language, facial expressions, proximity, and use of time. Nonverbal communication is different in different cultures. In a society made up of many cultural groups, we must be open-minded in interpreting nonverbal communication.

Generalization

Select from the following activities.

1. Direct students to observe and record proximity zones among family members and in the community. Help students raise their awareness of their own comfortable proximity zone with different people.

2. Direct students to examine family pictures and focus on the facial expressions and body language of family members. Suggest comparing actual feelings and feelings suggested in the pictures. Ask, "Why do you suppose our nonverbal messages in pictures are not always a true reflection of our personality? Or are they?"

3. Collect pictures of people from newspapers and magazines. Analyze body language and facial expressions.

ENRICHMENT

1. Encourage students to write a poem on an aspect of nonverbal communication (for example, personal space, eye contact, gestures).

2. Present the following scenario and discuss cultural differences in nonverbal communication and response to authority:

   The principal caught a group of male students smoking in the rest room. He suspended the whole group, including a Native American student. The principal explained to the student's mother that, although her son had not been seen smoking, he was assumed guilty because he would not make eye contact or assertively defend himself when questioned. The principal was surprised at the student's involvement because he was a good student and had never been in trouble prior to this incident.

Nonverbal Messages

Name: _____ Date:_____

Make a list of five nonverbal messages and their meanings. For example, if you make a circle with your thumb and your index finger, the message is "OK!"

1. _____
   _____

   The message is: _____

2. _____
   _____

   The message is: _____

3. _____
   _____

   The message is: _____

4. _____
   _____

   The message is: _____

5. _____
   _____

   The message is: _____

Figure 18

Get the Message?

Name: _____ Date:_____

Read the scenario, then circle the letter that best answers the following questions.

One day, Yolanda overheard two students whispering that they had seen her boyfriend Tony at the skating rink with Judy, Yolanda's best friend. Yolanda rushed over to Judy, seated nearby. She put her face 2 inches from Judy's face and accused her friend of stealing her boyfriend. At first, Judy raised her eyebrows; then she squinted her eyes and pressed her lips together. She eventually got up and ran out crying.

1. When Yolanda put her face close to Judy's, she:
   a. invaded Judy's personal zone.
   b. wanted to look at Judy's eyes.
   c. demonstrated appropriate proximity.

2. Yolanda's attitude and behavior was coming from her:
   a. Impulsive Me.
   b. Bossy Me.
   c. Thinking Me.

3. At the beginning of the confrontation, Judy was:
   a. angry.
   b. surprised.
   c. frustrated.

4. Judy's second facial expression (squinting her eyes and pressing her lips together) indicated that she was:
   a. trying to focus on Yolanda's face.
   b. letting Yolanda know that she was getting angry.
   c. thinking and trying to compose herself.

5. Judy's body language sent the following message:
   a. that she was happy to see her friend.
   b. that she was upset.
   c. that she wanted to study.

6. When Judy ran out crying, her body language was:
   a. assertive.
   b. nonassertive.
   c. aggressive.

Figure 9

SOCIAL NEEDS, SOCIAL DEEDS

GOAL

- To recognize social aspects of communication

OBJECTIVES

- Recognizing that communication fulfills a social need
- Recognizing that malicious gossip is a negative form of communication
- Identifying types of communication in different cultures and subgroups
- Understanding the role of technology in social communication

MATERIALS

- Communication Matching (Figure 20)
- Responsible Answers (Figure 21)

PROCEDURE

OPENING

Review

In our last lesson we learned that we can communicate without talking. We send messages through our body language, facial expressions, proximity, and use of time. Nonverbal communication is different in different cultures and may be misunderstood in a society that has many different cultural groups.

Follow up on any generalization activities assigned during the last lesson.

Stating Objectives

In this lesson we will learn that good communicators are aware of the social conventions of communication. Malicious gossip is a hurtful way of communicating and can destroy relationships. We will examine how different cultures communicate and look at how language and systems of communication have been influenced by technological advances.

INSTRUCTION

Teaching and Guided Discussion

● —————— **Recognizing that communication fulfills a social need**

Why do you think people need to communicate with one another?

Elicit responses and discuss.

Communication is a social need, a human need. Communication helps develop relationships. What are some social groups that you belong to?

Elicit responses and discuss—include school, home, and community.

Positive interactions make us feel part of a group. Contact with other humans lessens our loneliness, provides stimulation, and helps us grow and learn to know ourselves better. We establish friendships through communication. We talk about movies, ball games, and other topics. We tell jokes and laugh; we get hurt and cry.

We also get to know ourselves by communicating with others. If you keep telling me I'm no good, I might begin to believe I'm a loser. But if you tell me I'm great, I can try to live up to your expectations. The effects people have on one another come largely from the messages they send and receive.

● —————— **Recognizing that malicious gossip is a negative form of communication**

Negative talk takes many shapes and forms. Malicious gossip is idle talk or spiteful hearsay. Communicating malicious gossip can deeply hurt people. Some people are entertained by repeating or hearing gossip. Others gossip to be part of the group. They feel that they will not be accepted if they don't participate. Do you know of anyone who has spread malicious gossip? How would you feel if someone gossiped about you?

Elicit responses and discuss.

People who gossip with the intent to hurt others are immature and insensitive to the feelings of others. Malicious gossip creates bad feelings and can destroy relationships and reputations.

Before spreading gossip, we need to empathize—put ourselves in the other person's shoes. People who gossip frequently assume an Impulsive Me or a Bossy Me attitude. It is very important to use a Thinking Me attitude in social situations. We all like to talk about each other, but before we do we need to STOP and THINK about what we are about say. Will our talk negatively affect someone? If so, we need to PLAN to redirect our conversation toward something else. We need to CHECK our plan and our feelings.

Identifying types of communication in different cultures and subgroups

Members of every society adopt certain customs in communication. For instance, when meeting somebody for the first time you may shake hands, simply say hello, or say, "I'm pleased to meet you." In many cultures people may embrace, or hug, when meeting friends. The main thing is that we show polite signs of acknowledgment. When we meet people from a different culture, we make them feel welcome by communicating and including them in our social group. We can learn their ways of communicating as they learn ours.

Many people from different countries are able to speak two or three languages—they are bilingual or trilingual. Why is it an advantage to be able to speak more than one language?

Discuss, pointing out how being multilingual can increase understanding and appreciation of other cultures.

Every social group has its own "sublanguage," or slang. Slang is the common talk we use with our friends. When I was a teenager, the word "bad" meant "not good." What does "bad" mean to you now?

Let students respond. Elicit discussion and compare the slang vocabulary of your group with the slang vocabulary 15 years or so ago.

Past	Present
hip	cool
sunglasses	shades
neat	awesome
stereo	boom-box
groovy	bad

Understanding the role of technology in social communication

In the 1930s and 1940s the radio was regarded as a miraculous system of communication. Then in the 1950s came television. Now the computer is changing communication worldwide. Countries are now connected through the "information superhighway," or Internet. Many schools encourage the use of computers for communication. Sending electronic messages (e-mail) over the Internet is an exciting way to communicate across geographical boundaries. For instance, a professor at Cornell University had been using the Internet to communicate with children in Bosnia. He found out that they needed pencils and paper and other school supplies. The professor raised money, bought the supplies, and personally delivered them to the children in Bosnia.

In addition to computers, cellular phones, telephone answering machines, and beepers have also changed the way people communicate. Technology is good, but we must not forget that the oldest and best means of communication is person to person.

Monitoring Knowledge and Comprehension

Ask the following questions and discuss.

1. Name some positive outcomes of social communication.

2. How can you politely refuse to listen to malicious gossip?

3. Do you know people from a culture different from yours? How is their way of communicating different? How is it the same?

4. How has technology changed the way the world communicates?

Guided Practice

Read the following situations to the entire group and ask the related questions.

1. Once upon a time a man climbed to the top of a hill, carrying a feather pillow. He ripped open the pillow and spread the feathers all over the valley.

   How is this story like the spread of malicious gossip?

   Will the man be able to retrieve all the feathers? Why or why not?

2. Amelia calls Nicole. Nicole is not home, so Amelia leaves a message and says, "Guess what? I saw Tyrone and Consuela at the store and they were . . ." Then the answering machine cuts off. Nicole hears part of the message, invents the rest, and spreads the gossip.

   Who might be hurt?

   What could Nicole do to repair the damage?

   What could Amelia do?

Assessing Mastery

Distribute copies of Figure 20 (Communication Matching) and have students complete. Answers: 1–g, 2–d, 3–a, 4–e, 5–f, 6–b, 7–c.

RETEACHING

Independent Practice

Pair students and allow about 5 minutes of conversation per student. Instruct the students to take turns telling each other about a goal, a wish, or anything else they would like to share about themselves. Direct students to introduce their partners to the group.

Evaluation and Feedback

Distribute copies of Figure 21 (Responsible Answers) and have students complete as instructed. Evaluate for understanding of the need to communicate in a socially acceptable manner.

CLOSING

Summary

Effective communicators are aware of the social aspects of communication. Malicious gossip is a hurtful communication and can cause trouble and destroy friendships. Different cultures have different ways of communicating. Language and systems of communication are continuously evolving and have been greatly influenced by technology.

Generalization

Direct students to identify a person within their family, peer group, or neighborhood and to initiate a friendly conversation. Students should plan the conversation to find out what interests the person has, avoid gossip, and keep the conversation positive. Students then report their experiences to the class.

ENRICHMENT

1. Form small groups. Present each group with a topic and direct them to write a dialogue reflecting the principles of responsible social communication. Topics may include "A Camp Out," "A Sleepover," "A Birthday Party," "A Welcome Back to School Party," and so forth. Share dialogues.

2. Have students write and share an acrostic for the word *gossip*.

3. Present students with the following problem: "Ms. Clark is lost on a rural highway. She has a flat tire, and the road is deserted. Describe how technology could help her." This could be conducted as either an individual or small-group activity.

Communication Matching

Name: _____ Date:_____

Match each word to its definition.

1. gossip

2. interaction

3. customs

4. malicious

5. culture

6. evolving

7. slang

a. habits and modes of a social group

b. developing over time

c. common, everyday talk

d. a social communication

e. hateful and hurtful

f. a social group

g. rumor and slanderous talk

Figure 20

Responsible Answers

Name: _____ Date: _____

Provide a socially responsible answer you could give in each of the following situations.

1. Have you heard about Patty's reputation with the boys?

2. I'd like you to meet Ahmed, a new student from Egypt.

3. Can you believe Joshua dropped the pass in the game?

4. Honestly, Keisha, must you be such a creep?

5. Can you believe Trudy told that joke about James
    (a student with a learning disability)?

6. Matthew sent an e-mail message saying that he was 25 years old,
    but he's only 14.

Figure 21

107

UNPOLLUTED LANGUAGE

GOAL

- To recognize language taboos and learn the importance of using more acceptable words and expressions

OBJECTIVES

- Understanding what taboo language is and why it is used
- Examining the use of taboo language in various social groups
- Recognizing the link between taboo language and prejudice
- Finding acceptable substitutes for taboo language

MATERIALS

- What Would You Do? (Figure 22)
- A Kinder Way (Figure 23)
- Weekly movie supplements from the local newspaper
- Chalkboard or easel pad

PROCEDURE

OPENING

Review

In our last lesson we learned that effective communicators are aware of the social aspects of communication. Malicious gossip is a hurtful communication and can destroy friendships. Different cultures have different ways of communicating. Language and systems of communication have been greatly influenced by technological advance.

Follow up on any generalization activities assigned during the last lesson.

Stating Objectives

In this lesson we will learn about taboo language. Such taboos include curse words, which often cause students trouble. We will examine verbal taboos in various social groups. Certain language taboos promote prejudice and dissension. It is better to substitute more acceptable words and expressions.

INSTRUCTION

Teaching and Guided Discussion

● ———— Understanding what taboo language is and why it is used

Taboo language refers to verbal expressions unacceptable to or forbidden by society in general. Language taboos include curse words, slang words with derogatory connotations, negative references to family members, and insults to cultural and religious institutions.

When children first learn to talk, they imitate what they hear. They may hear unacceptable language but not understand its meaning. When they repeat these words, they receive plenty of negative attention from adults, which often causes them to say the taboo words again. Why do you think children continue to use these words in spite of the punishment they receive?

Elicit responses and discuss. Answers may include to draw attention, to make people laugh, to rebel against the punishment, and so forth.

Why do teenagers use taboo language?

Elicit responses and discuss. Answers may include to feel like part of a group, to rebel against authority, to hurt people, to express anger, to feel empowered, and so on.

● ———— Examining the use of taboo language in various social groups

Use of taboo language varies among people according to their age, gender, and social group. Adults have more freedom in the use of language than young people. For example, movies today are more explicit in their use of taboo language and the depiction of sex and violence. Ratings have therefore been assigned to certain movies to protect young people. Most societies allow men greater freedom in using taboo language. Males begin to use such expressions at an earlier age than females, although girls are increasingly using curse words. Why do you think this is happening?

Elicit responses and discuss. Answers may include the change in social expectations for women and the desensitization of society in accepting taboo language.

What social groups are less accepting of language taboos?

Elicit responses and discuss.

Formal groups at school, church, or the workplace generally strictly prohibit the use of this type of language. Other less formal groups, such as clubs, gangs, or cliques, may be more accepting. Acceptance also varies from family to family.

Everyone is exposed daily to taboo language, and I'm sure you already know a lot of these expressions. However, many students get in trouble or are even suspended from school because of their use of this kind of language. If you ever get the urge to use one of these expressions, you must STOP and THINK of the consequences. A Thinking Me attitude can give you a chance to consider where you are and who is around you. Make a PLAN to express yourself in an appropriate manner, then CHECK the results of your plan.

Recognizing the link between taboo language and prejudice

Taboo language involves not only cursing and swear words. Language offensive to people of certain races is called *racist* language. Language that degrades males or females is called *sexist* language. Demeaning language can also be directed toward older people (*ageist* language) or toward individuals from different countries, cultures, economic conditions, occupations, and religions. The use of such language reinforces negative stereotypes and prejudices.

Many confrontations begin because of the use of taboo language. Some people use these types of derogatory expressions to aggravate others and start trouble. These people are definitely not using the Thinking Steps. Instead, they are allowing their Impulsive Me attitude to control them.

The meaning of words changes over time, and we must become aware of these changes. For example, it is no longer appropriate to refer to someone as a "retarded person"; instead, we say a "person with a cognitive or mental disability." A person with a physical disability is referred to as being physically challenged, not crippled or handicapped. Can anyone tell me why?

Elicit responses.

Whenever we use the phrase "a retarded person," we imply that the retardation comes first and is more important than the person. However, when we use the expression "person with a mental disability," we put the person first. We are acknowledging that the person is a human being like everyone else who also happens to have a mental disability.

Finding acceptable substitutes for taboo language

If your language is causing you difficulties at home or in school, you can find alternatives for those problem expressions. If you can make up your own substitute words and phrases, they won't get you into trouble. For example, suppose you stub your toe and are inclined to say a curse word. What are some words you could use instead?

Elicit responses. Answers may include "Ow!" "Oops!" "Yikes," and any number of others.

The place and the situation will determine whether or not you get in trouble when using taboo expressions. By adopting a Thinking Me attitude, you will begin to monitor your speech when talking to teachers and other adults. When talking to your friends, you are less likely to be censored. However, it is good to avoid using taboo language to begin with, or it may become a habit that is hard to break.

Monitoring Knowledge and Comprehension

Ask the following questions and discuss.

1. Name some reasons people use taboo language.

2. Is it more acceptable for boys than for girls to use curse words? Why or why not?

3. Why is the use of derogatory words about people from different races, religions, or nationalities prejudicial and harmful?

4. When should you use a substitute word or phrase instead of a curse word or another taboo expression?

Guided Practice

Distribute copies of Figure 22 (What Would You Do?). Direct students to describe their reactions in writing to the situations. Discuss sample responses.

Assessing Mastery

Discuss the role taboo language plays in students' social world: at home, at school, and in the community. Evaluate students' understanding of the need to adjust language according to different social situations.

RETEACHING

Independent Practice

Select from the following activities.

1. For a month, collect the weekly movie supplement from the local newspaper. Distribute copies to students and direct them to make a list of the movies and their ratings. Discuss. Encourage students to express their opinions and guess the reasons for the ratings.

2. Explain that the words we choose to use often denote our feelings and beliefs. Distribute copies of Figure 23 (A Kinder Way) and direct students to substitute more appropriate words for those given.

Evaluation and Feedback

On the chalkboard or easel pad, list these words: sexist, substitutes, stereotypes, taboo, racist. *Read the following aloud and have students write down the word that completes the sentence. Discuss answers.*

1. _____ language is used to put down members of a certain race.

2. _____ language is used in reference to gender.

3. A language _____ refers to verbal behavior forbidden by society.

4. _____ are alternatives to inappropriate language.

5. Put-down language reinforces negative _____.

CLOSING

Summary

In this lesson we learned why people use taboo language. Taboo language often causes students trouble in schools. We examined verbal taboos in various social groups and learned that using certain words and expressions promotes prejudice and dissension. If we try, we can find acceptable substitutes for taboo language.

Generalization

Direct students to identify verbal taboos used in the home or in their peer group. Instruct students to develop substitutes for taboo words and to use them casually at home or at play without calling attention to the taboo alternatives. Explain how modeling more appropriate language can help others improve their language over time.

ENRICHMENT

1. Instruct students to use a journal to list their own problem expressions and more appropriate alternatives.

2. Have students find a solution to the following problem:

   > Your 4-year-old brother is quick to pick up inappropriate language from certain television programs. Your mother has tried talking to him and punishing him. She has even used soap to wash out his mouth every time she hears him utter a curse word. So far, nothing has worked. He enjoys the attention no matter how unpleasant it is. How can you help?

What Would You Do?

Name: _____ Date:_____

Describe how you would react assertively in the following situations.

1. You are in a group. Your friend is telling a racist joke.

2. A female student passes by, and a boy in your group makes a sexist remark about a particular part of her anatomy.

3. You slam the door on your foot and are about to yell out a swear word.

4. A group of your peers are using derogatory language to describe a student who has a physical disability.

5. Your group uses the word "mental" whenever someone acts silly. You have a cousin with mental retardation, and now someone calls you "mental."

6. Your friend makes fun of and imitates the accent of a student who has immigrated from another country.

7. On the playground, a student makes hurtful remarks about another student, who is overweight.

Figure 22

A Kinder Way

Name: _____ Date:_____

Think of a kinder, more appropriate way to word the following.

1. cripple_____

2. drop dead_____

3. babes _____

4. drug addict _____

5. fat _____

6. housewife_____

7. chairman _____

8. bum _____

9. old geezer _____

10. crazy _____

Figure 23

ROLE-PLAY: COMMUNICATION

CHARACTERS

Rose, Tulip, Daisy

SITUATION

Rose never listens unless the conversation involves gossip. Her comments are inappropriate, and her conversation is very self-centered. In addition, her voice is loud, and she stands very close to people when talking. She uses many taboo expressions and is constantly in trouble at school and at home. Rose is spending part of her summer vacation with her two favorite cousins, Tulip and Daisy, at their beach home. Upon arrival Rose can hardly wait to tell her cousins some juicy gossip.

*NOTE: Role-players should use "blankety-blank" or another acceptable substitute wherever
%#! appears.

Rose: Tulip, Daisy, did you hear about what happened to cousin Lily? She is in trouble because . . .

Tulip: Stop! We don't want to hear gossip. Lily is having a hard time. Let's talk about our summer plans. We . . .

Rose: *(Glaring at Tulip, with her hands on her hips)* *%#! you. *(Putting her face close to Tulip's)* You are such a goody-two-shoes. I heard the real story, and I know everything.

Daisy: *(Attempts to take Rose's arm and gently pull her away from Tulip.)* Rose, Rose, chill out. We are going to have fun. We love you, and we're glad you are here. Let's go inside, help you unpack, and decide what we are going to wear to the party tonight.

Rose: *(Not listening to a word)* I know about Lily, and she asked for it. She is a *%#!.

Tulip: Rose, back off and listen to Daisy. Let's have some fun.

A week later, Rose feels neglected by everybody. She is alone and unhappy. She wants to know why everybody is avoiding her, so she decides to ask Tulip and Daisy.

Rose: *%#!, I don't know why people don't like me.

Tulip: Hey, I hear you. You are unhappy because people don't like you.

Daisy: When you curse and stand too close to people, it makes them feel very uncomfortable.

Tulip:	Loud talking and negative body language are real turn-offs. Our friends don't go for that.
Rose:	Yeah, I've been trying to do better, but sometimes I forget. It's getting to be a habit with me.
Daisy:	I have an idea to help. Our counselor in school taught us to use substitute words for curse words. Maybe you could try that.
Tulip:	She told us to keep an arm's length distance when talking to people. She called that proximity control.
Daisy:	Yeah, and she told us that gossiping is not a way to make friends, especially malicious gossiping.
Rose:	Maybe all that stuff can help me. I'm glad you told me because I really want people to like me.

EVALUATION AND FEEDBACK

1. At what point in the conversation did Rose interrupt?

2. Explain how the cousins used active listening.

3. How was Rose's conversation inappropriate?

4. What type of nonverbal communication did Rose use?

5. How did the cousins respond to the gossip?

6. What advice did the cousins give Rose to help her eliminate her taboo language?

SKILL
AREA
3

RESPONSIBILITY

WHERE AM I GOING?

GOAL

- To plan long-term and short-term goals

OBJECTIVES

- Understanding the importance of independent goal setting
- Identifying global or long-term goals
- Developing short-term goals to reach global goals
- Recognizing the need for persistence and motivation in achieving goals

MATERIALS

- Goal-Setting Worksheet (Figure 24)
- Chalkboard or easel pad
- Paper and pencils

PROCEDURE

OPENING

Review

None needed.

Stating Objectives

In this lesson we will learn about goal setting. The ability to set and achieve goals helps us to grow in responsibility. Global or long-term goals can help us know which way we are heading. We can break up these global goals into smaller short-term goals to achieve success. Persistence and motivation are necessary to achieve the goals we set.

INSTRUCTION

Teaching and Guided Discussion

●————— **Understanding the importance of independent goal setting**

Goal setting is like following a map to reach a destination. A map gives us direction and purpose. So does goal setting. Teenagers often establish goals by following those of their peer group. Members of a peer group typically share similar goals. These goals may be productive or destructive.

To be able to make productive, independent goals, you need to STOP, THINK, PLAN, and CHECK. When in doubt, you may need to seek advice from experienced people who have your best interests at heart. But most of all, when it comes right down to it, you make your own decisions because you have to bear the outcomes of them. We all grow emotionally because of our experiences. I am still growing emotionally, even though I am not a teenager. Working to achieve constructive goals helps us to mature and become responsible.

●————— **Identifying global or long-term goals**

A goal is a target—an end to something that we want to achieve. We set global, long-term goals that may take a long time to accomplish and smaller short-term goals that help us perform daily tasks and eventually reach our major goals. Can you name some major goals you'd like to achieve?

Elicit responses and discuss.

Many teenagers plan global goals such as finishing high school, deciding on a career, going to college, becoming rich and famous, or getting married and raising a family.

Sometimes teenagers rebel against traditional goals set by their families. It is OK to set your own goals, but it is not OK if these goals are destructive, such as using alcohol or drugs or getting involved with a gang. It is OK to own your personal global goals, but it is also OK to be realistic, to listen and learn, and to examine all your options. It is also important to examine your strengths and limitations. *(Personalize the following example.)* For example, it would be foolish for me to set a goal to become a movie star because I don't have the acting talent.

Assertive people assume responsibility for achieving their goals. You must believe in yourself in order to achieve your goals. In setting goals you need to be realistic—otherwise you may get discouraged and give up. However, you can also have high expectations for yourself.

●————— **Developing short-term goals to reach global goals**

We need to set small or short-term goals to be able to achieve our global goals. To set goals, we need to be self-directed—to be our own person. We start by following the Thinking Steps. Our first step is to STOP and THINK of a goal. Then we make a PLAN to achieve the goal. We should examine all our alternatives before we put our plan into effect. Finally, we CHECK to see how the plan is progressing.

Suppose your global goal is to get along better with a family member (mother, father, sister, brother). How would you go about breaking that long-term goal into smaller steps?

Lead students in reducing the global goal of getting along with a family member into several smaller goals. Write students' responses on the chalkboard or easel pad, following the format given in the sample Goal-Setting Worksheet below.

Goal-Setting Worksheet

Global Goal   I will reduce the number of arguments with my mother by at least 50 percent for the next 3 months.

Short-Term Goals

1. I will do my daily chores.

2. I will follow my curfew time.

3. I will make time to listen to and visit with my mother at least three times a week.

4. I will make time to engage in a fun activity (lunch, movie, bowling, playing cards) with my mother once a month.

5. I will calmly discuss and find solutions to problems and will avoid yelling and name calling.

●————— **Recognizing the need for persistence and motivation in achieving goals**

Persistence and motivation are two ingredients necessary in achieving goals. Keeping a journal of your daily activities can help you to be aware of your progress. Evaluate your efforts periodically. Is your strategy working? If not, try an alternative one. Above all, don't give up. Whenever you feel discouraged, find a support group or a person who will listen to and encourage you.

Monitoring Knowledge and Comprehension

Ask the following questions and discuss.

1. Why is it important to set your own goals?

2. Harry says, "I never make global goals because I can never reach them." Is Harry correct in his assumption? Why or why not?

3. Break up the following global goal into short-term goals: "I will have enough money to buy a car by the time I am 18 years old."

4. At this point, you are 13 years old and only have 25 dollars saved toward your goal of buying a car. How can you keep up your motivation and persist to achieve your goal?

Guided Practice

Have students work individually or in small groups to develop a plan to reach the goal described in the following scenario.

Your goal is to buy a pair of roller blades. They cost 79 dollars, and you only have 25 dollars. How can you achieve your goal? Develop a plan. In your plan consider the following:

- *Time:* What is your target date? How much time do you have to raise the money?

- *Resources:* What can you do to raise the money?

- *Energy:* How much energy are you willing to exert to achieve your goal?

Assessing Mastery

Discuss the following ideas as a group.

1. What are the goals that you hope to accomplish by age 20, 30, 40, 50, 60?

2. You just won 10 million dollars in the lottery. What are some of your short-term and long-term goals?

3. You have a year to live. You feel fine and full of energy. What goals would you like to accomplish?

4. What goals have you accomplished this week?

RETEACHING

Independent Practice

Have students develop a career goal, considering the following factors. Stress the need to be creative and have high aspirations but also the importance of being realistic in choices.

- *Work environment:* indoors or outdoors, with many people or few

- *Personal values:* helping others, recognition, money, competitive or noncompetitive situation

- *Personality:* creative, logical, introverted, extroverted, organized, spontaneous, low energy, high energy

- *Education:* high school diploma, college degree
- *Special skills:* math, science, art, music, writing
- *Previous experiences:* past employment, volunteer work, school-related experiences

Evaluation and Feedback

Reconvene as a group and discuss students' career goals and specific plans to achieve them. Evaluate for self-understanding and realistic thinking; give feedback and have other group members give feedback on the plans.

CLOSING

Summary

In this lesson we learned that we can grow in maturity and responsibility by setting goals. We can set long-term, global goals and smaller short-term goals. Our short-term goals help us achieve our global goals. We need to be realistic and consider our strengths, energy, and motivation in developing goals. Persistence and motivation are necessary to reach goals.

Generalization

Direct students to choose two or three long-term personal goals and, using copies of Figure 24 (Goal-Setting Worksheet), break these goals into smaller steps. The goals may be cognitive (e.g., to get better grades), affective (e.g., to make more friends), or psychomotor (e.g., to excel in a sport). Direct students to make their choices according to their interests and motivation. Encourage students to keep a journal over the next several weeks (or longer) to document their progress toward their goals.

ENRICHMENT

Discuss the following sayings and poem. Develop a bulletin board to display students' own contributions on this theme.

> To accomplish great things, we must not only act, but also dream
> —not only plan, but also believe.
>
> *—Anatole France*

> The great thing in this world
> Is not so much where we are
> But in what direction we are moving.
>
> *—Oliver Wendell Holmes*

> Where there is a will, there is a way.

> Bury not your talent, but persist and you will succeed.

> Intelligence comes from your intellect, but motivation comes from your soul.

Goal-Setting Worksheet

Name: _____ Date:_____

Global Goal

_____

_____

_____

Short-Term Goals

1._____

_____

2._____

_____

3._____

_____

4._____

_____

5._____

_____

Figure 24

I Did It Myself

GOAL

- To complete assigned tasks independently

OBJECTIVES

- Recognizing that task completion requires self-direction
- Recognizing the need for self-discipline to complete tasks independently
- Developing and sustaining motivation to complete tasks
- Establishing helpful strategies to complete tasks

MATERIALS

- Your Emotional Quotient (Figure 25)
- Self-Direction Review (Figure 26)
- Chalkboard or easel pad
- Old magazines
- Art supplies (butcher paper, markers, crayons, glue)

PROCEDURE

OPENING

Review

In our last lesson we learned that we can grow in responsibility and become more productive by setting goals. We can set short-term goals and long-term goals. Setting short-term goals helps us achieve our long-term goals. We need to be realistic and consider our strengths, energy, and motivation in developing goals. Persistence and motivation are necessary to achieve goals.

Follow up on any generalization activities assigned during the last lesson.

Stating Objectives

In this lesson we will learn that task completion requires emotional intelligence as well as intellectual intelligence. We all need self-discipline to complete tasks independently, especially when we do not like a task. Motivation gives us the drive needed to complete tasks. We can develop strategies to help meet our responsibilities and complete tasks.

INSTRUCTION

Teaching and Guided Discussion

● ———— **Recognizing that task completion requires self-direction**

When required to complete a task, do you ever say, "I don't feel like doing it?" You may be able to do the job very well, but your emotional state is not "with it." Whenever you are emotionally involved in a task, you become more competent. Why?

Elicit responses and discuss.

You become more involved because you are interested in the task. The psychologist Daniel Goleman believes that people who are strong in emotional intelligence lead happier, more productive lives. Some people may have high cognitive intelligence (IQ) and low emotional intelligence (EQ). People with high EQ use their feelings to reach good decisions. They are able to manage anger and tolerate frustration. They know how to stay motivated and be upbeat in spite of setbacks. They are empathetic and get along with most people. They are able to delay gratification and consider consequences. Which do you think is more important, IQ or EQ?

Elicit responses and discuss. Emphasize the idea that both are important but that in many situations EQ may be even more important than IQ. Instruct students to complete Figure 25 (Your Emotional Quotient) and discuss.

The word *self* is important because no one can make you grow emotionally. You must do it yourself. Throughout life you will have to accomplish certain tasks. Some tasks you will like, and some you won't. You can train yourself to be independently productive by increasing your EQ.

● ———— **Recognizing the need for self-discipline to complete tasks independently**

Why do you suppose we procrastinate, or keep putting off, some tasks?

Elicit responses and discuss. Answers may include our belief that the task is not enjoyable or important or that the task is too difficult.

Note: The ideas presented here are drawn generally from Daniel Goleman's book *Emotional Intelligence: Why It Can Matter More than IQ* (New York: Bantam, 1995).

You need to be self-disciplined to overcome all of these barriers. When you were in elementary school, your teachers and parents often helped you complete tasks. You may have become dependent on that help and come to expect some external force to help you with all your work. As you mature, you are expected to develop an internal force. In short, you become your own parent. You must develop the willpower to accomplish tasks independently. Most teenagers want to be independent, but independence is paired with responsibility. Can you give me some examples?

Elicit responses and discuss. Some possible responses follow.

- To participate in a sports activity (track, basketball, swimming), you must train every day.

- To enjoy a leisure activity, you must first finish your homework.

- To avoid a last-minute rush completing a project, you must set and achieve smaller work goals.

Developing and sustaining motivation to complete tasks

I find it very difficult to complete a task when I don't particularly want to do it. When has this happened to you?

Elicit responses and discuss.

Nobody can motivate you. Adults and friends may help, your environment may help, and the task itself can help by being interesting. But only you can motivate yourself. I sometimes have to give myself a lecture to motivate myself to complete my work. I often self-talk, and I hear a recording of my Bossy Me saying, "Stop fooling around and get to work." Why do you think we need to avoid giving ourselves too many of these Bossy Me messages?

Elicit responses and discuss. Answers may include that we get not-OK feelings, that guilt doesn't help us get the task done, or that such messages are bad for our self-esteem.

My Caring Me attitude also gives me advice. It helps me to care about myself and urges me to get to work. But it is my Thinking Me attitude that helps me focus and develop a plan to complete my task. A Thinking Me attitude helps me develop a strong will. The stronger the force within me, the less outside control I need. I use my Thinking Steps: I STOP, THINK, PLAN, and CHECK to reach my goal.

Establishing helpful strategies to complete tasks

Eventually, you will adopt your own strategies suited to your own learning style and personality. But let's examine some basic strategies that can help you complete tasks within an expected time limit. One strategy is to identify all the tasks that have to be completed.

On the chalkboard or easel pad, write the heading, "Things I Have to Do Today." List a number of important tasks (for example, grading essays, meeting with the principal, making family phone calls, paying bills, picking up laundry).

After I make my list, I prioritize and number each task according to its importance. I think writing bills is the most important. My creditors will charge additional money if I don't pay my bills on time. So I move that to the top of the list. I think the principal really needs to meet with me, so I'll do that second. You may be disappointed if I don't get your essays graded, so I'll do that next. My family is important to me, so I make sure I call them on the phone. Last is picking up my laundry. I can do that on my way home. I rewrite the list to show the new order of importance, then check off each task as I complete it.

Illustrate.

Another strategy for school involves keeping a record sheet of weekly assignments. Identify the subject, the assignment, and the date the assignment is due. Check off each assignment as you complete it.

Illustrate on the chalkboard or easel pad. An example follows.

Subject	Assignment	Date due
Math	p. 44, do all even numbers	9/12, Period 3
English	Essay on field trip	9/14, Period 1
Science	Oral report/photosynthesis	9/16, Period 2

Monitoring Knowledge and Comprehension

Ask and discuss the following questions.

1. Why does task completion require self-direction?

2. Why do people who lack self-discipline procrastinate in completing tasks?

3. How can you develop the motivation to complete a task you don't particularly like?

4. Describe a strategy that can help you complete a task independently.

Guided Practice

Divide students into small groups. Give each group a sheet of butcher paper, old magazines, and other art supplies. Direct each group to develop a collage or a mural on a given theme. (Because the focus of this activity is the process, topics may be anything currently relevant to the class.) Each member of the group must assume responsibility for a specific task. Give the following planning steps.

1. Make a list of activities.

2. Prioritize your activities.

3. Decide who will do what.

4. Make a plan for how each activity can be completed independently.

Assessing Mastery

Reassemble in the larger group, share collages, and discuss students' experiences working together. How did the group prioritize activities? Who did what? Did each member contribute? What could have made the process more efficient?

RETEACHING

Independent Practice

Distribute copies of Figure 26 (Self-Direction Review) and have students complete.

Evaluation and Feedback

Discuss students' answers; evaluate for comprehension and give feedback as appropriate.

CLOSING

Summary

In this lesson we learned that to complete a task requires self-direction. Self-discipline and a Thinking Me attitude are needed to persevere and avoid procrastination. To complete a task independently, you need to develop internal control. Nobody can motivate you, but you can motivate yourself. We discussed strategies that can help you become responsible and self-disciplined in accomplishing tasks independently.

Generalization

Direct students to devise a plan to complete a home chore (mowing the lawn, cleaning the garage, folding clothes) or a community activity (picking up litter, helping the Little League team, or tutoring a younger child or a peer with a learning disability). Allow time for students to put their plans into effect, then guide classroom discussion of the outcomes.

ENRICHMENT

1. Direct students to respond to the following "Dear Ann Flanders" letter.

   Dear Ann Flanders:

   I am a 12-year-old boy, and I have a problem. My mother expects me to finish all my homework as soon as I get home. After finishing my homework, I am expected to empty the dishwasher and put away the breakfast dishes. My sister is responsible for cleaning up after dinner. I frequently procrastinate and get into trouble. What can I do to complete all my tasks and still have some time for fun?

   —*Funless in Seattle*

2. Divide students into groups of five. Instruct each group to devise a plan to complete a school assignment (for example, presenting a specific chapter from a history or science text). Explain that each member of the group is responsible for a specific concept or section and will need to research additional information and confer with the group prior to a general presentation.

3. Have students brainstorm mottos with the theme "Getting the Job Done." For example: "Don't put off until tomorrow what you can do today" and "If you want something done right, do it yourself." Encourage them to compose their own mottos to add to the list.

Your Emotional Quotient

Name: _____ Date:_____

Check the "Yes" or "No" box to show whether the following statements are true for you.

10 yes	= Very high EQ
8–9 yes	= Fairly high EQ
6–7 yes	= Average EQ
4–5 yes	= Low EQ
2–3 yes	= Very low EQ
0–1 yes	= Danger zone

	Yes	No
1. Can you wait for reinforcement (reward or praise) for at least 5 hours?	☐	☐
2. Do you empathize with people in trouble and understand how they feel?	☐	☐
3. Do you persist with a difficult task until it is done?	☐	☐
4. Can you motivate yourself, even if the task is boring or difficult?	☐	☐
5. Can you control your temper in a difficult situation?	☐	☐
6. Do you complete household tasks without getting paid or rewarded?	☐	☐
7. Do you find it easy to wait for your turn to speak without interrupting?	☐	☐
8. Can you work cooperatively in a group without always wanting your way?	☐	☐
9. When you are in a bad mood, can you act pleasant to others?	☐	☐
10. Can you analyze or think things through when you feel frustrated or angry?	☐	☐

Figure 25

Self-Direction Review

Name: _____ Date:_____

Answer the following statements true (T) or false (F).

_____ 1. Self-talk can help in thinking and planning to achieve goals independently.

_____ 2. Prioritizing activities is a waste of time.

_____ 3. Keeping a list is a helpful strategy for independently completing school assignments.

_____ 4. Intelligent people do not need a strong emotional intelligence because they are smart anyway.

Answer the following questions as instructed.

1. Name three ways you can develop your emotional intelligence.

2. Which of the following is an example of external control? *(Check one.)*

☐ The teacher helps you locate Australia on the map.

☐ You find a globe and locate Australia on the map.

3. Why is it important to use your Thinking Me to help you complete tasks independently?

Figure 26

UNDERSTANDING DIRECTIONS

GOAL

- To follow and give directions

OBJECTIVES

- Understanding the importance of following directions
- Learning how to follow directions
- Recognizing when to ignore directions
- Assuming leadership in giving directions

MATERIALS

- Understanding Directions (Figure 27)
- Chalkboard or easel pad
- Art supplies (poster board, buttons, construction paper, markers)

PROCEDURE

OPENING

Review

In our last lesson we learned that completing tasks independently requires self-direction. You need strong emotional intelligence to motivate yourself and persist when tasks are difficult. To complete tasks independently you need to develop internal controls and rely less on external controls. We discussed strategies that can help you become more responsible and self-disciplined in accomplishing tasks.

Follow up on any generalization activities assigned during the last lesson.

Stating Objectives

In this lesson we will learn the importance of understanding directions. It is better to follow directions without constant reminders; however, there are times when it is OK to ignore directions. We will talk about why it is important to give directions in a clear and understandable manner.

INSTRUCTION

Teaching and Guided Discussion

● ——— **Understanding the importance of following directions**

> We all follow directions from somebody else at one time or another. To be able to follow directions is important at every age and in every phase of your life. You will be expected to accept and follow directions at school, at home, and later on at work. Can you think of times it is critical to follow instructions?

Elicit responses and discuss. Answers may include following instructions from your physician or dentist, from rescue personnel during a fire or accident, from a map to find an address, and so on.

> Why should students follow directions in schools and adults follow instructions at work?

Elicit responses and discuss. Answers may include to learn, to show respect for authority, to maintain order, to accomplish tasks.

● ——— **Learning how to follow directions**

> Have you ever heard an adult ask, "How many times do I have to tell you to _____ ?" Taking the initiative means doing something without having to be told. To be responsible you must be able to follow directions without continual reminders. Can you follow directions without being told? *(Students respond.)* When do you think you need reminders?

Elicit responses and discuss.

> It is easier to follow directions when they are given clearly and directly. However, sometimes directions are difficult to follow. To follow directions, you need to listen attentively, be assertive, and ask questions whenever you do not understand. Ask the person to repeat the directions if necessary and then silently restate them to yourself. Show you understand, then follow through.

● ——— **Recognizing when to ignore directions**

> In some situations, it is unwise to follow directions. When should you ignore directions?

Answers may include directions from a peer to destroy property or engage in illegal activities. To emphasize this point you may wish to remind students that, after World War II, Nazi war criminals said they were just following directions from their superiors to excuse the murder of millions of Jews and other political prisoners.

> If directions result in harm to self or others, it is best to ignore them. Use your Thinking Me attitude and decide whether you are willing to follow the directions. Express your decision and explain your reasons if you decide not to follow the directions. Use self-talk and the Thinking Steps—STOP, THINK, PLAN, and CHECK—to help you analyze the situation. Remember to predict consequences of following or not following certain directions.

Let's suppose I have a terrible headache and my friend gives me her own prescription medicine to help me. She tells me to follow the directions on the bottle carefully. Should I take the medicine? Why or why not?

Elicit responses and discuss. Reasons not to take the medicine are that it was prescribed for the friend's use, not your own; that you don't know the side effects; and that you may have a medical condition your friend does not that would mean you should not take the medicine.

●——— Assuming leadership in giving directions

Assertive people are able to assume leadership and give directions to achieve goals and complete tasks. They are responsible and can assign responsibility without a Bossy Me attitude. Assertive leaders use the Thinking Steps to make a plan and accomplish parts of the plan.

If you are giving directions, you must make sure that the instructions are clear and understandable. Limit the number of directions—keep them short. Giving too many directions at once may be confusing and frustrating for all involved. Check to make sure everyone understands. If more than a few steps are involved, give reminders. Be considerate and willing to change the directions as long as they lead to the goal.

A good leader knows how to delegate responsibility. A "self-starter" is a person with initiative who does not need to be told constantly what to do. A leader can delegate responsibility to self-starters and have them show other group members how to follow directions.

Monitoring Knowledge and Comprehension

Direct students to answer the questions on Figure 27 (Understanding Directions). Discuss.

Guided Practice

Divide students into small groups. Give each group an assortment of art materials and ask them to create a new game. Each group must create the components of the game (game pieces, spinners, consequence cards) and write the complete game directions. Upon completion, have each group instruct class members on how to play the game. Students then play the games by following the directions.

Assessing Mastery

Ask students to tell which of the following directions is easier to follow and to explain their choice.

1. Read the play on page 43 to 56 together. You may discuss, but use very soft voices. Answer briefly, in one to two sentences, the five questions I have given you. *(Write "soft voice" and "five questions" on the chalkboard or easel pad as a reminder.)* When you are finished, you may read your library book. Do you have any questions?

2. Read the play together, but you may not use loud voices because that may disturb the class next door. We do not want to upset that teacher, do we? She certainly deserves some peace and quiet. You will answer all the questions I have given you, and I expect your answers to be acceptable, not like the last time. They were far too short.

RETEACHING

Independent Practice

Divide students into groups and direct each group to choose a leader. Take the leaders aside and tell them to give specific instructions to the group to complete a task. The leaders must take the initiative and direct the group to finish the task. Steps in decorating a bulletin board are given as an example.

1. Assemble your group and together decide on a theme (springtime).
2. As a group, decide on a design (flying kites).
3. List items needed to complete the design (kites, flowers, trees, grass, sun).
4. Make a list of materials needed and obtain (construction paper, markers, magazines).
5. Assign responsibilities to each member (creating borders, letters, figures).
6. Start work on the design.
7. Complete task.
8. Evaluate your project.

Evaluation and Feedback

Evaluate and discuss group members' ability to follow the leader's directions in the previous activity. Include consideration of the need to follow instructions, assume responsibility, and exhibit self-starting behaviors. Discuss when a leader should tell people what to do and when he or she should delegate responsibility and allow other group members to take the initiative.

CLOSING

Summary

We learned in this lesson that it is important to follow directions. Responsible people can follow instructions without constant reminders. Directions that are harmful to ourselves or others must be ignored. Good leaders make sure that their directions are clear. They keep their directions short and to the point, check to make sure their directions are understood, and give reminders when more than a few steps are involved.

Generalization

Direct students to identify an issue in the local or world community. Use newspapers, TV, or radio newscasts. Direct them to brainstorm possible solutions, choose a solution, and develop a plan. Evaluate how accurately the students followed your instructions.

ENRICHMENT

1. Have students unscramble a list of directions. For example:

   Parent Program

   Welcome the parents.

   Send invitations.

   Appoint an entertainment committee.

   Develop the program.

   Organize committees.

   Get a list of parents.

   Appoint a refreshment committee.

   Elect a chairperson for the program.

2. Direct students to develop a list of directions applicable to the work world. Share and discuss. For example:

   Babysitting

   Call and confirm beginning and ending times of the job.

   Agree on fee per hour and per child.

   Obtain a phone number where parents can be reached and other emergency numbers.

   Obtain a list of children's activities (appropriate games, snack time, storytime, bedtime).

Understanding Directions

Name: _____ Date: _____

Choose whether the following statements are true (T) or false (F).

_____ 1. To follow directions independently, a person must be constantly reminded.

_____ 2. Directions should be given clearly and in a limited number.

_____ 3. It is easy to complete a task when you ignore the directions.

_____ 4. A good leader must do all parts of the task.

_____ 5. Directions must be followed all the time.

Answer the following questions.

1. Why is it important to follow directions?

2. What can you do when you do not understand directions?

3. Name an instance when you ignored a direction. Why did you choose to ignore it?

4. Name two important considerations when giving directions.

Figure 27

LET ME CHECK

GOAL

- To identify and apply self-management skills

OBJECTIVES

- Understanding how self-instruction applies to various tasks
- Creating self-recording strategies
- Self-evaluating and modifying plans
- Self-rewarding when plans are successful

MATERIALS

- Self-Management Review (Figure 28)
- Scott's New Me (Figure 29)

PROCEDURE

OPENING

Review

In our last lesson we learned that it is important to follow directions. Responsible people follow instructions without constant reminders. To follow directions, you need to listen attentively, be assertive, and ask questions whenever you do not understand. Directions harmful to ourselves or to others must be ignored. Good leaders check the effectiveness of their directions. They keep their directions clear, short, and to the point; check to make sure the directions are understood; and give reminders when more than a few steps are involved.

Follow up on any generalization activities assigned during the last lesson.

Stating Objectives

In this lesson you will learn how to be your own teacher. You will also learn how to keep track of and record your own behaviors. When you manage yourself, you are able to evaluate your own behavior, make plans, and change your plans when needed.

INSTRUCTION

Teaching and Guided Discussion

●————— **Understanding how self-instruction applies to various tasks**

Self-instruction means teaching or instructing ourselves. Nobody can make you learn if you don't want to learn. A teacher is a facilitator of learning. What does that mean?

Elicit responses and discuss.

A teacher helps us, but we are really responsible for our own learning. We teach ourselves all the time and often use self-talk to help ourselves complete a task. Did you ever learn a task without having someone teach it to you?

Elicit responses and discuss.

(Personalize the following example.) I never learned how to type in school. When I bought a computer I realized that I needed the skill. I talked myself (self-talked) into buying the appropriate software program and taught myself how to type.

By becoming your own teacher, you are showing responsibility and taking the initiative for your own instruction. That's not easy, especially with difficult tasks. Most students are accustomed to having other people teach them and tell them what to do. This may be fine in elementary school, but now you are maturing and receiving less direct instruction. Adults expect you to assume more responsibility for your own learning. To be able to self-instruct you need to use your Thinking Me attitude and your Thinking Steps much more often. You also need to be assertive and make choices.

●————— **Creating self-recording strategies**

A part of self-management is self-recording. We are often unaware of our actions. The purpose of self-recording is to increase our awareness by providing ourselves with a record of how often we are performing a certain behavior. Self-recording gives us feedback on our behavior. It is a concrete way of looking at what we do.

For example, let's suppose your mom constantly reminds you to clean up your room. Cleaning up your room is your "target behavior." A target behavior is a specific behavior you want to change or improve. You can start keeping a daily record of how many pieces of clothing or objects are left out of place and record this information on a chart. Then you can look at the chart and make a plan to reduce the number. Another example is using curse words in school. Cursing in school is a problem behavior. How could you use self-recording to decrease cursing?

Elicit responses.

You can record the number of times you use curse words and make a plan to reduce and then completely stop cursing. You can use tally marks, a golf counter, beads, and so forth to record the number of pieces of clothing on the floor or the times you use a curse word.

Another type of self-recording can help you improve at a task by recording the time it takes to complete—say, washing the dinner dishes. You can use a clock, a kitchen timer, or a sand timer. You can make a plan and set a specific time for completion. Writing in a journal is another good strategy to keep track of behavior.

Self-evaluating and modifying plans

Both strategies, self-instruction and self-recording, teach us to STOP, THINK, and PLAN to change behaviors. In addition, we also self-evaluate when we CHECK our plans. By looking back in a journal, for example, I can evaluate my progress and decide whether I need to continue with my plan or try another plan to achieve my goal. It would be ridiculous to repeat the same plan over and over again if it did not produce success. If my plan does not show results, I must go back to the drawing board and find an alternative plan. When I make a plan, I usually also think of an alternative. If Plan A backfires or doesn't work out, I can go to Plan B.

Self-rewarding when plans are successful

We all feel terrific when our school wins the track trophy or some other kind of award. On a personal basis, I feel wonderful when the principal, parents, or my students praise me for doing a great job. We all like recognition and an occasional pat on the back, and that's OK. But it is even greater to be able to recognize and reward your own accomplishments. Remember, you are your own best friend and you can count on yourself for the rest of your life. When you feel that you achieve even little successes, pat yourself on the back and feel proud.

You may even reward yourself. For example, if you have a problem staying on task when you are doing your homework, you may make a pact with yourself to take a 15-minute break for every hour you stay on task. You may call your friend on the phone or do something else that is rewarding to you, but only for 15 minutes. Use a kitchen timer to keep track of time. What other strategies can you use to reward yourself?

Share and discuss. Answers may include setting aside an hour every day for yourself to do a favorite activity, treating yourself to a favorite snack, or earning money to spend on something for yourself.

Monitoring Knowledge and Comprehension

Distribute copies of Figure 28 (Self-Management Review) and have students answer the questions. In Part I, Items 1, 4, 6, and 8 are types of self-instruction. Answers to Part II are as follows: 1–self-reward, 2–self-recording, 3–target behavior, 4–self-talk, 5–self-evaluation, 6–self-instruction, 7–initiative.

Guided Practice

Choose a brief videotape for students to view (your school librarian may be a good resource for locating an apppropriate one). Preview the video and select a target behavior of a character for students to record. Compare students' findings and discuss. Using the same video, instruct the students to identify self-instruction, self-evaluation, and self-reward strategies that could help any of the characters.

Assessing Mastery

Ask the following questions with respect to the videotape.

> 1. What was the real cause of the conflict?
>
> 2. Did the characters demonstrate self-discipline?
>
> 3. How did they act out their feelings?
>
> 4. How could they have redirected their emotions?

RETEACHING

Independent Practice

Divide students into small groups. Distribute copies of Figure 29 (Scott's New Me) and have students follow the instructions.

Evaluation and Feedback

Allow students to report their solutions to Scott's problems. Did they identify the target behaviors (asking for instructions, complaints)? Did they develop plans to eliminate these two behaviors? Did they include a plan for recording the target behaviors? Did their stories show Scott evaluating his plan and rewarding himself?

CLOSING

Summary

> In this lesson we learned that self-management includes self-instruction, self-recording, self-evaluation, and self-reward. These strategies help you become responsible and prepare you for adulthood.

Generalization

Instruct students to select a behavior they want to change at school, at home, or in the community. Have them record the number of times the target behavior occurs over a specific period of time. Direct students to make a plan to change the behavior, implement the plan, and graph frequency data. Have students evaluate the results of their plan by comparing the two sets of data. Sample target behaviors are as follows.

- Nail biting

- Interrupting

- Aggression (fighting, cursing, teasing)

- Tardiness

- Failing to complete tasks

- Arguing with parents or siblings

ENRICHMENT

1. Demonstrate helpful gadgets for self-recording. These may include golf counters, kitchen timers, alarm clocks, sand timers, beads, charts, and graphs. Ask students to come up with their own ways to self-record.

2. Direct students to record the number of times they hear you say "OK" during a 15-minute lecture. Tape your lecture and play it back to establish reliability.

Self-Management Review

Name: _____ Date: _____

Part I

Place a check mark beside each of the items that is a kind of self-instruction.

☐ 1. Get a book to read.

☐ 2. Listen to a lecture from a teacher.

☐ 3. Follow a tutor's instruction of an algebraic equation.

☐ 4. Observe and learn from another person's performance.

☐ 5. Get directions from parents.

☐ 6. Choose appropriate clothes.

☐ 7. Follow a football play as directed by the quarterback.

☐ 8. Create your own way to remember facts.

Part II

Complete the following sentences. Words to use: self-instruction, self-recording, initiative, self-talk, self-reward, self-evaluation, target behavior.

1. I treat myself to 30 minutes of watching television after 2 hours of work. I am using _____.

2. I am counting the times I say, "Oh, no!" I'm using _____.

3. A behavior I want to change is called a _____.

4. I think aloud to figure out a problem. I'm using _____.

5. My plan didn't work. I look back to see what went wrong. I am using _____.

6. I carefully read and follow the recipe to bake a cake. I'm using _____.

7. I don't wait for my mother to tell me to start my homework. I get started and stay on task. I am showing _____.

Figure 28

Scott's New Me

What can Scott do to regulate his behavior? Develop a plan for Scott. In your plan include self-instruction, self-recording, self-evaluation, and self-reward.

Scott is very nonassertive. He depends on everyone to give him instructions. Every afternoon during the week, he calls his friend Ronaldo and spends 45 minutes getting his homework assignment. He shows no initiative and complains that the teacher does not explain the lessons. He admires his friend Ronaldo, who is assertive and does not rely on the teacher for everything.

Figure 29

147

TAKING RESPONSIBILITY

GOAL

- To assume responsibility for personal actions

OBJECTIVES

- Defining behaviors involved in responsibility
- Recognizing the reasons for teenagers' drive for independence
- Recognizing that independence requires personal responsibility
- Identifying personal responsibilities and strategies to meet them

MATERIALS

- Taking Responsibility (Figure 30)
- Chalkboard or easel pad
- Paper and pencils

PROCEDURE

OPENING

Review

In our last lesson we learned that self-management includes self-instruction, self-recording, self-evaluation, and self-reward. These strategies help you develop responsibility and prepare for adulthood.

Follow up on any generalization activities assigned during the last lesson.

Stating Objectives

In this lesson we will examine the behaviors involved in responsibility. Teenagers want to be independent. They are at a time when they feel they can assume control of their lives. But independence requires responsibility. We all have certain responsibilities, and often these bring on stress. We will examine strategies to reduce these stressors and still meet our responsibilities.

INSTRUCTION

Teaching and Guided Discussion

●——— **Defining behaviors involved in responsibility**

Responsibility is the willingness and ability to accept duties, accept consequences, and be accountable for personal behaviors. Responsibility is a kind of trust and a sign of maturity and competency. Responsibility must accompany freedom. When we accept responsibility we grow in character and emotional intelligence.

Self-discipline allows us to delay gratification. What does it mean to delay gratification?

Elicit responses and discuss.

Delaying gratification means being able to wait for something that you want, set goals, practice self-control, and manage your own behavior. For example, many adults overspend on credit cards because they cannot wait to buy the things they want. Can you think of other examples of immediate gratification?

Elicit responses and discuss.

The Thinking Steps—STOP, THINK, PLAN, and CHECK—can help in times when you need to delay gratification. When you feel you want something right now, STOP and take a deep breath. THINK whether waiting might be more productive and make a PLAN to achieve your goal in a responsible way. Then CHECK your plan. Are you being responsible? If yes, you are on your way to independence.

●——— **Recognizing the reasons for teenagers' drive for independence**

Teenagers are looking forward to the time they can be free from the directions, rules, and regulations that come from adults. This goal is normal and healthy. Human beings follow a certain pattern in their physical and emotional growth.

Adolescence is a journey from childhood into adulthood. Teenagers are searching for their own identity and want to separate from their parents. They often seek the support of their friends. The group becomes the center of their existence, and they are very conscious of what the group thinks of them. They don't want to look, act, or speak differently from their friends. Unfortunately, some teenagers follow a group of friends who are involved in problem activities such as taking drugs or engaging in illegal acts.

It is difficult to be your own person during adolescence because those who are different are often regarded as weird. How can you keep your individuality and still be part of the group?

Elicit responses and discuss.

●——— **Recognizing that independence requires personal responsibility**

With freedom and independence comes responsibility. What does that mean? Can you give some examples?

Elicit responses and discuss. Answers may include getting an extended curfew (freedom) but needing to respect that curfew (responsibility) or attending unchaperoned events (freedom) but needing to be your own chaperone (responsibility).

Some people refuse to accept responsibility for their actions. They may project blame on others for their failures and their behaviors. Why do you think this is so?

Elicit responses and discuss. Examples may include pride, fear of punishment, fear of hurting someone else, embarrassment, or denial.

People have different reasons for blaming others. By placing the blame on others, they are denying responsibility.

It requires a great deal of courage to self-evaluate, admit fault, and accept consequences. We all make mistakes—nobody is perfect. Assertive people accept responsibility and consider the good of others as well as what is good for them. This requires a Thinking Me attitude, not an Impulsive Me attitude.

Independence requires strong emotional intelligence. A responsible person empathizes with others and is self-motivated, self-disciplined, and able to self-manage. Being independent is difficult, but it also feels wonderful.

Identifying personal responsibilities and strategies to meet them

We each have major responsibilities in our lives. The main responsibility of teachers is to help students learn. Teachers also have personal responsibilities at home and in the community. Students' main responsibility is to learn and prepare for adult life. But many young people today shoulder too much personal responsibility and overlook the importance of their main duty. Home situations vary in every family. Many situations require teenagers to assume adult and multiple responsibilities; other home situations do not encourage responsible behaviors. Teenagers need to focus on their main goal—to stay in school and learn. What are some strategies to help us shoulder responsibilities?

Elicit responses and discuss.

Whenever you feel overwhelmed, you can use stress reduction strategies such as physical exercise, relaxation, or meditation. You can talk to a friend or seek help from a knowledgeable adult.

Lesson 3 in Skill Area 8 (Time Management and Organization) presents a detailed relaxation exercise.

Monitoring Knowledge and Comprehension

Ask the following questions. Discuss.

1. Define two behaviors involved in responsibility.

2. Why do teenagers want their independence?

3. Explain why independence requires personal responsibility.

4. Name some strategies to reduce the stress of meeting your responsibilities.

Guided Practice

Ask students to generate a number of freedoms (or privileges). List these on the chalkboard or easel pad, then ask them to identify corresponding personal responsibilities.

Freedom	Responsibility
Sleepover at a friend's	Observing curfews
Going out (dating)	Respecting your partner
Getting an allowance	Budgeting your money
Baby-sitting	Learning how to handle children
Getting new clothes	Comparison shopping

Assessing Mastery

Discuss the following hypothetical story and evaluate students' response in terms of their understanding of personal responsibility.

Both Miriam and Tony are 14 years old and are romantically involved. Miriam becomes pregnant and wants to move in with Tony in his parents' garage apartment and raise their baby. Both sets of parents are against the idea and are urging the teenagers to make an adoption plan instead. Miriam wants her independence from her parents, but Tony is not sure whether he wants to accept the responsibility of marriage and family.

RETEACHING

Independent Practice

Have students change the following excuses for shirking responsibility into assertive responses.

1. It's not my fault.
2. He made me do it.
3. I didn't think this work had to be turned in.
4. I didn't see it written on the board.
5. I'm always the one to do the dishes.
6. I didn't have enough time.

Evaluation and Feedback

Distribute Figure 30 (Taking Responsibility) and have students answer the questions. Evaluate for understanding of the need to assume responsibility for personal actions.

CLOSING

Summary

We learned in this lesson that responsibility is earned. Responsibility is the ability and the willingness to accept duties, accept consequences, and be accountable for behaviors. Adolescence is a time of searching; many teens want to be independent. To be free and independent, we must be responsible. Independence involves self-discipline and strong emotional intelligence.

Generalization

Direct students to list their current home responsibilities and to give corresponding freedoms. Examples may include observing a regular curfew (responsibility) and having the curfew extended on special occasions (freedom) or doing your homework (responsibility) and watching television (freedom). Next ask the students to list the consequences they may face for not meeting their responsibilities. Allow them the choice to discuss in small groups.

ENRICHMENT

1. Discuss the following statements:

    The devil made me do it.

    Each accomplishment, great or small, starts with the right decision: I'll try.

    The buck stops here.

    There are people who see nothing but their bright spots.

    If something goes wrong, it is with somebody else, and not with me.

2. Encourage students to write a poem or rap on the theme of responsibility.

Taking Responsibility

Name: _____ Date:_____

Read the scenario and answer the following questions.

> Aunt Sally blames Tonya for breaking the TV set. Tonya did not do it and does not know how the TV was broken. Tonya's 13-year-old cousin, Tyrone, broke the TV accidentally while bringing it back from the repair shop, but he lets Tonya take the blame.

1. Why do you think Tyrone is allowing Tonya to take the blame?

2. What is Tyrone responsibility?

3. Was Tyrone's old enough to be given the responsibility for bringing the TV back from the repair shop? Explain your answer.

4. Write a conclusion to the story.

Figure 30

ROLE-PLAY: RESPONSIBILITY

CHARACTERS

Menaksha, John, Hilda

SITUATION

Menaksha is new to Booker T. Washington Middle School, but she is a very assertive and motivated young lady. She has set out to become president of her class. To become elected, she realizes that she needs the support of the student body. However, she feels planning the campaign requires her special expertise, and she does not like to delegate and often assumes too much responsibility. Menaksha has designed a campaign platform that includes responsible changes in the school and does not want to procrastinate in implementing her plan. Menaksha is very well spoken, except that she uses too many "OK's" when she talks. She also feels stressed out by the responsibilities of the campaign. Menaksha addresses her support group.

Menaksha:	I appreciate your support and help. OK. I've gone over our campaign plan, OK, and figured out what we should do, OK? *(She passes out job descriptions.)*
John:	I don't quite understand.
Menaksha:	Sorry, John. OK, maybe I wasn't clear, OK? *(Clarifies directions.)*
Hilda:	Menaksha, we all believe that you will make a great president, but we feel we need to point out something that may prevent your listeners from concentrating on your message.
Menaksha:	Tell me, Hilda, OK. I want to know, OK. Anything that will make me a better candidate, OK?

The group members share their concern about Menaksha's use of "OK's" and her reluctance to share her authority.

Menaksha:	I had no idea that I used so many "OK's," but I have a solution. I've heard about how people use a golf counter to record and change their behavior. I'll get one and use it to record every time I use "OK" in my speech. I'm glad you told me. OK!! Oops, here I go again. I'm not blaming anyone for my problem and I will correct it. I had no idea that I wasn't letting anyone else be responsible. It's true—running for president sometimes feels like carrying a heavy burden. Sometimes I feel so stressed out.

Hilda: Menaksha, please share the responsibilities of the campaign with us. We will be happy to help you plan—please trust us. You may want to start an exercise program with us to reduce your stress. Mr. Jones and Ms. Phillips are starting a wellness program that includes physical exercise and relaxation strategies three time a week for 30 minutes after school.

Menaksha agrees to join the wellness group and makes a plan, with the group's help, to reduce her "OK's." She also includes the group in her campaign planning and actually feels relieved. With the group's help, she improves her speeches and is able to become more relaxed.

EVALUATION AND FEEDBACK

1. Identify Menaksha's short-term and long-term goals.

2. What were some of Menaksha's strengths and weaknesses?

3. Describe John's behavior.

4. What strategies did Menaksha use to improve?

5. How did Menaksha feel about sharing her authority in planning at the beginning of the story?

6. Would you vote for Menaksha? Why or why not?

SELF-ADVOCACY & ASSERTIVENESS

HELP! I NEED SOMEBODY

GOAL

- To ask assertively for assistance

OBJECTIVES

- Identifying reasons people do not ask for help
- Identifying situations in which help is needed
- Appropriately asking for help
- Identifying how to respond when help is given or denied

MATERIALS

- Who Can Help? (Figure 31)
- Helping Review (Figure 32)
- Chalkboard or easel pad
- Paper and pencils
- Telephone book yellow pages
- Index cards

PROCEDURE

OPENING

Review

None needed.

Stating Objectives

In this lesson we will learn that we may avoid asking for help for several reasons. We will learn that there are certain situations when it is necessary to ask for help. It is important to know how to request assistance. We will learn how to respond when help is given or when help is refused.

INSTRUCTION

Teaching and Guided Discussion

● ——— Identifying reasons people do not ask for help

There are times when everyone needs help. However, sometimes people have difficulty asking for help. I wonder why? What are some reasons that would prevent you from asking for help?

List the reasons students generate on the chalkboard or easel pad.

One reason is *pride;* some people feel that asking for help might make them look stupid or incompetent. But nobody is perfect, and asking for help is healthy. Another reason is *fear.* We may be afraid of rejection: What if we ask for help and are refused? It is possible our request will be refused, but we can always ask somebody else. *Poor self-concept* is another reason some people hesitate to ask for help. People who have a poor self-concept are often shy or feel embarrassed about asking for help. Eventually they give up seeking help. Another reason not to ask for help is *ignorance;* some people just don't know where to go for the help they need. That's OK—we can't know everything, but by using a Thinking Me attitude we can find out and learn.

● ——— Identifying situations in which help is needed

Were you ever in a situation when you avoided asking for help and were later sorry? What was your reason?

Elicit responses and discuss. Adapt the following example as appropriate.

My friend had to take a driver's test to get a driving license. He had trouble with parallel parking and planned to ask his sister for help, but he felt too embarrassed and proud. Well, he flunked the test. Then he felt sorry that he had allowed his pride to interfere with his plan.

Some people avoid asking for help. Others are always asking for help and are not willing to take risks, make mistakes, or learn from their mistakes. They lack self-confidence and are too dependent on others. We can use our Thinking Steps to STOP and THINK to help us evaluate a situation and PLAN on how and where to go for help. After we have done so, we can CHECK our plan to see whether we got the help we needed. Many people in our lives can and want to help—in our homes, school, and neighborhood. There are places in our community that can help young people with their problems. Are you aware of such places?

Discuss. Make students aware of the existence of community agencies that help youngsters with alcohol and drug problems, runaways, teen pregnancies, medical issues, conflict resolution, and other predicaments.

● ——— Appropriately asking for help

How do we ask for help?

Elicit responses and discuss.

There are many ways to go about asking for help. Requesting help means asking in a polite manner, without being demanding. When we assertively request assistance, we show a positive self-concept and a desire to be helped. When we assume an Assertive Me attitude, our words are respectful. Our voices are strong yet courteous.

When we request help, we must first explain our difficulties and why we need assistance. Let's practice. What are some situations in which you have needed help?

Elicit responses. Depending on the makeup of your group, students may discuss or role-play their own situations or the following examples.

- *Situation 1:* Your final math exam is in 2 weeks, and you are unsure about how to calculate percentages. Where can you find help?

- *Situation 2:* You are saving for a special gift for a friend's birthday. You are 10 dollars short but are willing to work for the money. Where can you find help?

- *Situation 3:* Your "friend" talked you into taking a CD from a store without paying for it. You feel guilty but are afraid to return it. Where can you find help?

- *Situation 4:* You are addicted to cigarettes. You want to quit smoking but can't shake the habit. Where can you find help?

If you are sincere and polite in requesting help, you have a better chance of getting what you need. You must also be willing to accept the help when it is given.

Identifying how to respond when help is given or denied

Our response when help is given or when it is refused is important. Whenever help is given, we need to show appreciation in words and deeds. What are some ways we can show appreciation?

Elicit responses and discuss.

We can express gratitude by telling the person how we feel. We can also write a thank-you note or do something nice for the person. But the best way to show our appreciation is to let the person know that the assistance "paid off." Suppose a student has a problem with drugs and seeks help from the school guidance counselor. How could that student show appreciation?

Elicit responses and discuss.

Remember that actions speak louder than words. When the student stops using drugs, the positive changes in the student's health and behavior indicate appreciation. The student could simply tell the counselor, "Thank you for your help—it's really working." Suppose you have a less serious problem—say, trouble with your math assignment. A friend helps you with your math work, and as a result you get an A on the test. You say thank you, but your behavior on the test was the real payoff for both you and your friend.

In some instances your request for help may be refused. What if you ask your brother to help you clean up the yard, and he refuses? Would you start a fight? Would you refuse the next time he asked you for help? What would a person using a Thinking Me attitude do?

Elicit responses and discuss.

Remember your Thinking Steps: STOP, THINK, PLAN, and CHECK. Fighting usually does not help. An alternative plan may include dividing the yard work, getting help from someone else, or ignoring the refusal and cleaning up the yard yourself. I know that's hard to do.

In a more serious situation the outcome may be different. Let's suppose you need help in English and your teacher is too busy to give individual attention. What should you do? Use your Thinking Me attitude. Where can you find assistance?

Elicit responses and discuss. Answers may include from a friend, a family member, another teacher, a school counselor, and so forth.

Assessing Mastery

Ask the following questions and discuss.

1. Why do people sometimes hesitate to ask for help?

2. I am just learning to use a new computer program. I am completely confused and frustrated. What should I do? *(Answers may include getting help from someone who knows the program, reading the program manual, using the "Help" command on the computer, or all of these.)*

3. Suggest how to ask for help in the following situations.

   I have a problem making friends.

   I have a problem getting to school on time.

   I am failing English.

   All my friends smoke, and I can't say no.

4. Identify appropriate responses to show your appreciation.

   Your neighbor helps you with your homework.

   Your teacher helps you understand the new math lesson.

   Your friend helps you with a personal problem.

5. Identify appropriate responses when someone refuses to help in the following situations.

   The store clerk is rude and ignores your request for help in finding an item.

   Your brother or sister refuses to help you carry out the garbage.

   Your friend refuses to listen to your problem and makes fun of you.

Guided Practice

Divide students into three smaller groups. Distribute a copy of Figure 31 (Who Can Help?) to each group. Assign one situation to each group and direct groups to propose and record a solution. Have the small groups present their solutions to the whole class and discuss.

Assessing Mastery

Ask students to generate a list of phrases conducive to receiving assistance, as in the following examples. List these on the chalkboard or easel pad.

- Would you please . . .

- I would appreciate . . .

- I need help. Would you . . .

- I have a problem, and I know you can help . . .

- I feel _____ and could use your help.

RETEACHING

Independent Practice

Divide students into small groups. Give each group the yellow pages of the telephone book and an index card on which you have written a problem in one of the following categories: substance abuse, weight problem, physical or sexual abuse, medical problem, psychiatric problem, family problem. Ask each group to use the yellow pages to locate and list the names and telephone numbers of agencies or individuals who can help with their assigned problem. Allow time for discussion.

Evaluation and Feedback

Distribute copies of Figure 32 (Helping Review) and have students complete as instructed. Evaluate for understanding of the need to ask for help.

CLOSING

Summary

In this lesson we learned that we sometimes avoid asking for help because of pride, fear, ignorance, or poor self-concept. We learned that there are certain times when it is necessary to ask for help. It is important to know when and how to request assistance. It is also important to show appreciation when help is given and to know how to react when help is refused.

Generalization

Select from the following activities.

1. Direct students to ask for help with a project or problem at home or in the community. Guide students in developing plans to ask for help and in thinking of options if refused. For example:

   Your friends wrapped toilet paper around the trees and bushes in your yard. The wind blew the paper all over the neighborhood. Your parents insist you are responsible for the clean-up. Who can help you? What can you do if your plan doesn't work out?

Your favorite teacher is retiring. You want to do something special for him. Who can help you? What can you do if your plan doesn't work out?

2. Have students keep a journal to record the times they hear someone asking for help at school or at home. Tell them to note who asked, who and what was asked, and the response.

ENRICHMENT

Direct students to find solutions for the following problems. Assist them in writing scripts and role-playing their solutions.

1. You are with a group of friends at a department store at the mall. One of your friends pockets an inexpensive watch. She later tells you, "The store won't miss this piece of junk." You feel what she did was wrong, but you do not want to get her in trouble. Explain to your friend what her problem is and why she needs help. Who can help?

2. Your best friend is smoking weed. He tells you that he heard it's not addictive, and besides it makes him feel good and helps him handle stress at school and home. You are concerned about your friend's health and the legal implications, but you do not want to get your friend in trouble. Explain to your friend what his problem is and why he needs help. Who can help?

Who Can Help?

Situation 1

Jay is in the sixth grade. He is 2 years older than his peers. Jay's problem is that he cannot read. He repeated third and fifth grades, but that didn't help. So far he has been able to pass unnoticed, but the work is getting harder. He wants to remain with his friends and does not want to go to a special class.

What is the reason Jay has not asked for help?

Who can Jay ask for help?

Situation 2

Monique has been physically abused at home by her father. She hides her bruises by wearing make-up and long-sleeved shirts, even in summer. You notice the bruises and confront Monique. She bursts out in tears and defends her father by saying that he only hits her when he has had too much to drink. She makes you promise not to tell anyone. Later, you feel sorry you made that promise.

What is the reason Monique has not asked for help?

Who can you ask to help?

Situation 3

You notice a change in your friend, who has suddenly lost a lot of weight. You suspect an eating disorder, but when you bring up the subject your friend becomes angry and denies having a problem. You love your friend and want to help.

Why has your friend not asked for help?

Who can you ask to help?

Figure 31

Helping Review

Name: _____ Date: _____

Answer the following questions.

1. You are an A student, but you are having problems with algebra. What could be your reason for not asking for help? Who can help?

2. You don't seem to be able to catch up with your homework. What could be your reason for not asking for help? Who can help?

3. You have a drinking problem. What could be your reason for not asking for help? Who can help?

4. You spent your weekly lunch money on a CD. You won't ask your mother for more money. What could be your reason for not asking for help? Who can help?

5. You did not understand your assignment. You would like to ask your teacher for help, but you don't. What could be your reason for not asking for help? Who can help?

6. Change the following to an assertive request for help: "Mom, come here right now and help me with this stupid zipper. It's stuck, and I can't get this dress on. You shouldn't have bought me this dumb dress in the first place."

Figure 32

TAKE THE FIRST STEP

GOAL

- To offer and give assistance

OBJECTIVES

- Recognizing why people are helpful

- Understanding reciprocal helping

- Understanding the difference between conditional and unconditional giving

- Recognizing when not to help

MATERIALS

- What Kind of Helping? (Figure 33)

- Let Me Help You (Figure 34)

- Index cards

PROCEDURE

OPENING

Review

In our last lesson we learned that we sometimes avoid asking for help because of pride, fear, ignorance, or poor self-concept. Knowing when and how to request assistance is important. We need to show appreciation when help is given and respond in a positive and assertive way when help is refused.

Follow up on any generalization activities assigned during the last lesson.

Stating Objectives

In this lesson we will learn different reasons people help. By helping someone, we often also receive. Whenever we help someone, we should do it unconditionally—that means without any "if's." There are occasions when too much help is undesirable and people should be encouraged to help themselves.

INSTRUCTION

Teaching and Guided Discussion

● ———— **Recognizing why people are helpful**

When there is a disaster somewhere in the world, like an earthquake, flood, or war, many people take the initiative to volunteer their help. Why do you think these volunteers want to help people they don't even know?

Elicit responses and discuss.

Some people identify or empathize with others who are in similar situations. Others help because they feel sorry and sympathize. In yet other situations people feel an obligation to help, or they may be looking for recognition. Sometimes selfishness comes into play, and people help only when they have something to gain themselves.

Many people are leaders in offering help. They model assertiveness and show others how to help. Do you know or have you heard of such people?

Elicit responses. Some examples follow.

- President Jimmy Carter: building affordable homes through Habitat for Humanity
- Jacques Cousteau: caring for the ecology of the sea
- Cesar Chavez: helping migrant workers receive fair treatment
- Chief Black Kettle "Peace Chief of the Cheyenne": trying to restore peace to his people
- Nelson Mandela: helping to change South Africa's policy of apartheid

There are also many "unsung heroes" in our communities, neighborhoods, and families. These are people who help without being recognized. Do you know of any unsung heroes? What are they doing to help?

Elicit responses and discuss.

● ———— **Understanding reciprocal helping**

We don't have to travel to another country to be helpful—we can begin right here. We can start with our family and friends, at home, in school, and in the community. We can help people we know and people we don't know. It's easy to help a friend, someone you know and like. It's not as easy to help someone you don't know or don't particularly like. However, by helping others we also help ourselves. What does the saying "It is in giving that we receive" mean?

Elicit responses and discuss.

When we help others we get a good feeling inside. We receive satisfaction. When we help someone we don't know, we may make a friend. We receive friendship. When we help someone with math, science, or history, our own skills become stronger. We receive knowledge. This is called *reciprocal helping*—you win and I win, too. This does not mean the helper always gets something material in return for the help. Understanding that not all rewards can be measured in dollars or other material things requires a great deal of maturity and a Thinking Me attitude.

When was the last time you offered to help someone? Were your intentions sincere? Did you expect anything in return?

Elicit responses and discuss.

Understanding the difference between conditional and unconditional giving

What does the saying "I'll scratch your back if you scratch mine" mean?

Elicit responses and discuss.

This expression is an example of *conditional giving,* meaning you expect something in return for the help you give. The word "if" places conditions on your help. The opposite of conditional giving is *unconditional giving,* or giving without any "if's." It is better to help someone unconditionally because when you do so, you will not feel used or disappointed if that person does not show appreciation. Unconditional giving is like saying, "I'll scratch your back—and I'll enjoy it."

When you help someone, it is important to use your Thinking Me and analyze your motives. Do you expect something in return? If so, there are conditions on your giving.

Recognizing when not to help

It is important not to take over and use a Bossy Me attitude when we offer help. We don't want to make anyone feel incompetent or inferior. It is a good idea to ask if help is needed before offering assistance. Many people feel resentful or insulted when being helped without their permission. For example, some may assume that all elderly people or all people with disabilities need or want assistance. This is not necessarily correct. Most people want to help themselves.

It is important for you to help yourself—to assume responsibility for your own actions. For example, if you want to improve your basketball skills, you can STOP wishing and THINK of your different options to improve. You can make a PLAN. Your plan could include asking the coach for help, watching basketball videos, and practicing shooting baskets. You can implement your plan, then CHECK it out. It is your responsibility to make your plan work—to practice and improve your game. As a teacher I can help you learn, but it is up to you to decide whether you want to learn or not. The adults in your lives can help you develop into a responsible human being, but the final decision is up to you.

Monitoring Knowledge and Comprehension

Ask the following questions and discuss.

1. Name some reasons people help one another.

2. Mother is teaching Paul how to cook. How is mother helping Paul, and how is Paul helping mother? *(Paul is learning to cook, and mother is learning to give cooking lessons.)*

3. Jane says, "I will help you tidy up the room if you help me clean the kitchen." Is Jane's help conditional or unconditional?

4. Father solves Harold's math homework problems every night. He believes he is helping his son make A's in math. Should Harold's father continue to do Harold's math homework? Why or why not?

Guided Practice

Divide students into small groups. Give each group an index card upon which you have written one of the following situations. After groups have completed the exercise described, have them discuss their experience and ideas with the larger group.

- *Situation 1:* Your mother is having a surprise birthday party for your father. Make a list of things you can do to help.

- *Situation 2:* It is almost Christmas and your neighborhood food bank is almost empty. Your parents are worried that there won't be enough food for everyone in the community. What can you do to help?

- *Situation 3:* A hurricane hits Florida. Many people's homes are flooded, and they have lost all of their belongings. What can you do to help?

- *Situation 4:* A student with a learning disability has been assigned to your classroom. He has trouble taking notes in the history class and is also very shy and withdrawn. What can you do to help?

Assessing Mastery

Distribute copies of Figure 33 (What Kind of Helping?). Have students complete as instructed, then discuss.

RETEACHING

Independent Practice

Select one or both of these activities.

1. Have each student write down the name of any person he or she knows who needs help, make a helping plan, then follow it. Direct students to record the plan and its outcomes. Let students know that this plan is personal and confidential—they do not have to share it with anyone.

2. Have students interview one another to learn how they have helped others with their problems. Encourage them to discuss how they felt when they were successful in their efforts to help.

Evaluation and Feedback

Distribute and have students complete Figure 34 (Let Me Help You). Evaluate for understanding of the need to offer and give assistance.

CLOSING

Summary

In this lesson we learned that it is important to recognize why people are helpful. Helping someone often results in mutual gain—by giving we also receive. It is best if our offer of help is sincere and unconditional. Finally, it is a good idea to ask if help is needed before offering assistance. We can also help others to help themselves.

Generalization

Choose from among the following activities.

1. Encourage students to generate ideas for helping out at school—for example, tutoring younger students, reshelving books in the library, or decorating hallways.

2. Assign students to help in the community. Involve parents to get suggestions on where help is most needed—for example, nursing homes, hospitals, Head Start programs, Special Olympics.

3. Encourage students to observe and record incidents of unconditional helping at home and in the community.

ENRICHMENT

1. Start a peer-tutoring program in your class. Coach students to provide help without "taking over." Allow students to reverse roles to experience being both tutor and tutee.

2. Organize a crew to clean up the schoolyard or perform any other helpful activity.

What Kind of Helping?

Name: _____ Date:_____

Fill in the blanks with the correct word. Words to use: unconditional, conditional, sympathy, empathy, resentful, assertive, reciprocal.
You may use some words more than once.

1. My help is _____ when I expect something in return.

2. My help is _____ when I don't expect something in return.

3. By helping you, I'm also helping myself. This is called

    _____ helping.

4. When I feel sorry for someone and want to help, I feel

    _____.

5. When I can identify with your problem and want to help, I feel

    _____.

6. When I am forced to help someone, I feel _____.

7. "You scratch my back and I'll scratch yours" is an example of

    _____ helping.

8. When I take the initiative and show leadership in helping, I am being

    _____.

9. I'll help you even if you don't help me because my help is

    _____.

10. I'll help because I feel sorry for you, and I don't expect anything in return.

    I feel _____, and my giving is _____.

Figure 33

Let Me Help You

Name: _____ Date:_____

Change the following sentences into statements that show an appropriate, unconditional offering of help. Two items do not need to be changed.

1. You're doing it all wrong—let me do it.

2. If I help in the food pantry, how much will I get paid?

3. *(To a blind person)* Here, let me help you. You can't cross this busy street by yourself.

4. What would you do without me? You're so helpless.

5. Can't you do anything right? Your right foot is in your left shoe. I guess I have to help you.

6. I know your back hurts, Dad. Do you need help mowing the lawn?

7. You poor thing, are you having trouble buttoning your shirt? Here, let me help.

8. Let me tutor you in math. I'm an honor roll student.

9. I'll help you with your homework because I promised Dad I would.

10. I can help you with your homework if you like. I know how it feels to be in third grade—I've been there.

Figure 34

173

WHY SHOULD I?

GOAL

- To analyze and discuss fair and unfair rules and practices

OBJECTIVES

- Recognizing the right to question and change unfair rules
- Recognizing the importance of empathy in changing unfair rules
- Recognizing the connection between freedom and responsible behavior
- Recognizing that fair rules are necessary in society

MATERIALS

- Responsibility and Empathy (Figure 35)
- Fair or Unfair? (Figure 36)
- Index cards

PROCEDURE

OPENING

Review

In our last lesson we learned that it is important to recognize why people are helpful. Helping someone often results in mutual gain—by giving we also receive. Our offers of help must be sincere. It is best if they can also be unconditional—that means we shouldn't necessarily expect anything in return. It is a good idea to ask if help is needed before offering assistance and to help others help themselves.

Follow up on any generalization activities assigned during the last lesson.

Stating Objectives

In this lesson we will learn that some rules are unfair but that we may be able to change unfair rules by questioning them assertively. We will discuss the importance of empathy in deciding whether rules are fair or unfair. We will also look at the connection between freedom and responsibility and discuss why fair rules are necessary in society.

INSTRUCTION

Teaching and Guided Discussion

● ————— **Recognizing the right to question and change unfair rules**

Citizens of a democracy have the right to practice freedom of speech to change unfair laws and practices. We make these changes not through violence, but through peaceful protest and voting to elect people who will represent our views. Sometimes it takes a long time for change to come. Can you name some people who have worked to make laws and people's lives more fair?

Elicit responses and discuss. Students may mention Abraham Lincoln, Susan B. Anthony, Martin Luther King, Mahatma Ghandi, and Sojourner Truth, among others.

What are some unfair rules or practices, past or present, in our society, our city, or our school?

Elicit responses and discuss. Historical examples include slavery, denying women the right to vote, child labor, internment of Japanese American citizens during World War II, and exclusion of people with disabilities from work opportunities.

● ————— **Recognizing the importance of empathy in changing unfair rules**

Changing unfair rules requires assertion and a Thinking Me attitude. It also requires *empathy,* or the ability to truly understand how another person feels. When people empathize, they are able to see things from another's perspective. Why do you think empathetic people might be more tolerant of differences and more likely to believe in fair rules for everyone?

Elicit responses and discuss.

Empathetic people are able to "walk a mile in another person's shoes." This ability allows them to see clearly that every human being must be treated with respect and that rules should be fair for all.

● ————— **Recognizing the connection between freedom and responsible behavior**

Having the freedom to change unfair rules and practices does not mean we can do whatever we want. With freedom comes responsibility. Responsibility means using the Thinking Steps before questioning rules. Before reacting, we need to STOP. We need to THINK to determine whether a rule is really unfair. If we believe the rule is unfair, then we can PLAN how to change it, put our plan into effect, and CHECK our plan once we have tried it.

Adapt the following discussion if an issue specific to your school illustrates the point.

For example, suppose the principal decides all students will wear school uniforms because two rival gangs have been wearing gang "colors" and harassing the rest of the student body. You may not like wearing a uniform, but if you use your Thinking Me attitude, you must be responsible and think of the benefits of this rule to the entire school. What are the benefits of wearing uniforms? Do the benefits justify the inconvenience?

Elicit responses and discuss.

Before we question a rule or practice and say, "It isn't fair" or "I won't follow this rule," we need to analyze the rule and discuss it with others. Basically, we need to understand the consequences if we didn't have that particular rule.

●——— **Recognizing that fair rules are necessary in society**

Fair rules are necessary for peace. Without rules, there would be anarchy and confusion. For example, imagine that tomorrow all the traffic lights in the city will be removed. What do you think will happen?

Elicit responses and discuss.

Now imagine that our school had no rules and that everyone could do whatever he or she wanted. What do you think would happen?

Discuss.

We cannot be free of rules unless everyone is responsible in using that freedom. Fair rules are necessary in society. Unfair rules need to be changed, but we also need to proceed in an assertive and thoughtful manner.

Monitoring Knowledge and Comprehension

Ask the following questions and discuss.

1. How would you go about questioning and changing an unfair rule?

2. How does empathy lead to a sense of fairness and justice?

3. What would happen to a family or a nation if the people wanted to be free to do what they wanted but rejected all responsibilities?

4. Why do we need classroom rules, family rules, and laws?

Guided Practice

Divide the class into small groups. Give each group an index card on which you have previously written one of the following situations. Direct groups to create scenarios in which they responsibly challenge the rule described. Role-play and discuss.

- *Situation 1:* A teacher has a rule that if one student misbehaves, the whole class is punished.

- *Situation 2:* Denolis wants to enroll in a home economics class so he can learn to cook. The school counselor tells him the class is full because girls have priority.

- *Situation 3:* The school dress code requires that boys wear a crewcut and girls wear their hair above the collar. The principal cannot empathize with the students because he had to wear a crewcut when he was a teenager.

- *Situation 4:* The school forbids wearing T-shirts with printed words of any kind, not just profanity or other taboo language.

- *Situation 5:* Your parents expect you to be home at 8 o'clock on weekends. You feel that was OK when you were in elementary school, but now that you are in middle school you would like your curfew extended.

Assessing Mastery

Distribute copies of Figure 35 (Responsibility and Empathy) and have students complete as instructed.

RETEACHING

Independent Practice

Divide the class into three groups. Assign each group a research topic focusing on a historical event reflecting responsible challenge of rules. Some topics to suggest include Mahatma Ghandi and India's independence, Martin Luther King and civil rights, voting rights for women, and equal access for people with disabilities. Ask each group to work cooperatively to research their topic. If computer resources are available, you can encourage students to use these to look for and research other examples.

Evaluation and Feedback

Distribute copies of Figure 36 (Fair or Unfair?). Evaluate student responses for understanding of the need to analyze, plan, and avoid being judgmental.

Generalization

Direct each student to generate a list of unfair practices in his or her community, home, or school. Students then develop solutions and specify how they can initiate change. Guide students in developing their own personal plans for change.

CLOSING

Summary

In this lesson we learned that people have the right to question and change unfair rules and practices. Empathy with others is important in deciding whether a rule is fair or unfair, as is an understanding of the need to exercise our freedoms responsibly. Fair rules are necessary in a civilized society.

ENRICHMENT

Guide students in writing aphorisms on the themes of democracy, fairness, equality, responsibility, and personal rights. If cooking facilities are available, have students write their aphorisms on slips of paper, wrap in fortune cookie dough, and bake. (If no such facilities are available, this could be a home assignment.) Share, enjoy, and discuss. Some sample aphorisms follow.

- He who mistreats others should not expect others to treat him well.

- Treating your friends with respect is good, but treating those who are not your friends with respect is even better.

- Every human being has the right to be treated with dignity and respect.

- A responsible person thinks of the rights of others as well as his or her own personal rights.

Responsibility & Empathy

Name: _____ Date:_____

Tell what you could do or say to show responsibility in the following situations.

1. You want to start baby-sitting.

2. You want to make money by mowing lawns in your neighborhood.

3. You want to borrow your friend's tennis racket, basketball, or baseball glove.

4. You want your own private telephone line.

Tell what you could do or say to show empathy in the following situations.

1. Your little sister has an unusual amount of homework, but it's her turn to do the dishes. That's the house rule.

2. Students with disabilities eat lunch in a separate corner of the cafeteria. That's the school rule.

3. Your friend Ken is excluded from playing football because he flunked English. He is a slow learner in English, but he is a terrific athlete.

4. Your neighbor's father had a heart attack. You understand how your neighbor feels because your father had a heart attack 3 years ago. Your father has since recovered.

Figure 35

Fair or Unfair?

Name: _____ Date: _____

Place a check mark in the box to indicate whether you think the following rules are fair or unfair.

	Fair	Unfair
1. Chewing gum is not allowed in school.	☐	☐
2. Corporal punishment for violation of rules is used in your school.	☐	☐
3. You are responsible for cleaning your room at home.	☐	☐
4. Teenagers must be accompanied by an adult to shop in a convenience store.	☐	☐
5. Male customers must wear shirts and shoes to dine at restaurants.	☐	☐
6. You may not buy cigarettes until you are 18 years old.	☐	☐
7. You must wear seat belts in a moving automobile.	☐	☐
8. Only boys are allowed to take auto mechanics courses.	☐	☐
9. You may not play your stereo very loudly.	☐	☐
10. You may not buy alcoholic drinks until you are 21 years old.	☐	☐

Figure 36

181

Develop a plan to change three of the rules you think are unfair.

Rule number:_____

Plan: _____

_____

_____

_____

Rule number:_____

Plan: _____

_____

_____

_____

Rule number:_____

Plan: _____

_____

_____

_____

Figure 36 continued

YES SIR, YES MA'AM, BUT...

GOAL

- To respond positively and assertively to authority figures

OBJECTIVES

- Showing respect while responding assertively
- Responding tactfully and politely to authority figures
- Responding to authority figures with empathetic assertion
- Knowing how to convince adults that you are responsible enough to participate in decision making

MATERIALS

- Understanding Empathetic Assertion (Figure 37)
- Help Harry (Figure 38)

PROCEDURE

OPENING

Review

In the last lesson we learned that people have the right to question and change unfair rules and practices. We discussed the importance of empathy in deciding whether a rule is fair or unfair and talked about the strong connection between freedom and responsibility. We said fair rules are necessary in society.

Follow up on any generalization activities assigned during the last lesson.

Stating Objectives

Sometimes communicating with adult authority figures can be difficult. Some adults may view younger people's assertive behavior as disrespectful. In this lesson we will learn how to show respect by responding tactfully, politely, and assertively to authority figures. We will examine the difference between direct assertion and empathetic assertion. Last, we will discuss how you can convince adults that you are responsible enough to participate in making decisions.

INSTRUCTION

Teaching and Guided Discussion

● ———— **Showing respect while responding assertively**

Acting assertively does not mean being impolite. When young people respond assertively to adults it is important for them to show respect. We should always be respectful of one another, regardless of age differences. Respect means appreciation and consideration. Respect can be earned but also lost. Your parents, teachers, and friends earn your respect by being considerate and supportive, and you can earn theirs by behaving responsibly.

● ———— **Responding tactfully and politely to authority figures**

Sometimes we must show respect to people we feel do not deserve it but who are in positions of authority. For example, suppose I had a job where I did not respect the boss. I would have to show respect if I wanted to keep my job or until I developed another plan, such as finding another job. In this case I would show respect to my boss simply because of his or her position and not because my boss had earned my respect. We show respect for many different reasons. I may respond respectfully because I want something from you, because I am afraid of you, because I admire your accomplishments, or because I simply like you.

Being tactful and polite does not mean that you are nonassertive. Nonassertive people do not consider their own feelings. They only pretend to agree with others. Tactful but assertive people can consider their own feelings and the feelings of others but can still get their message across. Tact involves being considerate, polite, and diplomatic. Tact involves being reflective and empathetic.

● ———— **Responding to authority figures with empathetic assertion**

Many people in authority do not like to be challenged, especially by young people. They may misinterpret an assertive attitude as defiance or disrespect. In our last lesson we discussed empathy. What does it mean to be empathetic?

Elicit responses; review as needed.

Empathetic people understand others' feelings and concerns. They can appreciate other opinions and are tolerant of differences.

When behaving assertively, you may choose to use direct assertion or empathetic assertion. When using *direct assertion,* you get directly to the point. For example, imagine you are trying to convince your parents that you do not need their advice. You can say, "I am no longer a child, and I have proven to be responsible. Please let me make this decision." With *empathetic assertion* you still assert yourself, but you also show understanding of other people's feelings or points of view. In this case your response to your parents would be "I know that you are concerned about me and that you love me, but I think I am responsible enough to make this decision." Adults are more likely to respond positively to empathetic assertion than to direct assertion.

● ——— **Knowing how to convince adults that you are responsible enough to participate in decision making**

Sometimes it is difficult for adults to give younger people choices, especially during adolescence. Teenagers have to convince adults by acting responsibly. Once you establish that you are responsible, then you have earned the right to be assertive and make your own choices and decisions. How can you act assertively and convince your parents, teachers, principal, or any other adult in authority that you have rights and can make choices?

Elicit responses and discuss. Stress the idea that the message must be assertive, not aggressive.

Remember, there is a big difference between being assertive and being aggressive. When you use direct assertion you are telling the other person how you feel. In addition, you convey your beliefs without taking away the rights of the other person. In a home, school, or society, people have rights, but to exercise these rights they must consider the good of the group as well as themselves. To become good citizens, we must think reflectively and consider how our behavior affects other people.

Monitoring Knowledge and Comprehension

Ask the following questions and discuss.

1. What is respect, and why is respect given?

2. Why is being tactful important when responding to authority figures?

3. What is the difference between empathetic assertion and direct assertion?

4. Why is it best to use empathetic assertion when dealing with adults?

5. Does having personal rights mean you have the right to do whatever you please? Why or why not?

Guided Practice

Divide the class into three groups. Direct each group to respond to the following problem situation. When groups are finished, have them get together as a class to discuss and compare their solutions.

Your school's principal has issued an edict banning any field trips for the rest of the school year. The last field trip, taken by that wild bunch in the seventh grade, resulted in complaints from community members. The principal is determined that this sort of thing will never happen again. Your class has been preparing for weeks to visit a special once-in-a-lifetime science exhibit. Your task is to convince the principal to change her mind.

Assessing Mastery

Distribute Figure 31 (Understanding Empathetic Assertion) and have students complete as instructed. Discuss.

RETEACHING

Independent Practice

Divide students into small groups. Distribute copies of Figure 38 (Help Harry) and have groups generate a solution to the problem. Direct each group to present their plan to the class.

Evaluation and Feedback

Ask the following questions and discuss. Evaluate for understanding of the need to be assertive yet diplomatic when dealing with authority figures.

1. How is empathetic assertion different from direct assertion?

2. What does it mean to be tactful and diplomatic?

3. Why is it difficult to convince people in authority to consider your point of view?

4. What is the difference between being polite and being nonassertive?

5. Why is it a good idea to consider the feelings of the people you are trying to convince?

6. Which of the following is empathetic assertion?

   Mother, I need my own room—please let me use the study.

   Mother, Jay is much younger than I am, and he doesn't understand that I need my privacy. May I use the study as my room?

CLOSING

Summary

In this lesson we learned that we can show respect while responding assertively. Sometimes communicating with adult authority figures can be difficult because some adults view assertive behavior from young people as disrespectful. We learned to respond tactfully, politely, and assertively to authority figures. We also learned that empathetic assertion, which considers the feelings and beliefs of others, works better with adults than direct assertion. Finally, we discussed ways you can convince adults that you are ready to participate in decision making.

Generalization

Direct students to visualize an unfair home or community situation in which an adult is in authority. Give the following instructions: "You would like to change this rule or situation. Close your eyes, take a few deep breaths, relax your mind and body, and feel positive. Picture yourself standing in front of the adult, talking and explaining your point of view." Give students a few minutes to visualize, then ask them to open their eyes. Discuss the experience as a group.

ENRICHMENT

Videotape a role-play situation in which students respond assertively to a teacher who has given an unfair assignment. View the videotape as a group and critique the dialogue. If videotape facilities are not available, divide the class into two groups and take turns role-playing and giving critiques.

Understanding Empathetic Assertion

Name: _____ Date:_____

Change the following direct assertive statements into empathetic assertive statements.

1. Please mother, I can do it myself.

2. Mrs. Jones, yesterday you told us the exam would only cover chapters 1 through 3.

3. Mr. Green (principal), because of the year-round school schedule, we should be allowed to wear shorts to class in the summer months.

4. Dad, I need a raise in my allowance.

5. I can't stop now. I'm late for practice.

6. Mrs. Jones, we need more time to finish our project.

7. I can't talk to you now—I'm very busy. I'll call you later.

8. Sorry, I can't lend you my new jacket.

9. Excuse me, but I was first in line.

10. Mother, the sweater you gave me for my birthday is not what I wanted. Let's exchange it.

Figure 37

Help Harry

Use your Thinking Steps (STOP, THINK, PLAN, CHECK) to help you devise a plan to get Harry out of trouble.

Harry was furious—he had rights, too. He did not cheat on the test. Harry was smarter than the average guy but hated to study for tests. He managed to get C's without cracking a book. "All this history stuff happened eons ago—who gives a hoot?" said Harry. But Harry started to care after a discussion with his father. Harry's father said he would hire Harry at the newspaper office if he would bring up his history grade. Harry's assignment at work was to research some facts on the Civil War for an article on multicultural education. Suddenly, history became very interesting. Harry made a 98 on his exam. His teacher did not believe he had done his own work and accused him of cheating. Harry lost his temper and called his teacher a liar. Now he is in deep trouble.

Figure 38

I CAN SAY NO TO YOU

GOAL

- To respond logically to peer pressure

OBJECTIVES

- Recognizing the negative influence of peers in decision making

- Recognizing the positive influence of peers in decision making

- Recognizing the dangers when saying no to negative influences

- Thinking reflectively and seeking support when resisting negative influences

MATERIALS

- Peer Pressure Situations (Figure 39)

- What Would You Say? (Figure 40)

- Say No? (Figure 41)

- Paper and pencils

PROCEDURE

OPENING

Review

In our last lesson we learned how to show respect while responding assertively. Sometimes communicating with adult authority figures can be difficult. Some adults may view assertive behavior as disrespectful. We learned to respond tactfully, politely, and assertively to authority figures. We examined the difference between direct assertion and empathetic assertion and discussed how to convince adults to consider the decisions of young people.

Follow up on any generalization activities assigned during the last lesson.

Stating Objectives

In this lesson we will recognize the negative and positive influence of peers in decision making. We will learn how to recognize disadvantages or dangers when saying no to certain people. In addition, we will learn to think reflectively and seek support when resisting negative peer influences.

INSTRUCTION

Teaching and Guided Discussion

●——————— **Recognizing the negative influence of peers in decision making**

"Just say no." We have all heard those words. What do they mean to you?

Elicit responses and discuss.

Saying no is easier said than done, isn't it? Sometimes we have difficulty resisting friends who may get us into trouble. We all want to belong to a circle of friends, and saying no may jeopardize or threaten our friendships. Our friends have a great influence on our behavior, especially when they are more assertive than we are. Why do you think we give in to peer pressure?

Elicit responses and discuss.

In most cases we give in to peer pressure because we want to be accepted, and that's OK unless giving in results in trouble. Before we give in, we need to STOP, THINK, PLAN, and CHECK. By using our Thinking Steps, we can avoid getting into trouble.

An assertive person can say no. Sometimes saying no requires empathetic assertion and sometimes it requires direct assertion. Can you give me examples of such situations?

Elicit responses and discuss. Review as necessary from the previous lesson.

●——————— **Recognizing the positive influence of peers in decision making**

Peer pressure can also be positive. Can you think of some times when peer pressure was helpful to you?

Elicit responses and discuss.

Your friends may convince you to join a sports club or to do something fun. Before you say no, STOP and listen to your inner voice. Talk to yourself. THINK and ask yourself some important questions: Are your friends being helpful, or are they taking advantage of you? Are they concerned about what could happen to you, or do they want to satisfy their own needs? PLAN on how you will resist their influence if the choice is not in your best interests. However, if the influence is positive, go for it. Then CHECK—did you make the right decision?

●————— **Recognizing the dangers when saying no to negative influences**

In some situations saying no may be hazardous to your health. Many gang members threaten young people into joining their gangs and breaking laws. Not saying no may also be hazardous to your health, however. People die every day of drug overdoses and gang-related activities. We may be placing our lives in danger when we allow others to influence us. What are some behaviors that are dangerous or could get you in trouble?

Elicit responses and list. Responses may include skipping school, shoplifting, using profanity, carrying weapons, drinking alcohol, taking drugs, and smoking.

It is not easy to say no. Many young people are afraid they will "lose face" with their friends if they do not follow the crowd. What does "losing face" mean? How can you "save face" and still say no?

Elicit responses and discuss.

Real friends care for one another. Nobody lives in a vacuum. We all influence each other, and we all need friends. You can have a positive influence on others by modeling assertion. Remember, assertion is not aggression. You can say no assertively, and your real friends will understand that you are still worth having as a friend.

●————— **Thinking reflectively and seeking support when resisting negative influences**

You must be reflective before you say no. To be able to say no, you need to use your Thinking Steps: STOP, THINK, PLAN, and CHECK. You must also act assertively and allow your Thinking Me and not your Impulsive Me to make decisions. Before saying no to a situation that might endanger you, seek support from people who can help you. You may need to get advice from family members or other adults, such as a school counselor or teacher—even the police if you feel physically threatened.

A strong group of friends can also be important when you are resisting negative pressure. When you say no to nonthreatening situations, you become more assertive and prepare yourself to resist peer pressure in more dangerous situations. People will then perceive you as being more confident.

Monitoring Knowledge and Comprehension

Ask the following questions and discuss.

1. Say no assertively to the following: "One drag of this joint won't hurt you."

2. Model a positive response without "losing face" to the following: "Those sneakers you're wearing are really out of it. Where did you get them, from your grandma's closet?"

3. An off-beat crowd in your school wants you to join them, but they require you to steal a six-pack of beer from a convenience store. What are the dangers of saying no in this situation?

4. Where can you go to get help in the situation just described?

Guided Practice

Divide students into small groups. Distribute Figure 39 (Peer Pressure Situations) and assign each group one of the situations. Have groups develop a role-play to demonstrate how to deal with peer pressure; conduct role-plays before the whole group and discuss.

Assessing Mastery

Direct students to write down a brief situation that would require saying no. Examples: "Aw, come on, let me copy your homework," "Let's dig up Mr. Smith's tomatoes—he's such a mean old creep," and "If you want to be my friend, you will have to break up with Neray. She's not our kind."

RETEACHING

Independent Practice

Distribute copies of Figure 40 (What Would You Say?) and have students complete as instructed. Discuss answers.

Evaluation and Feedback

Divide students into small groups and give each group a copy of Figure 41 (Say No?). Direct groups to discuss, decide whether saying no is advisable, and devise a plan to handle each situation. Discuss with the entire group.

CLOSING

Summary

> In this lesson we learned to recognize the negative influences of peers in decision making. We learned that friends also have positive influences on our behavior. We must say no to negative influences, but we must also recognize possible dangers when saying no. In such cases, we need to think reflectively and seek support from people we trust.

Generalization

Select from the following activities.

1. Direct students to list real-life situations in which they have received pressure from their peers. Next ask students to list situations in which the peer pressure was helpful. Discuss.

2. Direct students to practice saying no at home to something harmful to them—for example, eating junk food or watching too much TV.

ENRICHMENT

Encourage students to write a poem or rap about saying no in a peer pressure situation. An example follows.

Assert Yourself and Just Say No

Think of what is asked of you:
If you decide that it won't do
Turn to leave, but before you go
Assert yourself and just say NO.

Say no to alcohol, cigarettes, and drugs,
Say no to bullies, swindlers, and thugs.
Assert yourself and you will show
That you can always just say NO.

Peer Pressure Situations

Situation 1

You and your friend are browsing in a sports store. You see those baseball cards that are missing in your collection, but you don't have enough money to buy them. Your friend is trying to convince you to take them, and you are very tempted.

Situation 2

You and your family are on a trip. You meet another family from your home town and make friends with their daughter. She tries to persuade you to carry a bag of pot in your baby brother's diaper bag. She says it is worth a fortune back home.

Situation 3

You've been sick and missed several days of school. You tried to catch up, but you are in way over your head. Your friend knows where the teacher keeps her final exam, and it would be easy to get. Your school has a "no pass, no play" policy, and you know you'll be off the basketball team if you fail the exam.

Figure 39

What Would You Say?

Name: _____ Date:_____

What would you say in the following situations? Supply the missing dialogue.

1. Peer: Let's skip school. It's Friday—nothing's going on.

   You: _____

   _____

   _____

2. Peer: Aw, man, take a sip of this vodka. It'll make you feel great.

   You: _____

   _____

   _____

3. Peer: Look! Here are your dad's car keys—let's cruise.

   You: _____

   _____

   _____

4. Peer: Come on and join us. We're helping with the Special Olympics this year!

   You: _____

   _____

   _____

Figure 40

Say No?

Situation 1

Fred's father is authoritarian and abusive. Fred works hard delivering newspapers and has saved 500 dollars toward a car he plans to buy in a few years. One day, his father tells him to hand over the money because he needs to take a fishing trip with his friends. Should Fred say no?

Situation 2

Serina has moved to a new city and a new school. It was a slow process getting accepted by her peers, but it finally happened. Serina has been invited to games, parties, and sleepovers. One weekend at a sleepover she hears a knock at the window and sees two boys from school peeping in. The girls tell Serina that if she wants to be their friend, she has to go for a walk with the boys. She does not know the boys, and the idea makes her very uncomfortable. Should Serina say no?

Situation 3

Fourteen-year-old Laura's parents are constantly reminding her not to let anyone in the house while they are at work, except her friends Carla and Denise. One day, Laura answers the door and four kids she knows from school are standing on the doorstep. They tell Laura they need to make an emergency phone call. Should Laura say no?

Figure 41

ROLE-PLAY: SELF-ADVOCACY & ASSERTIVENESS

CHARACTERS

Reba, Troy, Polly, Ollie

SITUATION

The students at Holloway Middle School are upset. The principal, Mr. Reno, has announced that the soda machines will be removed from campus. The reason isn't a concern for the students' dental health but rather for litter. Soda cans have been dropped everywhere all over the school, in spite of repeated warnings. The students feel that removing the soda machines punishes everyone when the culprits amount to a handful of students. Reba, President of the Student Council, has called an emergency meeting to ask for help.

Reba: I called this meeting because I cannot do this by myself. I need everyone's help if we are to convince Mr. Reno that this rule is unfair.

Troy: But what can we do? We are all guilty in a way. We ignored the warnings, and none of us had the courage to stand up to the kids who were littering. We all know who the litterbugs are, but we don't want to rat on them.

Reba: Does anyone have any suggestions? How can we get these kids to stop littering, and how can we get our soft drinks back?

Polly: Let's invite them to our next meeting. We've always left them out before.

Ollie: Invite them? You're crazy! They're not interested in the Student Council or in anything else.

Polly: That's not exactly correct. Peer pressure can be positive as well as negative. Let's think of a plan to involve everybody.

Troy: You mean start a campaign and ask them to join.

Reba: I see what you're getting at. We can start a "Keep Holloway Middle School Beautiful" campaign to convince Mr. Reno that we are serious about getting rid of litter.

Ollie: We can ask the litterbugs to help us in our campaign.

Polly: You can start by not calling them names. Shame on you!
We've got to keep positive.

Ollie: Lots of luck, Ms. Positive Pollyana!

Reba: Arguing among ourselves won't help. Let's get serious. Let's offer our help to them and let them help us.

Troy: But how? I'm so confused.

Reba: Let's go all out—posters and public announcements. One of my dad's clients is a news anchor on television. He's always looking for human relations stories. I'll talk to Mr. Reno first and ask his permission to start the campaign. I'll be assertive—I'll say, "Mr. Reno, we can't blame you for removing the soda machines because littering the school grounds is not right. But we want another chance to prove that we are interested in keeping Holloway beautiful. Here is our plan."

Polly: We can ask several of the litterers to appear on TV speaking against littering schools. I know exactly which ones. They won't refuse.

Ollie: I get it—we can help them present a positive picture, as though they are helping. We could also start a recycling club and raise money to buy sports equipment.

Polly: I'm glad my Positive Pollyana is rubbing off. And Ollie, it's not "as though" they will be helping. They really will be. Your recycling club idea is awesome. I'm sure the parents will want to help.

Reba: Great! It looks like we have something going. Let's get started and make some specific plans.

EVALUATION AND FEEDBACK

1. Why did the Student Council group need the help of the litterers to achieve their goal?

2. How did the group plan to help the litterers?

3. How did Reba handle the problem?

4. Name instances of positive and negative outcomes of peer pressure in the story.

5. Did Reba plan to use direct or empathetic assertion in persuading Mr. Reno to change his mind? Explain.

6. In what ways did the group follow the Thinking Steps?

7. Which Me was Ollie coming from when he called the litterers "litterbugs"?

8. Which Me was Polly coming from when she rebuked Ollie?

9. Which Me was Reba reflecting?

CONFLICT RESOLUTION

SKILL AREA 5

I Can Say No to Me

GOAL

- To practice self-control

OBJECTIVES

- Identifying the consequences of losing self-control
- Recognizing how feelings affect behavior
- Recognizing the relationship between loss of self-control and physical and emotional distress
- Identifying strategies to regain self-control

MATERIALS

- Self-Control Assessment (Figure 42)
- Self-Check Chart (Figure 43)
- Chalkboard or easel pad
- Paper and pencils
- Pictures of conflict situations (cut from magazines)

PROCEDURE

OPENING

Review

None needed.

Stating Objectives

In this lesson we will learn the importance of practicing self-control. People who constantly lose control cannot consider the consequences of their actions. Feelings play an important part in how we react to conflict situations. Our actions often affect our well-being, both physically and emotionally, but there are a number of ways to keep cool under stress.

INSTRUCTION

Teaching and Guided Discussion

●———— Identifying the consequences of losing self-control

What happens when we lose self-control?

Elicit responses and discuss.

We allow our Impulsive Me to be in charge. We say or do things we may regret. People who are out of control have a hard time saying no. They may drink alcohol, fight, take drugs, eat too much or too little, or engage in irresponsible sexual behavior. When people are out of control they may hurt themselves and others. Individuals who cannot control themselves behave irresponsibly and do not think of the consequences of their behavior. They often behave foolishly or even turn to violence.

●———— **Recognizing how feelings affect behavior**

It is very hard to control our feelings when we are under stress or when people mess with us. It is OK to be angry, sad, even jealous, but it is not OK to lose control when you have these feelings. This is especially true when your actions result in harm to yourself or other people. How do you feel when you lose self-control?

Elicit responses and discuss.

Often certain feelings result in rash and impulsive behaviors. When people are impulsive they overreact and forget to use the Thinking Steps—STOP, THINK, PLAN, and CHECK. It takes courage and strength to control our feelings, to practice self-control, and to use the Thinking Me and not the Impulsive Me.

●———— **Recognizing the relationship between loss of self-control and physical and emotional distress**

Out-of-control behaviors often result in physical and emotional problems. People who cannot control their feelings and behaviors frequently don't feel or look good. Let's suppose Pete feels envious because Warren has a new pair of pump sneakers. Pete's feelings of envy may result in a stomachache, headache, or lack of appetite.

Aggressive people who are constantly out of control may have high blood pressure, shortness of breath, and stomach ulcers. People sometimes strike out in anger because it feels good at the time. However, later they may feel physically or psychologically bad. Did you ever lose control this way, then feel guilty or physically sick?

Encourage students to generate examples of out-of-control behaviors and associated physical symptoms. List on the chalkboard or easel pad. Some examples follow.

- Shouting: headache

- Exasperating: flushed face

- Hitting: rapid heartbeat

- Worrying: sweating palms

Identifying strategies to regain self-control

When I am about to lose control, I use *self-talk*. I say to myself, "STOP." I take a deep breath and talk to myself silently. I sometimes say, "I won't lose it—I'll keep calm." It takes me a while before I can talk about my feelings. What about you? What do you do to keep your cool?

Elicit responses and discuss. Answers may include taking a walk, counting to 10, turning away from what is tempting you to lose control, taking a shower, doing push-ups.

Self-talk is a strategy you can use to practice self-control. For instance, some people have a difficult time losing weight. When dieting, they can talk themselves out of eating a second helping of food or a piece of pie. Let me show you: "I would like to have that piece of chocolate pie—my favorite, yum. STOP! What am I saying? I bet there are 1,000 calories and 25 grams of fat in that pie. THINK! That's my entire day's fat allowance. No, I better not. PLAN! I can have a scoop of frozen chocolate yogurt instead. CHECK! Good plan."

Many teenagers diet unnecessarily. If you think the preceding example may not be appropriate for your group, you may want to substitute another scenario.

It is important not to fall into a Bossy Me attitude during self-talk. The Bossy Me attitude uses too many shoulds, musts, and oughts. In my example I did not tell myself, "You ought to be ashamed of yourself for wanting that piece of pie." Instead, I allowed my Thinking Me to reason and recognize the consequences of eating the pie.

Monitoring Knowledge and Comprehension

Ask the following questions.

1. What happens if you punch somebody at school (at home, in the neighborhood)?

2. Is it OK to feel angry, to yell, or to cry? When and why?

3. How might you feel physically if you lose your self-control?

4. What are some alternatives to hitting, cursing, or shouting?

Guided Practice

Divide students into small groups and give each group a magazine picture showing people in conflict. Direct students to describe the feelings, body language, and facial expressions of the individuals in the pictures and to write a brief story illustrating the conflict. Evaluate stories for understanding of the effects of conflict on feelings and physical symptoms.

Assessing Mastery

Check for comprehension and offer assistance as students write.

RETEACHING

Independent Practice

Distribute copies of Figure 42 (Self-Control Assessment) and have students complete.

Evaluation and Feedback

Discuss students' responses to the assessment. Ask the following questions.

1. Why is it better to control ourselves instead of having other people control us?

2. How can lack of self-control lead to the use of drugs, violence, or irresponsible sexual behavior?

CLOSING

Summary

We have learned in this lesson that lack of self-control leads to negative consequences. People who are out of control often behave impulsively. They allow their feelings to interfere with their good judgment. We can control our behavior if we use the Thinking Steps and a Thinking Me attitude. Sometimes it is difficult to keep cool, especially when we are under stress or when someone provokes us. Stress and angry feelings can cause certain physical symptoms, like headaches and stomachaches. Counting to 10, talking to someone, or walking away sometimes helps us regain control.

Generalization

Guide students in identifying a situation occurring at home or in the community in which they are experiencing problems establishing and maintaining self-control. Incidents may include lack of patience with parents, siblings, friends, and others; saying no to drugs or alcohol; or other detrimental involvements. Encourage students to devise a plan to practice self-control and take charge of the situation. Encourage students to implement their plans and let them know that if they wish they may share their experiences with the group later. Provide students with a Self-Check Chart (Figure 43) to record their plan and its outcome.

ENRICHMENT

1. Model rehearsing a plan to "keep cool" by practicing positive self-talk in front of a mirror. Ask volunteers to do likewise and to evaluate one another's performance. Were self-talk and the Thinking Steps a part of each plan?

2. Use newspapers to identify stories illustrating lack of self-control. Discuss feelings and consequences.

Self-Control Assessment

Name: _____ Date:_____

Check the "Yes" or "No" box to show which of the following things you would be likely to do.

1–3 yes:	You're OK
4–6 yes:	Watch out
7–12 yes:	Danger zone

	Yes	No
1. You are late for practice. You scream and yell at your father.	☐	☐
2. Your sibling (brother/sister) borrows your clothes without asking. You get mad and throw all your sibling's homework papers off the desk.	☐	☐
3. You make an F on your test. You blame the teacher.	☐	☐
4. You listen to gossip, then run to tell others.	☐	☐
5. You think of chocolate, then you run to get some.	☐	☐
6. Your friend has new jeans. You must have new jeans right now.	☐	☐
7. Someone cuts in line. You push to get your space back.	☐	☐
8. Your mother asks you to take out the garbage. You shout, "It's not my turn."	☐	☐
9. Someone jokingly punches you on the arm. You punch the person back.	☐	☐
10. Someone aggravates you, and you burst into tears.	☐	☐
11. You stub your toe on a rock, then you overreact (cry, swear, blame the rock).	☐	☐
12. Your science project partner forgets to bring his or her part of the work. You say, "I refuse to work with you on this or any other project ever again!"	☐	☐

Figure 42

Self-Check Chart

Name: _____ Date:_____

Answer the following questions now.

1. What is the problem?

2. Who is involved? *(optional)*

3. What is my plan?

Answer these questions after you try out your plan.

1. What happened when I tried my plan?

2. What, if anything, do I need to do to make my plan work better next time?

Figure 43

TRY & TRY AGAIN

GOAL

- To find alternative solutions in conflict situations

OBJECTIVES

- Identifying the roles of support people in resolving conflicts
- Recognizing the need to be honest in identifying causes of conflict
- Exploring alternatives through brainstorming to resolve conflict
- Using self-management to develop plans to resolve conflict

MATERIALS

- What Else Could I Do? (Figure 44)
- Real-Life Alternatives (Figure 45)
- Chalkboard or easel pad

PROCEDURE

OPENING

Review

In our last lesson we learned that the lack of self-control often leads to negative consequences. People who are out of control are often impulsive. They allow their feelings to interfere with good judgment. Can anyone give me an example?

Elicit responses.

Sometimes it is difficult to keep cool, especially when we are under stress or when someone provokes us. People who act out their angry feelings often suffer physical as well as emotional distress. We can learn to practice self-control by using self-talk to help us apply the Thinking Steps and keep a Thinking Me attitude.

Follow up on any generalization activities assigned during the last lesson.

Stating Objectives

In this lesson we will learn how to find alternative solutions in conflict situations. Certain people can become a support group to help us resolve conflicts. We can identify causes of conflict through self-examination and brainstorming. We can make plans to reach alternative solutions to conflict by practicing self-management.

INSTRUCTION

Teaching and Guided Discussion

● ——— **Identifying the roles of support people in resolving conflicts**

The first thing we need to do in a conflict situation is to STOP and gain self-control. What is the next step we need to take if we want to resolve conflict?

Elicit responses and discuss.

Our next step is to THINK of alternative ways of solving the problem. Then we need to PLAN. Without a plan we may fall back into bad habits, and the conflict will not be resolved. Finally, we CHECK the plan to see if it is working.

One plan may include a support group. A support group is made up of people who can help us solve our difficulties. It can include your parents, your school counselor, or any other adult who is understanding. Your support group can also include a good friend who is objective and who can be honest and helpful. An objective person is able to reason and "tell it like it is," not just say what you want to hear. An objective person will not take sides. Who would you choose to be in your support group when you need help resolving a conflict?

Discuss.

● ——— **Recognizing the need to be honest in identifying causes of conflict**

Examining the causes of conflict is helpful in coming up with alternatives. We need to be honest with ourselves to find the real causes of a problem. Sometimes we try to fool ourselves and blame others. Sometimes we justify our actions based on what we perceive or believe to be correct. For example:

> During class change in the hall, José bumped into Ken accidentally. Immediately, Ken allowed his Impulsive Me to overreact. He doubled up his fist and punched José, giving him a bloody nose. Ken felt justified in hitting José because José had bumped into him. However, Ken had held angry feelings towards José for months, ever since he heard that José liked Ken's girlfriend, Marissa. What was Ken's real cause for the conflict?

Discuss. To help students clarify the real cause, ask the following questions.

1. If Raul, Ken's good friend, had accidentally bumped into Ken in the hall, how do you think Ken would have reacted?

2. If Marissa had accidentally bumped into Ken in the hall, how do you think Ken would have reacted?

3. What could Ken have done instead of collecting bad feelings?

Exploring alternatives through brainstorming to resolve conflict

Brainstorming is a technique to find alternative solutions in a conflict. When you brainstorm, you come up with as many alternatives as possible without judging any of them. After you list all the alternatives, you combine similar ideas and eliminate those that aren't practical. In this way, you come up with one or more workable solutions.

Write the following on the chalkboard or easel pad.

1. Come up with as many ideas as possible.

2. Do not pass judgment on any ideas.

3. Join similar ideas together; eliminate impractical ideas.

4. Narrow the list to a few workable solutions.

Encourage students to brainstorm solutions to the conflict between Ken and José. List alternatives on the chalkboard or easel pad, accepting all ideas nonjudgmentally. Alternatively, brainstorm solutions to an actual school-related problem.

- Ken could ignore the bump.

- Ken could check the stories about José and Marissa.

- Ken could wait after school to get even.

- Ken could question José about his feelings for Marissa.

- Ken could trip José "accidentally."

- Ken could pour his soda down José's shirt at lunch "accidentally."

- Ken could discuss his concerns with his girlfriend or with José.

- Ken could say "Watch where you're going" and walk on.

Ask students to rule out impossible or impractical ideas, combine and improve on ideas, and choose the best alternative.

Using self-management to develop plans to resolve conflict

Sometimes it is necessary to make several plans before we find one that will work. A successful plan will work when we become aware of our behavior and decide to change. *Self-management* means handling our behavior ourselves. *Self-recording* means counting and writing down the number of times we exhibit a problem behavior.

First we decide to change, then we take action and make a plan. Many times we are unaware of how often we display a certain behavior. Let's suppose I frequently yell at my students to get their attention. I want to stop yelling. My first step is to count the number of times I yell per day and then find a way to reduce that number. How could I keep track of my yelling?

Elicit responses. On the chalkboard or easel pad, demonstrate how to tally incidents and how data can be graphed to show progress.

Can you think of any other behaviors that you can count and record?

Elicit responses and discuss.

You can choose an alternative behavior for the one causing the problem. An alternative is a choice. This choice behavior is part of your plan. Instead of yelling, I could flick the light on and off, fold my arms and stare at my students until I got their attention, ring a little bell, or count aloud from 1 to 10. What else could I do?

Elicit responses and discuss.

Monitoring Knowledge and Comprehension

Ask the following questions.

1. Why is an objective person so important in seeking alternative solutions to a conflict?

2. What are some ways we can go about finding the real cause of a conflict?

3. How can brainstorming help us find alternatives when we have a conflict?

4. What are some alternatives in the following situations?

    *   *Situation 1:* I am 13 years old, and I have a drinking problem. I have joined a support group, but I really want a drink.

        Alternatives: Call a member of your support group. Drink an alcohol-free drink. Get involved in an interesting activity to get your mind off your drinking.

    *   *Situation 2:* I am furious. My girlfriend/boyfriend dumped me. I am afraid to confront him/her, so I have decided to trash his/her new jacket.

        Alternatives: Talk about your anger and hurt feelings with a supportive friend. Use self-talk and tell yourself that it is OK to feel angry, sad, disappointed, and hurt, but life goes on. Make new friends.

    *   *Situation 3:* I want to get off drugs, but I'm addicted.

        Alternatives: Join a support group. Talk to your school counselor or any other adult who can help. Avoid people who use drugs. Inform yourself about the dangers of drugs. Use self-talk to express your Caring Me and your Thinking Me.

- *Situation 4:* I want to stop smoking, but all my friends smoke. I can't get rid of my hacking cough.

   Alternatives: Get the facts on smoking. Seek professional help, starting with the school nurse or counselor. Use candy or gum as an alternative. Use self-talk to express your Caring Me and Thinking Me.

- *Situation 5:* I am mean when I lose control. I fight and get even. Later, I feel sorry for the hurt I caused.

   Alternatives: Use the Thinking Steps and identify a plan to chill out, like counting, listening to music, walking, and so on. Practice being assertive instead of aggressive. Examine your Me attitudes.

Guided Practice

Arrange students in small groups and direct each group to develop a plan for Tanya in the following scenario. Direct the groups to use their Thinking Steps, brainstorm to come up with an alternative behavior, and include a self-recording strategy.

> Tanya cannot control her cursing. She uses curse words at home, in her classroom, in the schoolyard, and just about everywhere. She has been suspended often and is failing the eighth grade. Tanya wants to go to high school with her friends, but her cursing is preventing her progress. What can Tanya do?

Assessing Mastery

Have groups report on their respective plans. Assess plans for their inclusion of the Thinking Steps, a self-recording strategy, and an alternative behavior. Also consider whether the plans include the use of a support group to assist Tanya or to identify possible causes for Tanya's problem.

RETEACHING

Independent Practice

Ask students to complete Figure 44 (What Else Could I Do?) and Figure 45 (Real-Life Alternatives).

Evaluation and Feedback

Give feedback on the students' responses. Evaluate for understanding of the need for alternative solutions to conflicts.

CLOSING

Summary

In this lesson we learned that support groups or people we trust can help us through conflicts. Everybody needs help sometimes. We need to know how to be honest when looking for the real causes of our conflicts. We can explore alternatives through brainstorming and recognize that we may need to try several plans to reach a solution. We can use self-management, especially self-recording, to help develop plans to resolve conflict.

Generalization

Direct students to keep a journal for one week and to record how they practiced self-control in school, at home, and in the community.

ENRICHMENT

1. Have students close their eyes and think of a personal problem. Encourage them to visualize an alternative solution, their reaction, and the reactions of others. Follow with discussion.

2. Encourage students to observe and identify conflict situations in school. Direct the students not to interfere but to document the conflict and the outcome. Discuss alternative solutions.

What Else Could I Do?

Name: _____ Date:_____

Suggest an alternative behavior for each of the following situations.

1. Someone curses at me. I curse back.

   Alternative: _____

   _____

2. My mother yells at me. I yell at my little brother.

   Alternative: _____

   _____

3. Someone slaps my back. I punch his/her face.

   Alternative: _____

   _____

4. My teacher is annoyed because I am late. I come to class even later
   the following day.

   Alternative: _____

   _____

5. My little brother breaks my new CD. I break his favorite toy airplane.

   Alternative: _____

   _____

Figure 44

215

6. I'm stressed out, and my friend asks me for help. I shout out, "Can't you see I'm busy?"

   Alternative: _____

   _____

7. Someone insults my mother. I lose control and start a fight.

   Alternative: _____

   _____

8. I make an F on my science test. I tear the test paper to shreds.

   Alternative: _____

   _____

9. My parents ground me because I come home late. I slam the bedroom door and knock the handle off.

   Alternative: _____

   _____

10. Somebody makes a pass at my girlfriend/boyfriend. I shout out threats.

    Alternative: _____

    _____

Figure 44 continued

Real-Life Alternatives

Name: _____ Date:_____

Write five sentences describing out-of-control behaviors that you have personally experienced or witnessed. Then write a sentence describing an alternative, in-control behavior.

Behavior 1: _____

Alternative behavior:_____

_____

Behavior 2: _____

_____

Alternative behavior:_____

_____

Behavior 3: _____

_____

Alternative behavior:_____

_____

Behavior 4: _____

_____

Alternative behavior:_____

_____

Behavior 5: _____

_____

Alternative behavior:_____

_____

Figure 45   *217*

GIVE & TAKE & MEDIATE

GOAL

- To demonstrate understanding of the processes of negotiation, mediation, and compromise

OBJECTIVES

- Recognizing the positive aspects of conflict and differing opinions
- Recognizing the need for peaceful negotiation of conflict
- Demonstrating basic understanding of mediation
- Demonstrating basic understanding of compromise

MATERIALS

- Chalkboard or easel pad
- Newspapers or news magazines
- Art supplies (poster board, markers, glue)

PROCEDURE

OPENING

Review

In our last lesson we learned that to resolve conflicts we need to find alternative solutions. We also learned that a support group or an objective person we trust can help us. We need to examine the real cause of our problem honestly before attempting to find solutions. We can explore alternatives through brainstorming, recognize that several plans may be necessary to reach a solution, and use self-management, especially self-recording, to help develop plans to resolve conflict.

Follow up on any generalization activities assigned during the last lesson.

Stating Objectives

In this lesson we will learn to understand conflict and different opinions. We will learn the importance of negotiation to find peaceful solutions. We will also learn how mediation can help resolve conflicts and talk about how to reach a compromise.

INSTRUCTION

Teaching and Guided Discussion

●————— **Recognizing the positive aspects of conflict and differing opinions**

Conflict in itself is neither good nor bad—it's what we make of it. When people are in conflict, they perceive that others are interfering in their efforts to reach their goal. By using our Thinking Steps—STOP, THINK, PLAN, and CHECK—and a Thinking Me attitude, we can learn to appreciate others' opinions. Conflict can help us sharpen our thinking skills and broaden our understanding. We can use conflict situations to help us grow and mature.

Can you think of a situation in which you and another person had different opinions? Were you both right or wrong?

Elicit responses and discuss.

●————— **Recognizing the need for peaceful negotiation of conflict**

We must accept that people differ in their opinions and that everyone is entitled to his or her own beliefs. We cannot change someone's attitudes through force. However, there are occasions when we must stand by our convictions and say no, even when it involves a conflict. In these cases our behavior must be assertive and not aggressive.

Review assertive versus aggressive behavior from the Preliminary Lesson as needed. Ask for examples of conflict situations in which students must say no. Answers may involve drug and alcohol use, illegal acts, or irresponsible sex.

There are many wars and conflicts in the world today. *(Give examples of current conflicts.)* It is difficult for people to live in peace. Why do people fight in wars?

Elicit responses and discuss. Responses may concern power, boundaries, wealth, religion, and so forth.

It is important for countries and for individuals to solve conflicts through negotiating and not fighting. To negotiate means to bargain and reach a settlement by talking, listening, and being willing to understand. Years ago, several countries got together and started an organization to prevent wars and to negotiate peace. This is the United Nations. The function of the United Nations is to help nations negotiate and find peaceful solutions to their conflicts.

We also need to find peaceful solutions in our own lives, families, and communities. What feelings do you think interfere with people's peaceful negotiation?

Brainstorm and list students' answers on the chalkboard or easel pad. Responses may include pride, revenge, need to control, power, hurt feelings, and so forth.

●————— **Demonstrating basic understanding of mediation**

How can two people in conflict negotiate and settle a dispute? Remember the United Nations? Individuals in conflict must identify what they are willing to negotiate to reach a solution to the problem.

Mediation is sometimes necessary to help us negotiate a conflict. A mediator is a neutral person who helps others solve conflicts and find solutions. A mediator does not take sides but allows people to take turns talking about their feelings without interruption. When two countries are in conflict, the United Nations sometimes appoints a mediator from a third country to help find a peaceful solution. It is not much different when individuals are in conflict. For example, if you and your brother or sister are fighting, your mother may serve as a mediator to help you negotiate and find a solution to the problem. Can you think of other situations that might require mediation?

Elicit responses and discuss. Answers may include conflicts between ballplayers and team owners, singers and recording companies, management and labor, or husbands and wives.

● ———— **Demonstrating basic understanding of compromise**

Negotiation and mediation involve compromise. What does it mean to compromise?

Elicit responses.

To compromise means to find a solution that is acceptable to everyone involved. However, the solution may not be everyone's first choice. To reach a compromise we often need to give up something we want. For example, suppose two friends are going to the movies. One friend wants to eat pizza first and then go to the 9 o'clock show. The other friend would prefer to go to the 7 o'clock show, then eat at home and finish a school report. They have a conflict. How can they negotiate, reach a compromise, and find a solution?

Discuss. Answers could include the following.

- Go to the 7 o'clock show, then go home and order pizza.

- Go to the 9 o'clock show this time and the 7 o'clock show next time.

- Pick up a pizza from a drive-through restaurant and still make the 7 o'clock show.

- Have the second friend skip the pizza and eat at home, finish the report, and meet the first friend for the 9 o'clock show.

Monitoring Knowledge and Comprehension

Ask the following questions.

1. Why is it important to keep an open mind to differing opinions?

2. What would happen if no one negotiated (between countries, in communities, in families)?

3. How does mediation help resolve conflicts?

4. My boss wants me to come to work at 6 o'clock in the morning and leave at 2 o'clock in the afternoon. I would rather start work at 7 o'clock and leave at 3 o'clock. How can I compromise with my boss?

Guided Practice

Direct small groups of students to find information from newspapers or news magazines on current world conflicts. Distribute art materials and have students make a collage illustrating a specific conflict situation.

Assessing Mastery

Ask the following questions.

1. Why are the two parties in conflict?

2. Could mediation and compromise change the situation? If so, how?

3. Have the parties been willing to negotiate?

4. What will it take to resolve this conflict?

RETEACHING

Independent Practice

Direct students to research the formation of the United Nations and write or present an oral report to the group. Encourage the class to discuss the work of the United Nations.

Evaluation and Feedback

Ask the following questions; evaluate for understanding of the need for negotiation, mediation, and compromise. Answers will vary.

1. Why do you suppose gangs from different ethnic groups fight each other? How are gang wars the same as wars between countries? How are they different?

2. What kind of conflicts do we find in our cities and schools? What do you think causes these conflicts?

3. What can be done to resolve conflicts in schools, homes, and the community?

4. Why are organizations such as the United Nations important to world peace?

CLOSING

Summary

In this lesson we learned that conflict can be positive and that we need to be open to opinions, even when these opinions are different from our own. We learned the importance of negotiation in reaching peaceful solutions. Mediation and compromise are two strategies we can use to achieve peace. It is often necessary for parties to compromise to resolve a conflict.

Generalization

Direct students to review the newspaper over a week-long period for articles in which negotiation, mediation, and compromise are described. Examples may include current court cases, demands of workers from employers, disputes between countries, or conflicts within the country, state, or community. Encourage students to share their findings with the group.

ENRICHMENT

1. Start a schoolwide United Nations club. Train groups of students as peer mediators to resolve conflicts as they arise. A good training resource is *Peer Mediation: Conflict Resolution in Schools,* by Fred Schrumpf, Donna K. Crawford, and Richard J. Bodine (Research Press, 1996).

2. Develop a bulletin board with the theme of conflict resolution. Ask students to contribute mottos or compose their own. For example:

   To compromise does not mean losing face.

   Look before you leap.

   It is to a person's honor to avoid strife, but every fool is quick to quarrel.

   If you can't stand the heat, get out of the kitchen.

   Our work for peace must begin within the private world of each of us.

3. Have students write acrostics for the words *negotiate, mediate,* and *compromise.*

WORDS CAN SOMETIMES HURT

GOAL

- To respond appropriately to teasing

OBJECTIVES

- Recognizing the intent of teasing
- Distinguishing between friendly teasing and hurtful teasing
- Identifying and dealing with feelings provoked by teasing
- Identifying behaviors that reinforce or reduce teasing

MATERIALS

- Check Your Teasing (Figure 46)
- Hurtful or Friendly Teasing? (Figure 47)
- Index cards

PROCEDURE

OPENING

Review

In our last lesson we learned that conflict in itself is neither good nor bad—it's what we make of it. We must be open to different opinions. Successful negotiation is necessary for peaceful resolution of conflict. Mediation and compromise are two strategies we can use to resolve conflict.

Follow up on any generalization activities assigned during the last lesson.

Stating Objectives

In this lesson we will find out why people tease. We will also learn to distinguish between friendly teasing and hurtful teasing. We all react to and feel differently about teasing, but planning ahead and responding assertively to teasing can help us avoid conflict.

INSTRUCTION

Teaching and Guided Discussion

●———— Recognizing the intent of teasing

Teasing can be good or bad, depending on the intention of the person who is teasing and on the perceptions of the person being teased. Joking and kidding may be considered friendly teasing, whereas harassing and mocking are hurtful teasing. We don't like to be teased when we are sensitive about something. What are some situations when you were teased and didn't like it?

Elicit responses.

(*Personalize the following example.*) I don't like to be teased about _____. It hurts my feelings when someone teases me about it. However, I get a kick when someone teases me about _____ because I'm not sensitive about that and it doesn't hurt my feelings. I understand the person is kidding.

Why do people tease?

Elicit responses and discuss. Answers may include to be mean, cruel, cute, inconsiderate, sarcastic, friendly; to get attention or revenge; to feel superior or in control; or to start a fight.

●———— Distinguishing between friendly teasing and hurtful teasing

There is a difference between friendly teasing and hurtful teasing. The purpose of hurtful teasing is to belittle, annoy, or make fun of a person. Friendly teasing is done to make the teased person laugh and be happy or to get that person's attention. Have you ever felt happy about being teased?

Elicit responses.

It is OK to kid around, but you must understand how the teased person is feeling. If the feeling is unpleasant, then the teasing can result in conflict. If the teasing results in happy feelings, then it's OK.

Hurtful teasers "hit below the belt." They pick on something that they know is very sensitive. Some students will tease by saying something nasty about members of your family because they know they will get a reaction. If that happens, then the teasers win.

It is best to back off when a teased person is offended or shows signs of anger or sadness. Some people may misunderstand the intention of the teaser. The intention may be friendly, but if the other person views the teasing as hurtful, then it must stop.

Distribute copies of Figure 46 (Check Your Teasing) and have students complete. Discuss students' responses.

●———— Identifying and dealing with feelings provoked by teasing

What feelings result from hurtful teasing?

Elicit responses. Answers may include sadness, frustration, isolation, and anger.

It helps to use the Thinking Steps in response to our feelings. The steps STOP, THINK, PLAN, and CHECK can make us realize what is happening. Instead of feeling angry and responding with an Impulsive Me attitude, we can regain control and avoid the teaser's trap. By feeling confident and using a Thinking Me attitude, we can avoid conflict.

Assertive people can walk away from being teased without losing face—or confront teasers without feeling angry or hurt. An Impulsive Me would feel like getting even and respond with more hurtful teasing. Remember the saying "Sticks and stones may break my bones, but words can never hurt me"? Can words hurt your feelings?

Elicit responses and discuss.

It is important to choose our words wisely and to examine the situation before deciding on a plan of action. If the teasing is likely to make you feel sad or angry, it is wiser to walk away than to act on your feelings.

Identifying behaviors that reinforce or reduce teasing

Our behavior often determines whether teasing will continue or stop. If our behavior reinforces or pleases the teaser, then the teasing is likely to continue. On the other hand, we can stop the teasing by not reinforcing or paying attention to the teaser. Teasers often know exactly how to push your buttons and what your behavior will be (crying, fighting, cursing). You and you alone can prevent them from getting what they want. How could you behave to stop being teased?

Elicit responses and discuss. Answers may include using humor, ignoring, saying or doing something nice, appealing to the teaser's sense of fairness, explaining your feelings, and stating assertively that you do not want to be teased.

Before reacting, use your Thinking Steps. Tell yourself to STOP and THINK. Then make a quick PLAN to handle the situation. You can CHECK your plan later and use it in a future teasing situation if it was successful.

Monitoring Knowledge and Comprehension

Ask the following questions.

1. Why do you suppose people tease?

2. When is teasing hurtful and when is it playful?

3. List three feelings in response to hurtful teasing.

4. How can the teased person's behaviors reinforce the teaser?

Guided Practice

Select from the following activities.

1. Divide students into small groups and distribute index cards on which you have written typical responses to teasing—for example, "Get off my back," "I hate your guts," "You're a pain," or "Get out of my face." Ask each group to generate assertive alternative responses.

2. Direct small groups to write a scenario on one of the following topics.

> A friendly, playful teasing situation
>
> A vicious teasing situation
>
> A boy/girl romantic teasing situation
>
> An overreactive response to a teasing situation
>
> An assertive response to a teasing situation

Assessing Mastery

Direct groups to develop a plan using the Thinking Steps to respond to their written scenarios.

RETEACHING

Independent Practice

Direct students to complete Figure 47 (Hurtful or Friendly Teasing?). Discuss. Answers will vary—point out that this is the case because the nature of teasing (hurtful or friendly) can only be determined by the sender's intentions and the receiver's feelings.

Evaluation and Feedback

Ask the following questions.

1. When is it best to ignore teasing?

2. When is it best to assertively confront a teaser?

Ask students to react negatively and positively to the following teasing statements.

1. Your mama wears army boots.

2. If I had your face, I'd wear a paper sack.

3. What's the matter, skinny, are you afraid you'll break if you play football?

CLOSING

Summary

In this lesson we learned that we can respond to teasing without losing our cool. There is a difference between friendly teasing and hurtful teasing. We need to consider the feelings of the person being teased and adjust our behavior accordingly. When we are teased we can either ignore the teasing or we can assertively confront the teaser. Before we do either we need to consider the situation carefully. An assertive person can confront a teaser without becoming angry or hurt and can walk away from the situation without losing face.

Generalization

Direct students to interview a family member or a friend about a teasing situation and determine how that person feels about being teased. (The interviews should be anonymous.) The teasing situation may be being teased or teasing others. After 4 or 5 days, compile students' written interviews and, as a group, identify appropriate and inappropriate responses to teasing and the consequences of teasing. Stress the snowball effect of malicious teasing.

ENRICHMENT

1. Direct students to make one list of hurtful motives or reasons why people tease and a second list of various feelings a person experiences while being hurtfully teased. Discuss. Direct students to make two more lists. This time, inform them to list friendly motives for teasing and various feelings a person experiences while being teased in a friendly way.

2. Direct students to write an acrostic using the words *teasing* and *feeling*. Students may also write a free-form poem or rap on the subject.

Check Your Teasing

Name: _____ Date:_____

Check the "Yes" or "No" box to show which of the following are true for you.

	Yes	No
1. Are you sarcastic in your teasing?	☐	☐
2. When you tease, is everyone laughing but the person being teased?	☐	☐
3. Do you invalidate (put down, insult) the person you are teasing?	☐	☐
4. Does the teased person get angry?	☐	☐
5. Do you tease about something you envy (grades, clothes, popularity)?	☐	☐
6. Do you tease to make yourself look good?	☐	☐
7. Do you have the reputation of being a teaser?	☐	☐
8. When you tease, do you feel powerful?	☐	☐
9. Do you offend people with your teasing?	☐	☐
10. Are you reprimanded by adults (your parents, teachers) when you tease?	☐	☐

Figure 46

Hurtful or Friendly Teasing?

Name: _____ Date:_____

Decide which are examples of hurtful teasing and which are examples of friendly teasing.

	Hurtful	Friendly
1. You are as sweet as sugar candy, Candy.	☐	☐
2. Hey, shorty, how's the weather down there? Ha! Ha!	☐	☐
3. Did you get those sneakers at the city dump?	☐	☐
4. John never sleeps—that's why he gets all A's.	☐	☐
5. Hey, fatso, if you get any fatter we'll have to roll you.	☐	☐
6. You little devil, you. You sure know how to impress parents.	☐	☐
7. Wheeee! Watching you work makes me tired. You move like a tornado.	☐	☐
8. Da di da di da da, Mary loves Danny.	☐	☐

Write your own examples of hurtful and friendly teasing.

Hurtful: _____

_____

Friendly: _____

_____

Figure 47

ROOM FOR IMPROVEMENT

GOAL

- To accept and give constructive feedback

OBJECTIVES

- Defining the various meanings of criticism
- Recognizing the helpful effects of positive criticism
- Recognizing the harmful effects of negative criticism
- Examining various considerations when giving criticism

MATERIALS

- Johari Window (Figure 48)
- East's Dilemma (Figure 49)
- Negative Criticism or Positive Criticism? (Figure 50)
- Chalkboard or easel pad
- Paper and pencils

PROCEDURE

OPENING

Review

In our last lesson we learned that we can respond positively to teasing. There is a difference between friendly teasing and hurtful teasing. We need to consider the feelings of the person being teased and whether the teasing is pleasing or irritating. Hurtful teasing can cause conflict. We can ignore hurtful teasing, or we can assertively confront the teaser. Assertive people can confront a teaser without becoming angry or hurt; they can also walk away from a teasing situation.

Follow up on any generalization activities assigned during the last lesson.

Stating Objectives

In this lesson we will learn that there are two types of criticism, positive and negative. We will examine the helpful effects of positive criticism and the harmful effects of negative criticism. Considerations when giving criticism include timing, the other person's perceptions, and the way the criticism is given.

INSTRUCTION

Teaching and Guided Discussion

●————— **Defining the various meanings of criticism**

Who can define *criticism?*

Elicit responses.

Criticism can be defined as disapproval, rejection, and condemnation of an action or a person. It can also be defined as analysis, feedback, and a first step toward improving behavior. For example, a movie or art critic will analyze a movie or work of art and report on both positive and negative aspects.

Whenever we do something good, we like to be acknowledged, but rarely do we like to be criticized. We often view criticism as negative, and our first impulse is to reject what is being said or to strike back at the person giving the criticism. When someone criticizes us, we may feel that we've done something wrong or that the person doing the criticizing is wrong. Our first reaction places us on the defensive. Why do you think criticism places us on the defensive? Why would we want to strike back?

Elicit responses and discuss. Answers may include pride, guilt, poor self-esteem, or the way the criticism is given.

We use an Impulsive Me rather than a Thinking Me attitude when we are on the defensive. We can improve when criticism is positive and given as constructive feedback.

●————— **Recognizing the helpful effects of positive criticism**

One way to learn to accept constructive feedback is to know yourself. Two people, Joseph Luft and Harry Ingram, invented a technique to help people learn about themselves. They combined their own first names and called this technique the Johari Window.

Reproduce the four "windowpanes" of the Johari Window (see Figure 48) on the chalkboard or easel pad. In the first pane, write the word "open."

In this pane are things I know and others know about me.

In the second pane, write the word "blind."

Note: The Johari Window is described in *Of Human Interaction* (p. 13) by Joseph Luft, 1969, Palo Alto, CA: National Press Books.

——
234

This pane contains things I do not know about myself, but things other people know about me.

In the third pane, write the word "hidden."

In this pane are things that I know about myself but that others do not know about me.

In the fourth pane write the word "unknown."

In this pane are things I do not know about myself and neither does anyone else. These are things that I may have repressed deep in my mind.

(Point toward the "blind" pane.) In many instances I do not know things about myself, but others do. As I begin to participate in a group and interact with people, I send out information that I am not aware of but that other people are picking up. The information may be in the form of nonverbal cues, mannerisms, the way I say things, or the way I relate to others.

Have you ever known anyone who had an annoying habit but who had no idea he or she needed to improve in that area?

Elicit responses.

I once knew a lady who didn't realize she offended people by being overly critical. She was always giving advice about people's health. She would say, "Now, honey, you better not put so much butter on that—it will raise your cholesterol" or "Don't you know smoking can kill you? You'd better stop." She couldn't figure out why people started to avoid her. In which of these panes would I write her behavior?

Elicit responses. Put a check mark in the "blind" pane.

A good friend finally told her tactfully about her problem. The lady was surprised that her "good advice" offended people. She changed her behavior and only gave advice when she was asked for it. Where does her behavior belong now that both she and other people know about it?

Elicit responses. Erase the check mark from the "blind" pane and write it in the "open" pane.

What do you know about yourself? What do your friends know about you? What does your family know, and what don't they know? Do you think other people might know things about you that you aren't aware of yourself?

Discuss briefly, then distribute copies of Figure 48 (Johari Window) and have students fill in the squares with their own information. Allow students to share only what they wish.

● ——— **Recognizing the harmful effects of negative criticism**

Positive criticism is nonthreatening, helpful, and preferably solicited (asked for). On the other hand, negative criticism is often given to make one person look better and to hurt another person. It is demeaning and provides no constructive benefit. It creates bad feelings and prevents people from building positive relationships. Negative criticism is easy to give, but positive criticism is difficult.

People who give negative criticism may or may not be aware of being negative. They assume a Bossy Me attitude and may think they are being helpful when really they are not. For example, parents and teachers sometimes give negative criticism when they intend to improve a child's behavior. Can you give me an example?

Elicit responses and discuss.

Before giving any kind of criticism, use your Thinking Steps: STOP, THINK, PLAN, and CHECK. Ask yourself, "Am I sincere, or do I want to cause embarrassment?" Describe the behavior rather than attack the person, and avoid negative statements.

How would you feel if I said, "You are so nasty when you get angry—you better change your ways"? *(Students respond.)* Now, how would you feel if I said, "I understand that you are angry, but losing control is not helpful to anyone"? *(Students respond.)* In the first statement I was accusing, attacking, and demanding, whereas in the second I was understanding and gave you feedback on your behavior. I did not attack you personally or tell you to change—I merely described what I perceived. I left you the freedom of choice to change. When giving constructive feedback, your behavior must be assertive and not aggressive. You must also avoid a Bossy Me or an Impulsive Me attitude; these attitudes reflect negative criticism. Use your Thinking Me attitude.

Examining various considerations when giving criticism

When giving criticism you must consider various factors. Timing is important. I wouldn't give feedback to a person who is in the middle of a temper outburst; neither would I wait too long. The person might forget the behavior and say, "I didn't act that way—you're imagining things." Another important factor is whether your perception is shared by other people. Has everyone witnessed the behavior, or is it only your own perception?

It is helpful if the feedback is solicited (asked for). Before giving criticism, use the Thinking Steps and be reflective. STOP and THINK about what you are saying. PLAN your words and be tactful and diplomatic. Be careful not to give in to your Impulsive Me attitude and attack the person. CHECK your plan. How did the person react?

Usually people have specific ideas of what they want to hear when they ask for feedback. Before responding to the request, ask yourself, "Does the person really want feedback?" Your feedback should be honest and courteous. If the person rejects your feedback, then ask yourself, "What's going on? Is my feedback really wanted?"

Ask students to give feedback on the way the lesson has been conducted so far. Discuss.

Monitoring Knowledge and Comprehension

Ask the following questions.

1. What does it mean to criticize?

2. Change the following negative criticism into a positive criticism: "Your posture is awful. Stand up straight."

3. Change the following positive criticism into a negative criticism: "When students are late for class it disrupts my teaching. Let's develop a plan to start on time."

4. What are some factors you need to consider before you give constructive feedback?

Guided Practice

Choose from the following activities.

1. Ask students to write a paragraph about a negative criticism and the feelings and responses it evoked. Next direct students to write a paragraph about a constructive criticism and the feelings and responses it evoked. Discuss the differences.

2. Divide students into small groups and give each group a copy of Figure 49 (East's Dilemma)—or another hypothetical situation if one would be more appropriate for your setting. Ask each group to brainstorm ways to give East constructive criticism. Have groups share lists. Discuss the following questions:

   What can East change, and what can't he change?

   Which of your ideas do you think would convince East to change?

Assessing Mastery

Distribute another copy of Figure 48 (Johari Window). Direct students to complete the window including behaviors and perceptions from the scenario about East.

RETEACHING

Independent Practice

Distribute Figure 50 (Negative Criticism or Positive Criticism?). Answers: 1–NC; 2–PC, 3–PC, 4–NC, 5–PC, 6–NC, 7–NC, 8–PC, 9–PC, 10–NC.

Evaluation and Feedback

Check students' responses for understanding of negative versus positive approaches to criticism.

CLOSING

Summary

In this lesson we learned that criticism can be either negative or positive. There is a big difference between negative and positive criticism. We need to use our Thinking Steps when giving positive criticism. Timing and tact are also important when giving criticism.

Generalization

Direct students to identify the behavior of an adult (parent, relative, teacher, neighbor) that makes them feel defensive. Encourage the group to brainstorm responses to the identified behaviors. Ask students to identify the responses that would best avoid conflict.

ENRICHMENT

1. Divide students into groups of five. Ask them to visualize a situation in which a teacher is giving constructive criticism about grade improvement. Direct students to examine their feelings while they are listening to the teacher's criticism, then share responses with the group.

2. Direct students to make a plan, using the Thinking Steps, to give constructive feedback to a friend, sibling, parent, or teacher. For example: "I hate it when Helen bites her fingernails. Yuck! It is so disgusting, nobody wants to be around her."

   - **STOP!** I am being negative. I will stop having negative thoughts.

   - **THINK!** She needs help, not negative criticism.

   - **PLAN!** I'll tell her, "Helen, your nail-biting in public is making people avoid you. How can I help?"

   - **CHECK!** Good plan. We can ask the school nurse for advice—she is always so helpful.

Johari Window

Things I know · Things I don't know

	Things I know	Things I don't know
Things others know	1 OPEN	2 BLIND
Things others don't know	3 HIDDEN	4 UNKNOWN

Figure 48

239

East's Dilemma

East had problems making friends. He was good looking, a great athlete, and had a terrific sense of humor, but he had poor hygiene and an unusual name. His mother constantly nagged and criticized him, but her criticism made him even more stubborn. He insisted he was just fine and blamed her for giving him a weird name. He wanted to be part of the group, and several of his peers wanted to accept him, but his poor hygiene made them reject him instead.

Figure 49

Negative Criticism or Positive Criticism?

Name: _____ Date:_____

Identify the following as either negative criticism (NC) or positive criticism (PC).

_____ 1. You are constantly interrupting—be quiet.

_____ 2. When you interrupt, I lose track of what I'm saying.

_____ 3. Loud voices are very disturbing in the library.

_____ 4. OK, loudmouth, keep the noise down.

_____ 5. I bet nonsmokers get more kisses.

_____ 6. Quit smoking—it's bad for your health, and anyway who wants to kiss an ashtray?

_____ 7. Your head is full of dandruff—go and wash your hair.

_____ 8. I prefer the way you combed your hair the other night. It really flatters your eyes.

_____ 9. I would rather not be touched, thank you. I know you are a "touchy" person, but some people don't like to be touched.

_____ 10. Must you talk so much? You never shut up.

Figure 50

241

ROLE-PLAY: CONFLICT RESOLUTION

CHARACTERS

Wayne, Festus, Tisha

SITUATION

Wayne and Festus have been friends since kindergarten. They are now in seventh grade and share similar interests. Unfortunately, one of these interests happens to be a young lady named Tisha. Festus and Tisha have gone out together in a group, but they are not seeing each other regularly. One evening following the football game, Wayne asks Tisha if she wants to go see a new rap group called the Vanilla/Chocolate Twist playing at the youth club. Tisha eagerly accepts. As they are getting ready to leave Tisha's house, Festus shows up. He is obviously annoyed.

Festus: *(In a teasing, sarcastic tone)* Hey, wimp, what are you up to? Tisha needs a real man, not a loser.

Wayne: What's the matter, man—we are just going to check out the "Twists."

Festus: Oh, yeah? Then check this out! *(He punches Wayne, giving him a bloody nose.)*

Tisha: *(In a shrill voice)* Fool, is that showing your manhood? You should be ashamed of yourself.

Wayne: Hold it, cool it, this is getting out of hand.

Tisha: *(Kicks Festus in the shin)* Take that, you monster.

Festus: Hey, that hurts. *(He pushes her away from him.)*

Wayne: *(Trying to control his nosebleed)* Man, what's the matter with you?

Festus: I'll show you what's the matter! *(He raises his fist again, but then stops and thinks, muttering to himself.)* STOP! This is no good. I'm letting my jealous feelings get the best of me. *(He drops his fist.)* I am losing two good friends. I better get it together before things get worse.

Tisha: You two calm down. What's the problem, Festus? What made you hit Wayne? Wayne, Festus, look at each other and talk.

Festus: I guess I lost it, man. I'm sorry. Here, let me help you.

Wayne: Festus, I can't forgive you right now. I'm mad. I need time to chill out. Let's talk tomorrow. We can work this out later.

EVALUATION AND FEEDBACK

1. What words did Festus use to tease Wayne?

2. How did Festus respond to Wayne's teasing?

3. When did Tisha attempt to mediate? What did she do?

4. At what point did Festus practice self-control?

5. What does Festus plan to do after he regains control?

6. Why didn't Wayne accept Festus's apology right away?

7. Continue the script and supply an ending that includes negotiation and a compromise.

SKILL
AREA
6

COOPERATION &
COLLABORATION

TOGETHER WE WILL OVERCOME

GOAL

- To develop the concept of cooperative teamwork

OBJECTIVES

- Defining and discussing the meaning of cooperation
- Defining and discussing the meaning of competition
- Comparing and contrasting competition and cooperation
- Recognizing the role of interdependence in cooperative groups

MATERIALS

- Cooperative Group Rules (Figure 51)
- Art supplies (butcher paper, markers, construction paper, glue)

PROCEDURE

OPENING

Review

None needed.

Stating Objectives

In this lesson we will learn that members of a group must cooperate to achieve a goal. In a competitive situation, winning is more important than reaching a goal cooperatively. Highly competitive people have difficulty working on a team. We will compare competitive and cooperative behaviors. Finally, we will examine why members of a group must be able to be team players and depend on one another to achieve a group goal.

INSTRUCTION

Teaching and Guided Discussion

●————— **Defining and discussing the meaning of cooperation**

In many situations people must cooperate to complete tasks. Can you give me some examples of situations where you have had to cooperate to be successful?

Elicit responses and discuss.

Cooperation means being a team player. For instance, in a basketball game, players must cooperate to be successful. One person cannot play alone. The players on the team must work together as one.

Review Figure 51(Cooperative Group Rules). Adapt the following discussion to fit your own situation.

In life, we face many situations that require cooperation. For example, members of this faculty often engage in teamwork on many different projects, such as assembling the yearbook and organizing school programs. How do members of a family cooperate?

Elicit responses and discuss. Responses may include meal preparation, household chores, driving responsibilities, and so forth.

Cooperation requires a positive attitude and willingness to be a part of the team. Negative attitudes limit the ability of the group to cooperate.

●————— **Defining and discussing the meaning of competition**

Competition between people often involves challenges. In many competitive situations, the goal is to win at all cost. People who are highly competitive may be very aggressive. They may assume a Bossy Me attitude and have difficulty cooperating in a group.

There is a difference between aggressive competition and healthy competition. In aggressive competition the team spirit is lost and is replaced by conflict. In healthy competition a player is assertive and works at being a good sport. There is no room for aggression. For example, in a tennis match where healthy competition exists, players congratulate each other at the end of the game. What would happen if the players exhibited aggressive behaviors?

Elicit responses and discuss.

In many societies competition is encouraged, and that's OK as long as the competition is healthy. However, cooperation is also very important because it helps bring people together to accomplish tasks or solve problems.

Ask students to explain the following statements: "In unity there is strength" and "No person is an island." Discuss.

Comparing and contrasting competition and cooperation

Competition and cooperation are learned behaviors. We learn very early how to compete and how to cooperate. Highly competitive people are often self-centered and only think of their own goals. In a cooperative group, people work together to achieve a common goal. Cooperative people assume Caring Me and Thinking Me attitudes. They use their Thinking Steps—STOP, THINK, PLAN, and CHECK—to help the group accomplish goals.

Visualize a society or a situation where cooperation never takes place and competition is the common practice. What do you think would happen?

Elicit responses and discuss, then ask students to imagine the reverse—a world where cooperation dominates.

Recognizing the role of interdependence in cooperative groups

Interdependence means relying on one another to reach a goal. One person cannot do all the work. Every member of the group has a specific task and needs to accept responsibility for the completion of that task. The other members can support but may not do the work for another member. When we depend on one another, we do not compete—instead, we give encouragement. The group works to achieve a common goal, but every worker must contribute a part.

Interdependence is like a puzzle—it requires teamwork. Have you ever tried to put a puzzle together and found some pieces missing? The puzzle cannot be completed, just as a task cannot be completed if some members of the group fail to finish their parts.

Can you think of some activities that require interdependence?

Elicit responses and discuss. Answers may include the following.

- Sports team: Players, coach, umpire or referee, cheerleaders, equipment person

- Medical team: Internists, medical technicians, nurses, anesthesiologists, surgeons

- Construction team: Architect, contractor, plumbers, carpenters, bricklayers, landscapers

Can you think of activities that do not require interdependence?

Examples may include various sports (golf, tennis, track and field, kayaking, skiing), reading, walking, cooking.

Is auto racing an interdependent sport?

Discuss. Point out that auto racing may seem like an individual sport, but in reality it requires a great deal of cooperation and interdependence to put together a winning race team.

Are there any group activities that do not require interdependence?

Discuss. Point out that once more than a single person is involved, interdependence comes into play.

Monitoring Knowledge and Comprehension

Ask the following questions and discuss.

1. Name a situation where cooperative behavior is essential. *(for example, during a fire, earthquake, or other emergency; when marching in a parade; when leading cheers at a sports event)*

2. Discuss the following statements in terms of the difference between healthy and unhealthy competition:

   I will have my friends beat up Tom, the spelling champ, so that I can win the spelling bee this year.

   I will study hard and defeat Tom, the spelling champ.

3. How are cooperation and competition similar? *(Both are learned behaviors, both are part of society.)*

4. How are they different? *(Competition is self-oriented, whereas cooperation is team-oriented.)*

5. How can interdependence be achieved in a cooperative group? *(by depending on one another to reach a goal)*

Guided Practice

Distribute art supplies. Have students plan and complete a mural with the theme of cooperation, with each member of the group taking responsibility for completing a part. Group size may vary; however, all students must participate.

Assessing Mastery

Encourage students to analyze their own behavior while working on the mural by referring to the Cooperative Group Rules. Were the students interdependent? Did they cooperate or compete?

RETEACHING

Independent Practice

Divide students into triads. Assign a story topic to each group. Each member of the group will be responsible for the introduction, the body, or the conclusion of the story. Sample topics include the following.

- Saving for a future purchase
- Organizing a party
- Planning a vacation trip
- Preparing for a special date

Evaluation and Feedback

Have students describe how the following situations can be changed to be more interdependent. Evaluate for understanding of interdependence.

- *Situation 1:* Jody is a new student and wants to be a member of the chorus. Her teacher tells her that she needs to learn five songs in a week. Jody feels overwhelmed.

- *Situation 2:* It is a week before the holidays, and Mom must decorate. She also has to bake and wrap presents. Mom feels stressed out.

- *Situation 3:* The yard person of the community center has quit. The grounds need to be maintained. You have been given this responsibility for a week.

CLOSING

Summary

In this lesson we learned that members of a group must cooperate to achieve a goal. In a competitive situation, winning is more important than cooperating with others to reach a goal. Highly competitive people may have difficulty working cooperatively. We compared competitive and cooperative behaviors. We also learned that interdependence means offering support and depending on one another to achieve a goal.

Generalization

Direct students to select a home chore and to work cooperatively with a sibling. If a sibling is not available, students may ask a friend to help with a home project. Have students discuss their experiences: Were decisions about who would do what made in a cooperative fashion, or did one person make all the decisions? How did it feel to share the work with another person? Was it easier or more difficult?

ENRICHMENT

1. Discuss and compare the following sayings:

    Two heads are better than one.

    Too many cooks spoil the broth.

    When spider webs unite, they can tie up a lion.

2. Ask students to visualize a situation in which interdependence was involved in a project (schoolwork, homework, cooking, cleaning, and so on). Have them describe the situation in writing, responding to the following questions:

    In what ways did you need the other person or people?

    How did you work together and share responsibilities?

    Could you have done the work by yourself?

    Was it easier doing the work with someone else? Why or why not?

3. Have students explain how the following activities could be either individual or cooperative:

> Reading a book
>
> Jumping rope
>
> Studying for a test
>
> Playing video games
>
> Planning a class party
>
> Singing a song

4. Divide the class into small groups. Each week, assign a group to decorate a bulletin board or wall inside or outside the classroom. You may assign a theme or allow the group to decide on a theme. Establish criteria for judging the displays. These criteria may include artistic qualities, creativity, information, cooperation, and utility.

Cooperative Group Rules

1. **Participation:** Be an active member of the group.

2. **Democracy:** Every member of the group has an equal voice.

3. **Empathy:** Open your mind to other members' opinions.

4. **Communication:** Listen actively and allow others to speak without interruption.

5. **Collaboration:** Work together as team players to achieve the group's goal. Allow each member a turn and refrain from Bossy Me attitudes.

6. **Assistance:** Help one another and use your particular strengths to compensate for weaknesses within the group.

7. **Reinforcement:** Encourage one another and acknowledge one another's contributions. Be proud of your accomplishments.

8. **Interdependence:** Depend on one another to achieve the group's goal. Gather your special skills and support one another.

9. **Problem resolution:** Solve problems as a group. Use the Thinking Steps: STOP, THINK, PLAN, and CHECK.

10. **Cooperation:** Work together as a team. Take on individual and group responsibility.

Figure 51

PATIENCE IS A VIRTUE

GOAL

- To learn to delay gratification and practice patience

OBJECTIVES

- Defining and discussing the meaning of patience
- Identifying the importance of turn taking
- Identifying factors leading to impatience
- Identifying strategies to increase patience

MATERIALS

- Patience Dilemmas (Figure 52)

PROCEDURE

OPENING

Review

In our last lesson we learned that members of a group must cooperate to achieve a goal. In a competitive situation, winning is more important than cooperating with others. Highly competitive people may have difficulty working cooperatively. We compared competitive and cooperative behaviors and also learned that interdependence means offering support and depending on one another to achieve a goal.

Follow up on any generalization activities assigned during the last lesson.

Stating Objectives

In this lesson we will learn the meaning of patience and the importance of taking turns. There are many reasons people may be impatient. These include lack of self-control, lack of empathy, pain, and length of waiting time. We will examine different strategies to help us wait for things we want.

INSTRUCTION

Teaching and Guided Discussion

●————— **Defining and discussing the meaning of patience**

(Personalize the following example.) Driving to work this morning really tried my patience. The traffic was bumper-to-bumper, and it seemed that I got in the wrong lane every time I changed lanes. Drivers were getting very impatient. Waiting and taking turns requires patience; you wait in line at the grocery store, you wait in a car at a stoplight or in heavy traffic, you wait in line at a movie theater or when you pick up a pizza. Practicing patience is not easy even for adults. What is patience?

Elicit responses and discuss.

Very young children cannot wait for a reward—they want their candy or ice cream right away. It is difficult for young children to take turns playing and speaking. Wise parents teach their children to be patient, to wait and to take turns. Parents teach young children in small steps because children have not yet developed much emotional maturity. It is normal for young children to want something right away because they don't have a clear concept of time and they lack internal controls. As we grow older we develop self-control and other social behaviors. It is important for teenagers to continue practicing patience because this is an important skill in adulthood. Impatient people can often hinder cooperation and success.

●————— **Identifying the importance of turn taking**

Being patient makes it easier to take turns, and taking turns is a skill we use throughout our lives. We need to learn cooperation, self-control, and empathy to acquire this skill. When we wait for a turn we can listen and evaluate a situation. By taking turns we delay or put off our immediate desires. We show respect and empathy for other people. Turn taking is also very important for effective communication. We often need to wait to make a statement, to reply, or to ask a question. What would happen if we all spoke at the same time?

Elicit responses and discuss.

In some cases a moderator, or a third person, is needed to give each party a chance to speak. A moderator is often necessary at debates or on television talk shows.

Many misunderstandings result when people do not take turns. What could happen if you broke into a long line of people waiting to buy tickets at a movie theater?

Elicit responses and discuss.

●————— **Identifying factors leading to impatience**

Can you recall situations in the community in which you had to practice patience? How did you feel? What do you think made it difficult for you to wait?

Elicit responses and discuss. Emphasize the following factors.

- *Self-control:* People with poor self-control want what they want immediately—they cannot delay gratification. Because they have an Impulsive Me attitude, they cannot STOP, THINK, PLAN, and CHECK.

- *Empathy:* People who cannot empathize have difficulty being patient because they are unable to relate to others involved in the situation.

- *Pain:* Pain often causes us to be impatient. For example, my patience is very limited when I am waiting in a dentist's office with a painful toothache. My pain adds to my impatience.

- *Time:* Finally, time is a factor. My patience wears thin when waiting for a long time or when waiting interferes with something else I need to do.

Identifying strategies to increase patience

Listening to the radio or to a tape while you are waiting in line or in your car helps you practice patience. You could also use the waiting time as thinking time to sort out problems you have or to make plans for the future. What other suggestions do you have?

Elicit responses and discuss.

Because lack of self-control is a factor leading to impatience, we can use our Thinking Steps to help us wait. I can STOP complaining and redirect my thinking. Control over my attitude can help me regain self-control. I can THINK: Getting upset and impatient does not help—I can delay whatever it is I want. I can make a PLAN to make waiting less stressful. I can think of past happy moments, like my trip to Disney World. If I am in a group, I can wait for my turn to speak by listening carefully to what the speaker is saying. If I am in pain at the dentist's office, I can use empathetic assertion and explain that I need to see the dentist as soon as possible. Remember, when you PLAN, you may develop more than one option. CHECK your plan. Do you need to use an alternate plan?

Monitoring Knowledge and Comprehension

Ask the following questions and discuss.

1. Why is patient behavior necessary in achieving cooperation?

2. What does appropriate turn taking demonstrate?

3. Name some factors that cause people to be impatient.

4. Name some strategies that can help you become more patient.

Guided Practice

Divide students into small groups. Distribute copies of Figure 52 (Patience Dilemmas) and have students complete as instructed. Share and discuss the strategies students develop.

Assessing Mastery

Evaluate students' solutions for their understanding of ways to facilitate waiting and turn taking.

RETEACHING

Independent Practice

As a class, read and discuss the fable of the tortoise and the hare. Have each student write or illustrate a part of the story depicting patience. Share and discuss.

Evaluation and Feedback

Discuss the following situations from students' own experience. You may want to depersonalize the situations by asking the students to recall incidents involving others.

1. Identify a situation in which you were impatient. What was the outcome, and how would the situation have been different if you had demonstrated patience?

2. Identify a situation in which you did not practice turn taking. What was the outcome, and how would the situation have been different if you had taken turns?

CLOSING

Summary

In this lesson we learned that life is full of waiting experiences. We learned the importance of taking turns. Many factors contribute to impatience; these include lack of self-control, lack of empathy, pain, and length of waiting time. We examined different strategies to help us learn to be more patient.

Generalization

Direct students to visualize the following situations then brainstorm ways to facilitate patience and turn taking.

1. You are riding in a car pool, and you are stuck in traffic.

2. You are at a doctor's office—you've been waiting for an hour.

3. You are in the car with your parents on an 8-hour drive to Seaworld. You can hardly wait to get there.

4. You are waiting in line at a grocery store, and the person in front of you has several items without marked prices.

5. You want to check out a book at the school library, and the librarian is on the phone. You have 4 minutes to get to class.

6. You are in class, and you are getting very hungry. It's only 10 o'clock, and your lunch break is at noon.

ENRICHMENT

1. Have students write a limerick or another poem on the topic of turn taking.

2. Discuss the following sayings:

    How poor are they that have not patience.

    —*William Shakespeare*

    Patience will achieve more than force.

    —*Edmund Burke*

    Good things come to those who wait.

    He who is first shall be last, and he who is last shall be first.

    Patience is a virtue.

Patience Dilemmas

Name: _____ Date:_____

Develop strategies to deal with the following dilemmas.

Situation 1

You are engaged in a heated discussion. The other person dominates the conversation. After listening patiently for 10 minutes, you want your turn to speak. How can you practice patience, and what can you do to regain speaking time?

Situation 2

You are baby-sitting for two young children. Both children want to play with the same toy. You are about to lose your patience with both of them. What can you do to empathize with the children, and how would you teach them to take turns?

Situation 3

Your boyfriend or girlfriend is away at camp for the summer. You can hardly wait to be together again. What can you do to make the waiting time more tolerable?

Situation 4

You've been waiting for an hour at the movie theater, and when it's your turn to buy tickets you find that the movie is sold out. What can you do to keep your cool?

Figure 52

WE'RE IN THIS TOGETHER

GOAL

- To learn how to interact successfully with others

OBJECTIVES

- Recognizing the benefits of successful interactions
- Identifying the skills needed for successful interactions
- Identifying the different roles of team members
- Identifying roadblocks to successful interactions

MATERIALS

- Will This Group Succeed? (Figure 53)
- Chalkboard or easel pad

PROCEDURE

OPENING

Review

In our last lesson we learned that life is full of waiting experiences. We learned the importance of taking turns and practicing patience. People may lose patience because of lack of self-control, lack of empathy, pain, or length of waiting time. We examined different strategies to help us be more patient.

Follow up on any generalization activities assigned during the last lesson.

Stating Objectives

In this lesson we will learn that there are many benefits to working together. We need to learn many skills to interact successfully with others. Sometimes certain roles will be assigned to members of a group. These roles should be flexible, shared, and assigned in a fair manner. Sometimes roadblocks occur and can prevent successful interactions between group members.

INSTRUCTION

Teaching and Guided Discussion

●————— **Recognizing the benefits of successful interactions**

There are many benefits of successful interactions. When people interact positively, tasks are made easier, new things are learned, and new friendships are developed. Can you give an example of a successful interaction?

Elicit responses and discuss. Personalize the following example.

Recently, I worked in a group of three people at the food bank. We were able to sort the canned goods, box the food items, and distribute the food in one-third the time it would have taken if one person had done the task alone. I also made new friends and learned new information by talking with my fellow workers.

●————— **Identifying the skills needed for successful interactions**

What are the skills necessary for successful interactions?

Elicit responses and discuss.

Some important skills are goal setting, positive communication, problem solving, and a good sense of humor.

- *Goal setting:* We need to know how to set goals as a group. I may not like your goal, but the idea is to reach a goal that all the members of the group can accept. Together, group members must work toward achieving the goal.

- *Positive communication:* Members also need to communicate positively by listening to one another and by delivering their messages in a positive way.

- *Problem solving:* Whenever group members disagree, they need to use the Thinking Steps to solve their problems. They need to STOP and THINK about ways to agree. Then they can brainstorm and make a PLAN. They can CHECK their choices and settle their difficulties.

- *Humor:* A good sense of humor promotes successful interactions because it establishes a positive climate. People feel freer to contribute to the group if they can laugh together.

Review rules for active listening and positive communication from Skill Area 2 (Communication) and for mediation, negotiation, and compromise from Skill Area 5 (Conflict Resolution) as needed.

●————— **Identifying the different roles of team members**

Different roles are sometimes assigned to members of a team. A leadership role is sometimes necessary to encourage successful interactions. The leader should not assume a Bossy Me attitude, but rather be assertive in guiding the group to reach the goal. The leader must be fair. What does this mean?

Elicit responses and discuss.

To be fair, the leader encourages everyone to express an opinion. Group members should express their opinions to help the group achieve the goal, not to cause argument.

Another role in the group is that of recorder or reader, when appropriate. The recorder can take notes about what is going on, and the reader can read directions or whatever else is necessary.

When each member assumes responsibilities and participates, goals are achieved, and everybody can feel good about a job well done.

Identifying roadblocks to successful interactions

Roadblocks are behaviors that can keep interactions from being successful. When members refuse to participate, you can't have successful interactions. Team members who do not get along can wreck the team effort. Not understanding what is required can delay the group from reaching its goal. A group member who cannot empathize will not be willing to consider the opinions of others. Can you think of other roadblocks?

List students' responses on the chalkboard or easel pad. Discuss. Stress the idea that to interact successfully, group members must accept responsibility and avoid roadblocks.

Monitoring Knowledge and Comprehension

Ask the following questions and discuss.

1. What are the benefits of successful interactions?

2. What skills should I as a teacher develop to interact with other teachers?

3. What skills should you as a student develop to interact with your peers?

4. What are some different roles of group members?

5. Sheldon refuses to participate in the group. How would you handle that roadblock?

Guided Practice

Divide the class into groups of four or five students each. Assign each group one of the following activities, or make up your own activities.

1. Plan a Halloween or other holiday party. Every member of the group should be given a role. Identify the role and the responsibility of each member.

2. Design a "junk band" of homemade musical instruments. Each member must contribute and play one musical instrument.

3. Construct a mural, collage, or pinata with a theme. Identify roadblocks that interfere with successful interactions and find ways to deal with these roadblocks.

4. Participate in a scavenger hunt. Either provide the group with a list of items or allow the group to develop their own list. Students are responsible for deciding who will obtain which items.

Assessing Mastery

Ask the following questions.

1. How did members of the group participate and interact?

2. What different roles were assigned?

3. Were there any roadblocks? If so, how were they handled?

4. What new information did you gain from this experience?

5. Did working in the group help you reach the goal? Why or why not?

6. Were friendships established or strengthened? Why or why not?

RETEACHING

Independent Practice

Distribute copies of Figure 53 (Will This Group Succeed?) and have students complete as instructed.

Evaluation and Feedback

Ask and discuss the following questions.

1. What can you do as group leader to ensure positive interaction from the class clown, the school bully, the cheerleader, and the shy student? *(Brainstorm with the group and find out their interests and strengths.)*

2. What should be done next? *(Make a plan and use the Thinking Steps. Involve each member in a task based on his or her interests and abilities.)*

3. What is the main roadblock in this situation, and how might it be handled? *(Characterizations of group members keep them from expressing their individual strengths. Leader could assign a team name to help motivate members to work together.)*

CLOSING

Summary

In this lesson we learned that there are many benefits to successful interactions. We can complete tasks more efficiently, gain new information, and develop friendships. Many skills are involved in successfully interacting with others. Sometimes certain roles are assigned to group members. These roles should be assigned in a fair manner. Roadblocks are problems that can keep interactions among group members from being successful, but group members can use their problem-solving skills to overcome roadblocks.

Generalization

Select from the following activities.

1. Select three different television situation comedies and ask students to identify positive interactions and roadblocks among the characters. Discuss as a class.

2. Direct students to make a list of successful interactions with family members or friends. Have them identify the major roadblocks to successful interactions with these people.

ENRICHMENT

1. Divide students into small groups. Direct each group to write a scenario showing successful group interactions in one of the following situations. Have students act out their scenarios and discuss how they included positive interactions among group members.

   Sports (football, baseball, basketball, and so on)

   Garage sale

   State fair

   Graduation party

2. Videotape students working in any group situation. Before viewing the tape with students, preview it and list the positive interactions and roadblocks. Guide students in identifying these behaviors and making suggestions for improving their interactions.

3. Survey your community and make a list of places that would welcome students' help (for example, hospitals, nursing homes, tutoring labs for younger students). With parental involvement, assign groups of students to volunteer their time. Prior to the community assignments, review appropriate interactions for each setting.

Will This Group Succeed?

Name: _____ Date: _____

Read the following situation, then write a paragraph answering the questions at the end.

You are the leader of a group, and your goal is to decorate a float for the school parade. Four classmates have been assigned to your group. Besides yourself, the other group members could be described as follows:

Class clown

School bully

Cheerleader

Shy student

1. Is this group likely to interact successfully?

2. Why or why not?

Figure 53

A BALANCING ACT

GOAL

- To become aware of the importance of equality

OBJECTIVES

- Defining and discussing the meaning of equality
- Recognizing that equality does not imply equal division of tasks
- Recognizing that each person's contribution should be equally valued
- Recognizing that authoritarian behavior destroys equality

MATERIALS

- Different Abilities, Equal Value (Figure 54)

PROCEDURE

OPENING

Review

In our last lesson we learned that there are benefits to successful group interactions. We accomplish tasks more efficiently, gain new information, and develop friendships. There are also many skills we need to learn to interact successfully with others. Sometimes certain roles are assigned to members of a group. These roles should be assigned in a fair way. Roadblocks often occur; however, group members can use their problem-solving skills to overcome roadblocks.

Follow up on any generalization activities assigned during the last lesson.

Stating Objectives

In this lesson we will discuss the meaning of equality in groups. Equality does not necessarily mean equal division of tasks—there are times when it is fair to be unequal. What equality means in a group is that each person's contribution is equally valued. Whenever people abuse power and become authoritarian, they destroy equality.

INSTRUCTION

Teaching and Guided Discussion

●────── **Defining and discussing the meaning of equality**

We hear the statement that all individuals are created equal. What does that mean?

Elicit responses and discuss.

Do you think this statement means that we are all born with the same talents, the same potential, or the same strengths and limitations?

Discuss.

We are equal in a most important way—our humanity. We are all human beings. We all have feelings, we all have needs, we all have hopes and dreams, and in a democracy we all have certain rights. In this country, we have the right to vote and to worship in the place of our choice. What rights do we have simply as human beings?

Elicit responses and discuss. Responses may include the right to happiness, to our own thoughts and opinions, to a safe environment, and to an education.

Many times countries go to war because of differences in religion, nationality, or race. Many times students don't empathize with and even dislike others simply because they are different. We need to STOP, THINK, PLAN, and CHECK before we decide that these differences cause us to be unequal. We need to STOP thinking about differences and start to THINK about what we have in common instead. We need to PLAN to put aside prejudices that justify our feeling of superiority. We need to work on our plans and CHECK to see if they are good ones.

●────── **Recognizing that equality does not imply equal division of tasks**

In a group, equality does not necessarily mean being the same or doing equal work. Group members may have different strengths and limitations, and to be effective in reaching the group goal, they may have to work differently. Sometimes it may be necessary for group members to have unequal tasks. For example, let's suppose four students are working on a history project. Their goal is to make a presentation to the entire class on the Civil War. Their tasks include researching information, writing a paper, illustrating a poster, and delivering a presentation. The group includes one student who has difficulty reading but who is artistic, someone in the drama club, and two more-or-less academically average students. In this case it is not best for the work to be equally divided. How would you divide the tasks in such a case?

Elicit responses and discuss. Ask the following questions.

1. Will every member contribute equal time to the project?

2. Is each task equally difficult?

3. Is it fair to give some members easy tasks and others more difficult ones?

4. How could a group leader fairly divide responsibilities?

● ———— **Recognizing that each person's contribution should be equally valued**

Who has made the greatest contribution to society—Michelangelo, Einstein, Elvis Presley, Beethoven, Abraham Lincoln, Martin Luther King, Marie Curie, or Babe Ruth? How has each contributed, and how has society benefited?

Elicit responses and discuss. Distribute copies of Figure 54 (Different Abilities, Equal Value) and have students complete as instructed. The "abilities" listed here are the same as the "intelligences" described in Lesson 1 of Skill Area 1 (Awareness of Self and Others). If desired, teach or review the information from this lesson.

People's contributions may be very different, and work within a group may not be equally shared, but it is important for every group member's contribution to be equally valued. Each person has equal rights within the group, and no member should be put down. Individual effort and differences should be recognized.

● ———— **Recognizing that authoritarian behavior destroys equality**

A Bossy Me attitude does not show respect for equality. People with Bossy Me attitudes want to dominate and do not want to work with a group in a supportive manner. These people feel superior to the group and don't show respect for the equality of other members. Messages of superiority and power are authoritarian and interfere with the group's reaching its goal.

Some teenagers join youth gangs because they want to belong to a group. In many gangs the equality of members is not respected. Gang leaders are authoritarian and do not consider the contributions of the gang members. Leaving the gang may not be an option, and members give up their individual rights. This type of group membership is destructive because members sacrifice their freedom and individuality to be part of the group.

Monitoring Knowledge and Comprehension

Ask the following questions and discuss.

1. What does the phrase "equal in our humanity" mean?

2. Should all tasks in a group project be equally divided? Defend your answer.

3. How can each member of the group contribute his or her special talents?

4. How does an authoritarian leader destroy equality within in a group?

Guided Practice

Divide the class into two groups. One group has the responsibility of defending Fred's father. The other group must defend the opposing view. Direct groups to appoint a leader to make sure everyone's viewpoint is heard and a recorder to write down the group's position.

Fred's father was angry because he could not find a parking place. The areas reserved for handicapped parking were available. Fred's father felt that he had a right as a motorist to park in any available area. Do you agree with Fred's father?

Assessing Mastery

Compare and contrast each group's recorded responses. Did each group work together cooperatively and fairly? Were members' contributions equally respected?

RETEACHING

Independent Practice

When a natural disaster occurs (hurricane, earthquake, tornado), relief workers must take orders from a leader and cooperate to provide assistance. Have students write a short essay describing the importance of group leadership in such situations. Ask them to address the following questions.

1. Does taking orders from a leader make the relief workers less equal?

2. Will the workers be assigned jobs that are equal in terms of difficulty or time spent on the job? Why or why not?

Evaluation and Feedback

Ask students to collect data over a weekend about situations in which equality is expressed. These situations could include interactions on television programs and in films, in family situations, or during other activities. Ask students to identify and share a situation of their choice with the group.

CLOSING

Summary

> In this lesson we learned that although people are not created equal in all aspects, we all deserve to be treated equally as human beings. Equality in a group does not mean equal division of tasks. There are times when it is fair to make allowances for individual strengths and weaknesses. Each person's contribution should be equally valued within a group. Authoritarian behavior abuses power and destroys equality within the group.

Generalization

Direct students to interview teachers and other school staff (librarian, school nurse, cafeteria worker, bus driver, custodian) and write an article on how faculty and staff perceive equality among the adults at the school. This exercise may be repeated within a home or community situation. Direct students to share and discuss their findings.

ENRICHMENT

1. Invite a speaker (fire fighter, police officer, paramedic, factory worker) to talk to students about the importance of equality and leadership on the job.

2. Discuss the following statements:

   > It's not fair to allow students with learning disabilities to take extra time to complete exams. They just need to study like the rest of us.

   > Girls should not play football. They are weaker than boys and can't take the hard licks.

   > We live in a democracy, so we do not have to follow the rules our state and national leaders dictate.

   > Men should do the tough jobs around the house, like mowing the lawn and painting the house. Women should take care of the cooking and the babies.

3. Assign a library assignment to research the social contributions of notable figures, past and present—for example, Marie Curie, Amelia Earhart, Martin Luther King, Sir Edmund Hillary, Leonardo da Vinci, Edgar Allan Poe, Sir Winston Churchill, John F. Kennedy, Eleanor Roosevelt, Thomas Edison, Vincent Van Gogh, Aristotle, Helen Keller, Frederic Chopin, Admiral Matthew Perry, Jim Thorpe, Spike Lee, and Cesar Chavez.

Different Abilities, Equal Value

Name: _____ Date:_____

Name an individual who is outstanding in each ability.

Ability   **Individual**

Logical/mathematical
(scientist, mathematician) _____

Visual/spatial
(artist, sculptor)_____

Body/kinesthetic
(athlete, ballerina)_____

Musical/rhythmic
(musician, singer) _____

Interpersonal
(philantropist, politician) _____

Intrapersonal
(philosopher, psychologist) _____

Verbal/linguistic
(writer, news broadcaster) _____

Figure 54

WHAT'S YOUR TYPE?

GOAL

- To understand how one's own and other people's personality types influence group interactions

OBJECTIVES

- Identifying four basic personality types

- Understanding that people are not a single type but have a combination of personality characteristics

- Understanding how conflict may arise between different personality types

- Adapting to other people's personality types

MATERIALS

- What's Your Type? (Figure 55)

- Identifying Personality Types (Figure 56)

- Chalkboard or easel pad

- Butcher paper

- Markers

PROCEDURE

OPENING

Review

> In our last lesson we learned that people have certain rights. People are not created equal in all aspects, but we all deserve to be treated equally as human beings. Sometimes equality in a group does not mean equal division of tasks; however, each person's contribution should be equally valued within a group. Authoritarian behaviors interfere with the group's goal achievement.

Follow up on any generalization activities assigned during the last lesson.

Stating Objectives

In this lesson, we will learn about four basic personality types. Although people are a combination of these types, conflicts can arise between people who have very different personality characteristics. It is important to understand our own basic personality type and to be able to adapt or "flex" to the personality types of others. A group needs all the personality types to succeed.

INSTRUCTION

Teaching and Guided Discussion

●————— Identifying four basic personality types

There are four basic personality types. Knowing about these different personality types can help us understand ourselves and appreciate a variety of people.

Write the following four categories on the chalkboard or easel pad.

Dependable/Organizing

Dependable/Organizing people are task oriented and responsible. They tend to like structure. They learn new information one step at a time and are careful and methodical. New ideas and new inventions are not generally appealing to them. They resist change, but when they eventually accept a change they stick to it like glue. Their motto is "If it's not broken, don't fix it." They respect tradition and feel comfortable with schedules and routines. In a group situation, they want to know what is expected of them, and then they will perform. They may not be flexible, but they get the work done. Dependable/Organizing people are not necessarily boring or dull. This personality type enjoys parties but needs to be told ahead of time to feel ready. Most Dependable/Organizing people like the structure and organization of school. They are usually on time and the first to turn in their assignments. They tend to assume a Bossy Me attitude and seldom show an Impulsive Me attitude.

Knowing/Inquisitive

People who are Knowing/Inquisitive enjoy learning new information. They love to take charge and lead people to accomplish goals. They are logical, independent, and enjoy exciting discussions. They are curious and constantly searching for knowledge. They want reasons and answers before they do something. Many Knowing/Inquisitive people feel more comfortable being around adults because they may become impatient with what they feel are their peers' immature questions and answers. They discourage emotional or irrational thinking and tend to be objective in their decisions. They enjoy parties, especially when the guests include one or more other Knowing/Inquisitive people. Knowing/Inquisitive people generally assume Thinking Me or Bossy Me attitudes.

Note: The four categories described here are based generally on the work of Isabel Briggs Myers, *Gifts Differing: Understanding Personality Types,* 1995, Palo Alto, CA: Davies-Black.

Loving/Devoted

Loving/Devoted personalities love to be with people. They show their feelings openly. They are understanding and intuitive. They tend to rely on gut feelings rather than logic in making decisions. Loving/Devoted people are loveable and treat others the way they would like to be treated. However, in trying to please too many people, they may feel pulled in a thousand directions. They cannot say no because they are afraid to hurt other people's feelings. They are optimistic and tend to see the best in people and situations. People often take advantage of Loving/Devoted individuals. However, they are usually popular and enjoy a good party with lots of people. They are the ones who most frequently show a Caring Me attitude.

Carefree/Flexible

Carefree/Flexible personalities like to be the center of attention. They are fun people and, if they are interested and motivated, can adapt to anything. They tend to "march to the tune of a different drummer" and perform well in competitions where there is lots of action. Other people often feel exhausted by the energy Carefree/Flexible personalities project. As their name suggests, they are flexible and can adapt to situations on the spur of the moment. They do not like to plan too far ahead, and they tend to do too many things at once. However, they sometimes manage to get a lot accomplished. They are nonconformist and enjoy trying new things and meeting new challenges. They are fun-loving and like to party. Carefree/Flexible personalities tend to assume Enthusiastic Me or Impulsive Me attitudes.

● Understanding that people are not a single type but have a combination of personality characteristics

People generally differ in the degree to which they possess the personality characteristics of each of these four types. Different characteristics of our personalities merge like the colors of a rainbow. We may shift back and forth from Dependable/Organizing to Carefree/Flexible according to the situation. *(Personalize as appropriate.)* For example, I tend to be more Dependable/Organizing in a faculty meeting and am more Carefree/Flexible at a party. I tend to be more Caring/Devoted when a student is suffering emotional or physical pain. Basically, however, I am a Knowing/Inquisitive person.

● Understanding how conflict may arise between different personality types

Suppose you knew two sisters who were completely opposite. One was a Carefree/Flexible type, and the other was a Dependable/Organizing type. The Carefree/Flexible sister would probably call the Dependable/Organizing sister "a stick in the mud" and always be telling her to lighten up. The Dependable/Organizing sister would probably call her sister impulsive and hyperactive, and always be telling her to slow down. Have you ever known two people who got into conflict simply because their personalities were so different?

Elicit responses and discuss.

By understanding our own and others' basic personality types, we can make sense of the personal differences that exist in many social relationships.

Adapting to other people's personality types

The saying "opposites attract" is true in the case of couples who have very different temperaments. But what do you think happens when people cannot accommodate differences?

Elicit responses and discuss.

Once people understand one another's personalities they can become more tolerant and accepting. If the two sisters in the example we just discussed understood each other's different personality types, they would probably be able to stop being so critical and get along better.

When working in a group, we must accommodate or "flex" to each others' personality types. Some people may prefer to work alone but must flex and participate in teamwork. A group needs a Dependable/Organizing person to organize tasks and keep track of the time. Carefree/Flexible people need to adapt to Dependable/Organizing people, or their group will have difficulty completing a project. A Loving/Devoted person needs to adopt a Thinking Me attitude and be more like a Knowing/Inquisitive person when making decisions. Knowing/Inquisitive individuals sometimes need to be more like Loving/Devoted people and adopt a more Caring Me attitude in considering how other people feel.

We need all four personality types to work in a group. No characteristic is better than another: It took Carefree/Flexible and Loving/Devoted people to dream up the idea of reaching the moon, and it took Knowing/Inquisitive and Dependable/Organizing people to interpret the data and make it happen.

Monitoring Knowledge and Comprehension

Ask the following questions and discuss.

1. Name the four basic personality types.

2. True or false: If you are one personality type, you don't have any of the characteristics of any of the other types.

3. What can happen in a relationship when people have very different personality types but don't know it?

4. Why does a group need all of the personality types to succeed?

Guided Practice

Distribute copies of Figure 55 (What's Your Type?) and have students answer the questions true or false. After they have done so, have students note the abbreviation for the basic personality type reflected in each statement. On the basis of their answers, students can speculate on their own dominant personality characteristics. Discuss, emphasizing the idea that the inventory gives only a general idea of one's personality type. Answers: 1–DO, 2–LD, 3–CF, 4–KI, 5–KI, 6–LD, 7–CF, 8–DO, 9–LD, 10–DO, 11–CF, 12–KI.

Assessing Mastery

Based on the results of the inventory, group students with similar personalities and direct each group to solve the following problems. Have groups outline their solutions on a large sheet of butcher paper. Display and compare solutions. Contrast the sequential, detailed outlines of the Dependable/Organizing personalities with the global solutions of the Carefree/Flexible personalities.

Your class has won a trip to Disneyland. Your task is to plan and prepare for the trip.

Your class has been given the responsibility of organizing a book fair to raise money for your library.

RETEACHING

Independent Practice

Distribute copies of Figure 56 (Identifying Personality Types) and have students complete.

Evaluation and Feedback

Evaluate students' responses for understanding of the basic personality types. Discuss and give feedback. Answers: 1–LD, 2–KI, 3–CF, 4–DO, 5–KI, 6–DO, 7–LD, 8–CF, 9–CF, 10–DO. In the final question, Tina is flexing her CF to adapt to Fred's DO.

CLOSING

Summary

In this lesson, we learned about the four basic personality types. People are a combination of these types, but conflicts can arise between individuals who have very different personality characteristics. It is important to understand our own basic personality type and to be able to adapt or "flex" to the personality types of others. A group needs all the personality types to succeed.

Generalization

Direct students to observe their family members or friends and to notice the different personality types of each person. Have students keep a journal and note if and how the people observed adapt or "flex" to one another.

ENRICHMENT

Encourage students to read and discuss Are You My Type? Or Why Aren't You More Like Me? *by Claudine G. Wirths and Mary Bowman-Kruhm (Davies-Black, 1992). Other references for professionals and students are listed in the bibliography.*

What's Your Type?

Name: _____ Date: _____

Make a check mark in the box to show whether the statement is true or false for you.

DO = Dependable/Organizing
KI = Knowing/Inquisitive
LD = Loving/Devoted
CF = Carefree/Flexible

	True	False
1. I feel comfortable when my teachers clearly define what I have to do.	☐	☐
2. I feel best when my teachers show they care about me.	☐	☐
3. I love fun and exciting classroom activities.	☐	☐
4. I enjoy new ideas that challenge my curiosity.	☐	☐
5. I prefer to work independently.	☐	☐
6. I love to work in cooperative groups.	☐	☐
7. I adapt well to last-minute changes.	☐	☐
8. I do my best if I have a lot of structure and clear directions.	☐	☐
9. I feel bad when another student is punished.	☐	☐
10. I feel frustrated when things are disorganized.	☐	☐
11. I feel bored with the same old routines.	☐	☐
12. I feel annoyed when my peers ask questions I think they should already know the answers to.	☐	☐

Figure 55

Identifying Personality Types

Name: _____ Date:_____

Write the abbreviation for the basic personality type in the space to the left of each statement.

> DO = Dependable/Organizing
> KI = Knowing/Inquisitive
> LD = Loving/Devoted
> CF = Carefree/Flexible

_____ 1. John likes to work in groups.

_____ 2. Maria is analytical and uses all her senses to obtain information.

_____ 3. Celeste is full of energy and new ideas.

_____ 4. Rory follows a schedule and keeps lists of "Things to Do."

_____ 5. Norma is independent and reserved.

_____ 6. Paul is punctual, organized, and traditional.

_____ 7. Janina is sensitive to the feelings of others.

_____ 8. Tony is popular at parties.

_____ 9. Tina has many projects and participates in six extracurricular activities.

_____ 10. Tina's boyfriend Fred is involved in only one school organization and completes one project before tackling another.

Answer the following question.

To please Fred, Tina organizes her schedule and gives up four activities. Tina is flexing her _____ to adapt to Fred's _____.

Figure 56

279

ROLE-PLAY: COOPERATION & COLLABORATION

CHARACTERS

Teacher, Stephie, Lou, Chris, Randy, Anne, three other class members

SITUATION

Randy has a learning disability. He is a slow reader and has been receiving special education services in reading. He is very creative and very kind and loves to be with people. At Randy's recent IEP meeting it was decided that Randy would receive social studies instruction in the general education classroom.

Teacher: Class, tomorrow we will have a new student. His name is Randy, and I want you all to welcome him. He will sit next to you, Stephie. You can help him get started since you are so well organized.

The next day, Randy arrives.

Teacher: Class, look at your board work and complete it in 10 minutes. I will be assigning group projects, and you are to work cooperatively.

Stephie: *(To Randy)* You better hurry up—you are slowing us down. I'm running out of patience. What's the matter? Are you mental?

Lou: Ha, ha, ha—you've got a dummy sitting next to you. I hope he's not in my group.

Chris: *(Whispering to Randy)* Don't worry about it. You'll get the hang of it pretty soon.

The teacher assigns the groups. Lou is the leader of Group A, and Chris, Randy, and Anne are members. Stephie is the leader of Group B, with three members. Each group is assigned an activity to develop a mural. Every member of the group must contribute a part.

Teacher: We'll begin our group project tomorrow. Now let's begin today's lesson. Randy, will you read the title of chapter 8, please?

Randy: M m mon monray d d d doctor.

Stephie: Monray doctor!! *(Class laughs.)* It's the Monroe Doctrine. Did you lose your batteries or something?

Chris: Aw, come on Steph, lay off. Give him a chance.

Teacher: *(Calling Stephie aside)* Stephie, we need to have a talk. I think I better explain before we have any more unpleasant incidents. As citizens we all have an equal right to a free and appropriate public education. A committee including Randy, his parents, and the principal decided that this class was the most appropriate setting for Randy. We will follow the rule, and we will all help Randy. Randy can help us, too. He is very creative and has won several awards for his artwork. Any group would be lucky to have him. I expect each student to show respect, patience, and understanding.

Stephie: OK. I understand. *(Returns to her seat.)*

The class continues without further incident. At the close of school, Lou grabs Stephie's hand.

Lou: *(In a whisper)* Stephie, I don't want that fool in my group. He'll ask dumb questions. Help me talk to the teacher and get him out. He belongs in special education and not with normal kids.

Stephie: No way—I'm already in trouble! Besides, the teacher says Randy is very artistic and can really help us with our assignment.

Chris: *(Leaning over to Lou)* Now, aren't you sorry for your unkind remarks?

Lou: Yes, I really am. I'll apologize and ask Randy to contribute his talent to the mural. If we all cooperate, I'll bet we'll have the best mural. *(To Randy)* Oh, Randy, I need to talk to you . . .

EVALUATION AND FEEDBACK

1. Is the rule placing Randy in the social studies class reasonable? Why or why not?

2. Which student practices patience?

3. How does the teacher encourage interdependence?

4. Randy has a learning disability. Does he have equal rights to an education in the regular classroom?

5. What is the reason for Lou's change of attitude and his willingness to cooperate?

6. What is Stephie's basic personality type?

7. Can you guess Chris' and Lou's basic personality types?

NOTE: Stephie is probably a Dependable/Organizing personality. The teacher notes that she is well organized. She decides she wants to exclude Randy because she wants to finish the project in a timely manner and thinks Randy will slow the group down. Chris is probably a Loving/Devoted personality. She is sympathetic to Randy from the beginning. Lou is probably a Knowing/Inquisitive personality because he is worried that Randy will "ask dumb questions."

SKILL AREA 7

LOVE & CARING

•

Lesson 1

UNDERSTANDING OUR DIFFERENCES

•

Lesson 2

A WALK IN YOUR SHOES

•

Lesson 3

MANY FACES OF LOVE

•

Lesson 4

LOVE & RESPONSIBILITY

•

Lesson 5

WITH OR WITHOUT CONDITIONS

UNDERSTANDING OUR DIFFERENCES

GOAL

- To show tolerance, respect, and understanding for differences

OBJECTIVES

- Defining and discussing prejudice
- Recognizing the need for tolerance
- Recognizing the importance of understanding differences
- Demonstrating respect for differences

MATERIALS

- Different but the Same (Figure 57)
- Chalkboard or easel pad

PROCEDURE

OPENING

Review

None needed.

Stating Objectives

In this lesson we will examine the roots of prejudice. We will learn that prejudice can be destructive and divisive. We will also learn that tolerance is important in a society made up of different cultures. Through knowledge and understanding we can respect what we have in common and appreciate differences.

INSTRUCTION

Teaching and Guided Discussion

● ──────── **Defining and discussing prejudice**

Prejudice is an unfavorable attitude about a person or a group of people, without just cause or sufficient knowledge. What do you think causes prejudice?

Elicit responses and discuss.

Some people are suspicious of differences or feel threatened because they have grown up in homes that have promoted prejudice. Lack of knowledge, or ignorance, also causes prejudice. Ignorance often results in fear, which may cause people to react in an unreasonable manner.

What are some of the differences that are involved in prejudice?

Elicit responses and list on the chalkboard or easel pad. Answers may include the following: skin color, weight, facial features, religion, gender, age, customs and traditions, language, socioeconomic status, education, disability status, or general appearance.

How many of you have felt discriminated against at one time or another?

Elicit responses and discuss.

There are many ways people discriminate, or show prejudice. One is by stereotyping, or "putting people into pigeonholes." For example, some may hold the stereotype that all women are terrible drivers. Some may believe that all old people are helpless. Stereotypes of people are not based on facts. Before we stereotype or prejudge anyone, we should STOP, THINK, PLAN, and CHECK. We must STOP and THINK about the consequences of our negative attitudes. School fights, riots, and other violent acts have resulted from prejudicial attitudes. We must PLAN to become more informed and seek out friends who are different. We must CHECK our plan to see if it is working.

● ──────── **Recognizing the need for tolerance**

When people are intolerant, their Bossy Me and Impulsive Me attitudes show through. When people are tolerant, they accept others' differences. Tolerance is having the patience to get to know people and look for their strengths. *(Personalize the following example.)* For example, I knew a student—I'll call him Frank—who was disfigured in a fire. He was a beautiful person, but his peers didn't give him a chance because of the way he looked. But as they became more tolerant, they understood what a fighter he really was. Frank had to fight to survive, and that made him strong.

People who are tolerant understand and respect differences. When people respect differences, they don't make jokes about cultural differences or believe their own culture is superior to other cultures.

Recognizing the importance of understanding differences

Instead of focusing on differences, we can look at what we have in common. Many countries are like a mosaic—every little piece is different, but when we put the pieces together we understand what a beautiful picture they create.

Some people believe in the "melting pot" idea—that everybody living in a country should be the same and adopt exactly the same customs. In this view, the different cultures are like vegetables in a delicious soup. When you make vegetable soup, all the vegetables melt down. They lose their shape and become one dish. Other people believe that a country made up of different cultures should be more like a delicious salad. The vegetables are mixed together but are not melted down. Each piece keeps its shape and contributes to making the salad. These two examples help us understand the way differences are commonly viewed. Which idea do you think is better—the soup or the salad?

Elicit responses and discuss.

Demonstrating respect for differences

The world is made up of different people from different races, nationalities, and religions. There are rich people, poor people, not-so-rich people, and not-so-poor people. People in different cultures have their heros, heroines, and universal contributions. We all have different abilities and limitations, but we must work to respect these differences. What does it mean to respect differences?

Elicit responses and discuss.

We all are equal in our humanity. We all feel the same emotions, and we all want to be happy. Together, our differences can make us stronger and more beautiful, like a beautiful mosaic.

Monitoring Knowledge and Comprehension

Ask the following questions and discuss.

1. What do you think causes people to become prejudiced?

2. Why is tolerance important in any society?

3. How can you start showing that you understand differences?

4. Why is it important to respect people who are different from yourself?

Guided Practice

Divide the class into five groups. Distribute a copy of Figure 57 (Different but the Same) to each group. Assign one situation to each group; direct groups to analyze their situation and suggest solutions.

Assessing Mastery

Have groups report their solutions. Did the solutions include an understanding of prejudice, tolerance, and respect for differences?

RETEACHING

Independent Practice

Choose from the following activities to illustrate how different cultures combine to make an interesting whole.

1. Divide students into small groups and direct them to cut pieces of paper of different colors, textures, and sizes to create a unified picture or scene. A group reporter explains this mosaic to the larger group.

2. Have small groups arrange a bouquet of flowers in which each flower makes an important contribution to the whole arrangement. Students may make their own paper flowers or use artificial flowers. A group reporter explains the arrangement to the class.

Evaluation and Feedback

Divide students into two groups. Conduct a debate in which one group argues for the "melting pot" concept of cultural diversity and the other advocates the "salad" idea.

CLOSING

Summary

In this lesson we learned what prejudice is and discussed the need for tolerance and understanding. Stereotyping categorizes certain people. Prejudice and discrimination create inequality. People are different, but we are all the same in our humanity. We need to understand and respect differences.

Generalization

Direct students to interview their parents or relatives to discover their ethnic and cultural roots. Have students share their findings with the class. As they do so, help students identify likenesses and differences among families and reinforce the need for understanding and respect.

ENRICHMENT

1. Arrange a multicultural party for your class. Celebrate customs, foods, and traditions from various cultures. Involve parents and other classrooms.

2. Direct students to assemble a multicultural cookbook.

3. Assign students to research the immigration movement at the turn of the century and report to the class.

Different but the Same

Situation 1

Belinda has a reading difficulty and has been placed in special education classes. She is mainstreamed for math and science but does not have many friends in those classes. How can Belinda earn her peers' respect and understanding, and make friends? How can the other students help Belinda?

Situation 2

Raymond speaks English with a different accent, and he sometimes uses the wrong words. This causes the class to laugh. Raymond feels bad and refuses to participate in class. What can the teacher, students, and Raymond do to solve the problem?

Situation 3

Mary loves to shoot baskets, and she is good at it, but she is excluded when the boys play during recess. She is tall for her age and a year older than her peers because she repeated a grade. Help Mary solve her problem.

Situation 4

Kisha is an African American student who attends a predominantly white middle school. She is an honor-roll student and a good athlete. She attends services at an Islamic mosque and is very religious. She does not use make-up or wear blue jeans. Kisha also has a hearing impairment, uses sign language, and reads lips. Her language is sometimes difficult to understand. Kisha loves to sew and is also very artistic. How is Kisha different from her peers? How is she the same? How can you help her fit in the group?

Situation 5

Imagine you lived in a subdivision where all the houses are alike, and all the neighbors wear tan slacks and white shirts all the time. For fun they get together at the subdivision club house and barbecue chicken every Saturday night. On Sunday they all attend the same religious service, and after the service the men and boys go to the school playground to play baseball. The women and girls go home and cook spaghetti and meatballs. What is wrong with this picture? How would you change it?

Figure 57

A WALK IN YOUR SHOES

GOAL

- To show empathy

OBJECTIVES

- Improving emotional understanding of self and others
- Developing empathy
- Identifying feelings associated with empathy
- Recognizing that a lack of empathy can lead to self-centered behaviors

MATERIALS

- Paper and pencils
- Classroom furniture (chairs, desks, tables, and so on)
- Blindfolds
- Yellow ribbons (optional)

PROCEDURE

OPENING

Review

In our last lesson we learned that prejudice is destructive. We also learned that tolerance is especially important in a society made up of different cultures. Through knowledge and understanding, we can respect what we have in common and appreciate our differences.

Follow up on any generalization activities assigned during the last lesson.

Stating Objectives

In this lesson we will examine how empathy can improve our emotional understanding of ourselves and of others. We will examine what is needed to develop empathy. We will discuss feelings associated with empathy and how a lack of empathy can lead to self-centered behaviors.

If students have previously studied Lesson 4 in Skill Area 4 (Self-Advocacy and Assertiveness), you may wish to review its teachings on empathetic assertion.

INSTRUCTION

Teaching and Guided Discussion

● ———— **Improving emotional understanding of self and others**

Having empathy means understanding the concerns and feelings of other people. It means being sensitive to the differences of others and being able to see things from other people's points of view. Empathetic people understand and accept that different individuals will feel differently about things.

Empathy is not the same as feeling sorry for someone; rather, it is the ability to place yourself in that person's situation and experience similar feelings. Empathy involves being compassionate. For example, let's suppose your friend has been grounded and cannot attend the school dance this Friday. If you have ever experienced a similar situation, you can empathize and relate especially well to your friend's feelings. Can you think of situations in which you empathized with someone?

Elicit responses and discuss.

● ———— **Developing empathy**

To develop empathy, we need a Caring Me attitude. An empathetic person is understanding and, above all, open-minded. A closed-minded person will have difficulty empathizing. Why?

Elicit responses and discuss.

To empathize we also need a Thinking Me attitude to examine the situation and circumstances and, whenever possible, to find solutions. We can use our Thinking Steps to help us understand how other people feel. Let's examine your grounded friend's situation. First, STOP and examine the situation. Then THINK: What if I were grounded? How would I feel? Next PLAN: You could talk on the phone with your friend (if allowed) or write a short note expressing your support and understanding. CHECK your plan—is it helping your friend deal with the situation? If so, great! If not, try another plan.

To empathize, we must also be assertive. Sometimes you may be teased by your peers for showing empathy. If this happens, you must be able to disregard the criticism and go on with your plan.

● ———— **Identifying feelings associated with empathy**

By being empathetic we are able to offer help without feeling pity. You often hear people say, "I know how you feel—I've been there." Feelings are sometimes difficult to understand, and showing empathy takes sensitivity and a willingness to examine our own emotions. As we grow older we collect experiences. These experiences can make us more empathetic, or they can make us more cynical and distrustful. The decision is up to each one of us.

Even if you have not experienced something exactly like what someone else is experiencing, you can imagine what the other person is going through and identify the feelings involved. For example, let's suppose your best friend just broke up with a boyfriend or girlfriend. What would you say to show empathy? What could you do to cheer your friend up?

Elicit responses and discuss. Answers may include talking with the friend, taking him or her out for a treat, writing a short note, calling on the telephone, and so forth.

Sometimes constant exposure to a condition robs us of our empathy and sensitivity. For example, there was a famine in an African country, and many children were starving. Television news shows displayed these hungry children day after day. People empathized and sent money for food. After a while, however, viewers became "desensitized." They got used to seeing these skeleton-like figures and stopped empathizing. To keep feeling empathy, we may need to keep reminding ourselves of how our own experiences relate to what others are going through.

●————— Recognizing that a lack of empathy can lead to self-centered behaviors

People who do not empathize have difficulty understanding other people. They are insensitive and closed-minded. They adopt a Bossy Me attitude and do not allow their Caring Me and Thinking Me to come through. They are self-centered—their actions show that they think only of their own feelings.

We have a right to pursue happiness, but not at the expense of other people's happiness. People who cannot feel empathy may have been mistreated, never shown love, or never taught to empathize. Do you think such people can change? What could make them become more empathetic?

Elicit responses and discuss.

They might change by working to improve their Thinking Me and Caring Me attitudes. They might also change if they could experience empathy and caring from others.

Monitoring Knowledge and Comprehension

Ask the following questions and discuss.

1. How can empathy improve our emotional understanding of others?

2. John uses a wheelchair. How can you empathize with John's situation?

3. Identify feelings associated with empathy. *(Answers may include sadness, happiness, gratitude, remorse.)*

4. Why do some people fail to empathize?

Guided Practice

Set up an obstacle course in the classroom, using chairs, desks, tables, and other classroom furniture. Pair students and have one of the students wear a blindfold. The student without the blindfold leads the other student through the obstacle course, then reverses roles with the blindfolded student. This exercise can be repeated to simulate other conditions (writing with a nondominant hand, walking with a crutch, using a wheelchair, wearing earplugs, or reading by holding a book in front of a mirror).

Assessing Mastery

Assemble the entire group and encourage students to recount their feelings when experiencing their temporary disability. How did they feel when helping their temporarily disabled partners? How did the experience affect students' ability to empathize?

RETEACHING

Independent Practice

Choose from the following activities.

1. Direct small groups of students to write and act out a scene based on one of the following situations. Discuss the scenes in the larger group.

   > Harry likes the Oilers, but Myrna likes the Saints. The Oilers are losing to the Saints. How can Myrna empathize with Harry?

   > Kerry likes Tom, but Tom does not like Kerry. How can their friend Tina empathize with Kerry?

2. Have half of the students in class pin a yellow ribbon to their shirts. Divide the class into small groups, including some ribbon wearers in each group. Direct each group to assemble a jigsaw puzzle or to play a group game. Privately, tell the students who are not wearing ribbons to ignore or speak only harshly (no cursing allowed) to the ribbon wearers. After 10 minutes, reverse roles. Reassemble the class and ask students to verbalize their feelings. What role did empathy or a lack of it play?

Note: The second activity is based generally on the work of Jane Elliott, an elementary teacher who in the 1960s led students in a participatory classroom experiment on discrimination. For discussion, see "The Eye of the Storm," by Jane Elliott, in *Answering Children's Questions on Prejudice,* edited by Peter Jennings, 1992, New York: ABC Special Production.

Evaluation and Feedback

Ask and discuss the following questions.

How would you want to be treated if:

- You had a learning disability.

- You couldn't speak English.

- You were a girl/boy.

- You were of black/white/Hispanic/Asian descent.

- You had a physical disability.

- You just came from a different country.

CLOSING

Summary

In this lesson we learned how empathy can improve our understanding of ourselves and of others. We examined what is needed to develop empathy. We need to be sensitive, caring, and open-minded to appreciate the feelings of others. We discussed feelings associated with empathy and how a lack of empathy can lead to self-centered behaviors.

Generalization

Choose from the following activities.

1. Invite students to visualize and discuss one of the following situations:

    You are in the shoes of your parent or main caregiver, with all that person's responsibilities. How would you handle two of these responsibilities?

    You are the parent of a teenager hooked on drugs. You love your child very much. How do you feel? What would you do to help your child?

2. Have students select a home chore to do to relieve a parent of a specific responsibility (baby-sitting, mowing the yard, cooking, and so on). Encourage students to discuss how they can empathize with their parents' responsibilities.

ENRICHMENT

1. Have students read *Bury My Heart at Wounded Knee* (Dee Brown), *The Grapes of Wrath* (John Steinbeck), *Rosa Parks: My Story* (Rosa Parks), or any other book depicting discrimination. Open discussion by asking students how they would feel if they were in one of the character's shoes.

2. Pair students and ask them to interview each other. How would each one feel if he or she had to switch parents and homes for a day?

3. Ask students to research a country and write an essay entitled "If I Lived in _____" (China, Australia, Mexico, Egypt, Russia, and so forth).

MANY FACES OF LOVE

GOAL

- To recognize that love can be felt and expressed in many ways

OBJECTIVES

- Identifying self-love
- Identifying love expressed in friendships
- Identifying love expressed in families
- Identifying love expressed for animals, the environment, and humanity

MATERIALS

- Paper and pencils
- Art supplies (markers, poster board, glue, construction paper)

PROCEDURE

OPENING

Review

In our last lesson we learned how empathy can improve our understanding of ourselves and of others. We examined what is needed to develop empathy. We must be sensitive, caring, and open-minded to appreciate the feelings of others. We discussed feelings associated with empathy and how a lack of empathy can lead to self-centered behaviors.

Follow up on any generalization activities assigned during the last lesson.

Stating Objectives

In this lesson we will learn how love can be expressed in many ways. Before we can give love, we must first love and accept ourselves. There are many different kinds of love. Our love for friends and family is different from our feelings for acquaintances. We also feel and express love for animals, the environment, and humanity.

INSTRUCTION

Teaching and Guided Discussion

●———— **Identifying self-love**

What does it mean to love yourself?

Elicit responses and discuss.

> Before we can give love, we begin by learning to love and accept ourselves. We are our own best friends. I love me, but that does not mean I am selfish. What does it mean?

Elicit responses and discuss.

> It means that I care enough about myself to nurture myself physically, emotionally, and mentally. A Caring Me attitude cares about me and also cares about you. A Bossy Me attitude, however, is self-centered. Loving involves responsibility and work. Real love does not involve hurting ourselves and others.

> When you truly love yourself, you want to take care of yourself, and that requires a Thinking Me attitude. Before doing anything to hurt yourself—like smoking, drinking alcohol, or taking drugs—you need to use the Thinking Steps: First ask yourself to STOP and put out that cigarette. THINK of the consequences of your behavior. What does nicotine do to your body? If you are already addicted to nicotine, PLAN to get help to kick the habit. Follow your plan and CHECK—did it work? Do you need another plan?

●———— **Identifying love expressed in friendships**

The information in this section reprises material originally presented in Lesson 3 of Skill Area 1 (Awareness of Self and Others).

> There are many different levels of love, and we express love differently with different people and in different situations. One type of love is expressed in friendships. There are different levels of friendship.

Acquaintanceship

> Acquaintanceship means we know someone and that person knows us. We are friendly with acquaintances, but we do not spend time with them outside of the situation where we know them. What kind of person would be an acquaintance?

Elicit responses. Answers may include a person in a class at school or a neighbor.

Casual friendships

> We spend time with casual friends and like them, but we do not expect a deep bond. We enjoy listening to the same music, having fun together, and just plain hanging out with our casual friends. The bond is not close in this relationship—it may best be described as liking instead of loving someone. Can you name some people who would be casual friends?

Elicit responses. Answers may include teachers, peers, and special people in the neighborhood.

Deep friendships

In a deep friendship, we exchange secrets or confidences as well as enjoy the person's company in many different situations. We expect these friends to be loyal and trustworthy, and they expect the same of us. We establish a close bond of love with these special friends. To do this, we have to be willing to give of ourselves, to compromise, and to enjoy being together. Close friends may disagree but are able to resolve their conflicts. A special kind of bond exists. Do you have any deep friendships?

Discuss.

Intimate friendships

Deep friendships are very special, but they are not intimate. We have intimate friendships with a boyfriend or girlfriend—someone we love in a romantic way.

Lesson 4 in this Skill Area discusses romantic love and sexuality in young adolescents. If you plan to follow this lesson with Lesson 4, you may want to tell students at this point.

●———— **Identifying love expressed in families**

What does the saying "Blood is thicker than water" mean?

Elicit responses and discuss.

That means the bond between blood relatives is stronger than the bond between unrelated people. Some families have a mother and a father and brothers and sisters living together. Some have only one parent, or a grandparent, as the primary caregiver. Regardless of how the family is made up or whether the people are biologically related, what defines it and keeps it together is love. We love and are involved with our families very deeply. It is fine to love family members differently—brothers and sisters, parents, grandparents, and other relatives.

●———— **Identifying love expressed for animals, the environment, and humanity**

Love can also be expressed for animals, the environment, and all of humankind. All living things need love to be healthy. If we do not protect animals in the wild, some species may become extinct. Our pets also need caring, nurturing, and protection. Pets respond to the way they are treated. If they are loved, they love us back. What is the meaning of the saying "A dog is a person's best friend"?

Elicit responses and discuss.

In addition, we need to care for and protect our environment. When we hurt the environment we really hurt ourselves. What are some ways this can occur?

Elicit responses and discuss. Responses may include the following.

- Littering and graffiti destroy the beauty of the environment.
- Air pollution (including smoking) contaminates the air we breathe and causes many illnesses.

- Forest fires carelessly started by people deplete our forests.

- Pollution of rivers, lakes, and oceans contaminates our water supply.

When we love humanity, we love not just one person or a few people, we love all of humankind in a general sense. The ancient Greeks called this *agapé*, as opposed to *eros*, which referred to sexual love. How are some ways you could show love for humanity?

Elicit responses and discuss. Answers may include volunteering your time at a food bank, collecting donations for the homeless, making charitable contributions, and treating others as you yourself would like to be treated.

Some people love inanimate objects more than they love humanity. Material things are not bad in themselves. We all enjoy nice clothes, good food, beautiful cars, and the latest in electronic equipment. These things are meant to be enjoyed. However, if we value material objects more than people, we need to STOP and THINK about what is really important in life. We need to PLAN to shift our priorities and CHECK to be sure our plan is working.

Monitoring Knowledge and Comprehension

Ask the following questions and discuss.

1. Miriam hates herself because she is overweight. She does not pay attention to her grooming and dress. What can she do to develop self-love?

2. How are casual friendships different from deep friendships?

3. Why is it important for families to develop a deep bond of love?

4. Name one way you can show love for each of the following: animals, the environment, humanity.

Guided Practice

Have students brainstorm to create a list of people in their lives: self, family members, relatives, friends, teachers, neighbors, other adults. Direct students to categorize as acquaintances, casual friends, deep friends, or family.

Assessing Mastery

Consider students' lists and how they categorized their relationships. Discuss results as a group.

RETEACHING

Independent Practice

Choose from the following activities.

1. Distribute art supplies and have students make a poster with the theme "Every Day Is Valentine's Day."

2. Encourage students to write a love poem or song for someone they care about. Share in the group if students wish.

Evaluation and Feedback

Direct students to write an essay on the following topics: "I Am My Own Best Friend," "People I Love," "Pets I Love," or "Love and Respect for the Environment." Instruct them to express both how they feel and how they show their love. Read essays aloud and discuss. Evaluate for understanding of lesson concepts.

CLOSING

Summary

In this lesson we learned about different kinds of love. Before we can give love, we must first love and accept ourselves. There are many different kinds of love. Love for friends and family is different from feelings for acquaintances. We also feel and express love for animals, the environment, and humanity.

Generalization

Direct students to select a family member and do something extra-nice to show love. Have students continue for several days, observing and recording the family member's response. Encourage students to share and discuss their experiences with the group.

ENRICHMENT

1. Plan an activity to show love and respect for the environment—for example, picking up litter, recycling cans or newspaper, planting a flower bed, or conserving paper. Instruct students to record their feelings before, during, and after the activity.

2. Purchase two identical plants or start plants from seed. Assign a different group of students every week to take care of the plants. Plant A and Plant B should receive identical amounts of water, fertilizer, and sunlight. Direct students to talk nicely and occasionally caress only Plant A. Have them collect data on and compare rates of growth. There may or may not be a difference in growth; regardless of outcome, discuss students' feelings towards Plant A and Plant B.

LOVE & RESPONSIBILITY

GOAL

- To identify behaviors and responsibilities associated with intimate relationships

OBJECTIVES

- Understanding platonic relationships
- Identifying the consequences of irresponsible sexual behavior
- Recognizing the effects of drugs and alcohol on sexual behavior
- Identifying behaviors associated with responsible love relationships

MATERIALS

- Three Dilemmas (Figure 58)
- What Should I Do? (Figure 59)

PROCEDURE

OPENING

Review

In our last lesson we learned that there are many different kinds of love. Before we can share love, we must first love ourselves. Love for friends and family is different from feelings for acquaintances. We also feel and express love for animals, the environment, and humanity.

Follow up on any generalization activities assigned during the last lesson.

Stating Objectives

In this lesson we will learn what a platonic relationship is. We will discuss the consequences of irresponsible sexual behavior, the effects of alcohol and drugs on intimate behavior, and the meaning of responsibility in a love relationship. We will learn the importance of being well informed about the consequences of sexual behavior and that responsible love is not based on sex alone—it requires a great deal of maturity.

INSTRUCTION

Teaching and Guided Discussion

●————— **Understanding platonic relationships**

Adolescence is a time of sexual awakening. In addition to physical changes, teenagers experience social and emotional changes. How do you think you have changed emotionally since elementary school?

Elicit responses and discuss.

During adolescence, boys and girls view each other as they never did before. Holding hands, hugging, and kissing are early experiences of sexual love. Teenage love is wonderful, but young people must be cautious about how they express their love.

Have you ever heard of a platonic relationship? What does that mean?

Elicit responses and discuss.

A platonic relationship is a close relationship between two people of the opposite sex that exists without sexual intimacy. Having this kind of relationship requires teens to use their Thinking Me attitude. If you are involved in an activity that could lead to sexual intimacy before you are ready, STOP. Walk away and THINK about the possible consequences. PLAN another course of action, such as keeping the relationship platonic. Continue to evaluate your relationship and CHECK your plan.

●————— **Identifying the consequences of irresponsible sexual behavior**

Today boys and girls are sexually active at a younger age than the previous generation, so it is especially important to be able to foresee the negative consequences of sexual intimacy at an early age. What are some of these consequences?

Elicit responses and discuss. Responses may include the following.

- Unplanned pregnancy

- Sexually transmitted diseases (including AIDS)

- Emotional problems (getting "in over your head" in a relationship before you are ready)

- Loss of self-respect

- Loss of the respect of others (family, peers, other adults)

Teenagers can get into real problems if they are promiscuous, or if they have more than one sexual partner. Besides possibly getting a bad reputation, promiscuity greatly increases the chance of getting a sexually transmitted disease. The AIDS virus is out there, and it is a killer.

It is difficult for many teenagers to think about these consequences. For some reason, they believe the "personal fable" that nothing bad can ever happen to them. Another problem is misinformation about sex and sexuality. For example, some young people believe that you can't get pregnant the first time or that if someone looks healthy, that means the person can't be infected with the AIDS virus. What are some other myths you have heard?

Elicit responses and discuss.

You may or may not get accurate information about sex from your friends. Books may give you only part of the story. If you want to get the real facts, you need to talk to a responsible adult. Who would be a good person to ask if you have a question about sex?

Elicit responses. Answers may include a parent, school counselor, health teacher, medical professional, and so forth.

● —— **Recognizing the effects of drugs and alcohol on sexual behavior**

Some teenagers drink alcohol or take drugs. Alcohol and drugs can be deadly. Alcohol and drugs travel quickly to the brain and impair judgment. They shut out the Thinking Me. As a result, these teens behave irresponsibly—they may not choose to abstain from sex, even if that is best for them. If they do have sex, they may not use reliable contraception to prevent a pregnancy or a condom to provide protection from sexually transmitted diseases.

Education is critical in preventing drug and alcohol abuse. Many adolescents get their information on drugs and alcohol through the media—magazines, television, the movies, and music. This information is often incorrect and biased. How do you get your information?

Elicit responses and discuss. Reemphasize the importance of reliable sources (parents, teen programs on drugs and alcohol, school counselors, medical professionals, and the like).

● —— **Identifying behaviors associated with responsible love relationships**

Responsible love between two people is not just passion. Responsible intimate love goes far beyond the sexual act to a relationship that is satisfying for both people on many levels.

What does the saying "Love is blind" mean?

Elicit responses and discuss.

In romantic love, the couple see each other through rose-colored glasses—and sometimes not at all! They acknowledge only each other's strengths and ignore any weaknesses. As time goes by and the novelty of the relationship wears off, they may suddenly realize that their beloved is imperfect. What do you think happens next?

Elicit responses and discuss.

In responsible love, neither party tries to possess, manipulate, or use the other. Each partner acknowledges the other's strengths and weaknesses, and allows the other to be free to grow and develop. When two people share a responsible love relationship, they accept difficult experiences as well as pleasurable ones. The passion of responsible love and the passion of sex are not the same. In responsible love, the couple work out difficulties and accept each other. Responsible love is very difficult for teenagers to achieve—many adults have difficulty being truly responsible in a love relationship.

Monitoring Knowledge and Comprehension

Ask and discuss the following questions.

1. What is a platonic relationship?

2. Name two consequences of irresponsible sex.

3. What are the effects of drugs and alcohol on sexual activity?

4. What does responsible love involve?

Guided Practice

Divide students into small groups. Distribute copies of Figure 58 (Three Dilemmas). Direct groups to discuss and present their solutions to the class.

Assessing Mastery

Evaluate each group's solutions. Did they reflect and analyze the situation? Did they consider the responsibility required of the intimate relationship?

RETEACHING

Independent Practice

Distribute copies of Figure 59 (What Should I Do?) and have students complete as instructed.

Evaluation and Feedback

Evaluate students' responses for understanding of the need for responsible sexual behavior. A sample answer follows.

Dear Concerned:

Telling your parents about your sister could cause hard feelings that could go on for years. Approach your sister kindly and urge her to talk to the school nurse or counselor. If that doesn't work, tell your sister that you love her (in spite of your jealousy) and that you want to help her. Explain firmly but kindly that you will go to the school nurse or counselor to get her the help she needs. If your sister still won't accept help, you will need to go to your parents—but be sure to tell your sister that you intend to talk to your parents before you do. Good luck!

—*Ann Flanders*

CLOSING

Summary

In this lesson we learned what a platonic relationship is. We also discussed the consequences of irresponsible sexual behavior, the effects of alcohol and drugs on intimate behavior, and the meaning of responsibility in a love relationship. We learned that teenagers need to be well informed about the consequences of sexual behavior. Responsible love is not based on sex alone—it requires a great deal of maturity.

Generalization

Assign students to interview an adult of their choice on the responsibilities of marriage and parenthood. Direct them to document the interview and their reflections in a written report. Share in the group.

ENRICHMENT

1. Divide students into small groups. Instruct each group to write a paper on one of the following topics and to present their findings to the class: "AIDS Can Kill You," "Sexually Transmitted Diseases," "Sexual Abstinence and Contraceptives: Whose Responsibility?" "The Responsibilities of Teenage Parenthood," "Sex Education," and "Drugs and Sex Don't Mix."

2. Invite a guest speaker (school nurse, doctor, psychologist, professor, spiritual leader, human sexuality counselor) to discuss the physical, psychological, and spiritual aspects of sexuality.

Three Dilemmas

Dilemma 1

Charlie is 14 years old and is the quarterback of the junior football team. He is very popular with girls, and he knows it. He has had many sexual experiences with several girls and believes those who made out with him are sluts. His new girlfriend, Patricia, refuses to have sex and wants to keep their relationship platonic. When Charlie insists, Patricia calls him promiscuous. Charlie says he thinks she's wrong because he really loves her, and, anyway, only girls can be promiscuous. What do you think?

Dilemma 2

Shara is 13 years old, and Adolf is 15 years old. They are in love. At the beginning of their relationship, they just kissed and petted a little. One evening, after a movie, their petting led to sexual intercourse. Shara didn't think she could get pregnant at her age, but she did. Who is responsible for the pregnancy? How do you think this story will end?

Dilemma 3

Tenay is teased by her friends because she is a virgin. She succumbs to peer pressure and becomes intimate with a boy she hardly knows. When the word gets around, she becomes very popular with other boys. Tenay doesn't enjoy the sex—in fact, she doesn't like it at all. She wants to remain popular and be part of the group. What can Tenay do?

Figure 58

What Should I Do?

Name: _____ Date:_____

Answer the following letter, pretending you are the advice columnist.

Dear Ann Flanders:

I am a 14-year-old girl. All my life I've been overweight and have had to compete with my gorgeous, popular, and skinny 16-year-old sister. My parents think she is perfect. Well, I know she isn't—she sleeps around with just anybody. In fact, I know she has a sexually transmitted disease and is afraid to tell my parents. I feel it's my duty to tell them because she may pass this disease on to others. What do you think?

—*Concerned*

Figure 59

309

WITH OR WITHOUT CONDITIONS

GOAL

- To distinguish between expressions of unconditional versus conditional love

OBJECTIVES

- Identifying unconditional love
- Identifying conditional love
- Responding assertively to pressure situations
- Seeking and using information about sexual decision making

MATERIALS

- Conditional or Unconditional? (Figure 60)
- What's Wrong Here? (Figure 61)
- I'll Love You If . . . (Figure 62)

PROCEDURE

OPENING

Review

In our last lesson we learned about platonic relationships, the consequences of irresponsible sexual behavior, the effects of alcohol and drugs on intimate behavior, and the real meaning of responsible love. We learned that teenagers need to be well informed about the consequences of sexual behavior. Responsible love is not based on sex alone—it requires a great deal of maturity.

Follow up on any generalization activities assigned during the last lesson.

Stating Objectives

In this lesson we will learn about unconditional and conditional love. Unconditional love does not place any restrictions on love. Conditional love means affection may be withdrawn if certain conditions are not met. We will also learn about relationships, social pressures, and assertive responses you can use to respond to pressure situations. Finally, we will consider how to seek and use information to make decisions about sex.

INSTRUCTION

Teaching and Guided Discussion

●———— **Identifying unconditional love**

Scientists have shown that without human nurturing and love, babies die or grow up to become very disturbed adults. When parents love their infants, they establish a bond. Their love is unconditional, or without conditions. What does that mean?

Elicit responses and discuss.

To love without conditions means that I love you for yourself and not because I want something from you. When love is unconditional, it can never be taken away. When two people love each other unconditionally, they empathize with each other and are in tune with each other's attitudes, beliefs, and values. They respect each other and will not place each other at risk.

●———— **Identifying conditional love**

When we love conditionally, we place restrictions on our affection. A parent may tell a child, "I love you when you are good." What happens to this child if the child misbehaves? A husband may tell his spouse, "I love you because you have such a beautiful face." What happens to this woman if her face is disfigured or when she becomes old and wrinkled?

Elicit responses and discuss.

Conditional messages like these put up a barrier to love. You are saying that you will only take down the barrier when and if the other person meets your expectations. Your real message is "I love you for what you can give me to make me happy."

Frequently, when two young people are in love, their love is conditional. One partner may say to the other, "If you really love me, you will have sex with me." Many young people are pressured into having sex because they don't want to lose their partner's love. They submit to the condition. When someone puts conditions on love, it is best to back off. Have you ever been pressured in this way?

Elicit responses and discuss.

Responding assertively to pressure situations

●————

You and you alone can control your decisions about your sexual activity. This is where knowing how to be assertive can help. You can get in touch with your feelings first by being honest with yourself. Practice self-talk and rehearse assertive refusals. Can you think of such statements?

Elicit responses. Some examples follow.

- I am really not comfortable doing it.

- I don't believe we should do that.

- I hope you understand, but I've promised myself not to.

- I trust you to respect my decision.

- I realize how you feel, but no.

Plan ahead. What would you do if you found yourself in a compromising situation? For example, suppose you found yourself at a party and several of your friends and their partners were having sex. If your partner started making sexual advances, would you feel too embarrassed to assert yourself? Could you control your own desire? These are questions you can ask yourself before you get into this kind of situation.

We said earlier that good relationships are based on unconditional love and respect. Many teenagers have sex because they believe everybody else is doing it and they don't want to feel left out. They give in to social pressures because they fail to STOP, THINK, PLAN, and CHECK. Peer pressure may be greater on boys than it is on girls—a boy virgin is often ridiculed by his peers. In many situations, however, girls also are pressured by the group into having sex. In addition, girls usually have most of the responsibility when they get pregnant. Who do you think is responsible when a girl gets pregnant?

Elicit responses and discuss.

Both boys and girls are responsible. Boys as well as girls must act assertively and practice self-control. Both boys and girls must learn to make responsible decisions about sexual relationships and resist pressure to have sex if they are not ready.

Seeking and using information about sexual decision making

Many teenagers are misinformed. Some appear to know the facts about sex. Their parents have talked to them, they have taken sex education courses in school, and they have learned a lot more from their friends. However, these same teenagers do not use their knowledge, and pregnancy and disease are often the result. In addition, both partners are at risk for psychological harm. When premarital sex goes against your value system, it can cause you great anxiety and pain. If your partner decides not to be with you anymore, you may suffer low self-esteem.

Before engaging in sexual behavior, it is important to assume a Thinking Me attitude and STOP and THINK about the sex information you have received, about what you can do in specific situations, and about the consequences of your actions. You need to PLAN whether to abstain from sex or to protect yourself from pregnancy and sexually transmitted diseases. People must make choices and CHECK their own personal beliefs and values about sex; however, the only way to be completely safe from pregnancy and disease is to abstain from sex.

Many teenagers read magazines, listen to their peers, and watch TV—some even watch sexually explicit videos or movies. These are not reliable sources of information. To get the facts, you can begin at home with your parents. If you feel you have a problem communicating with your parents, then find another adult you trust. Many schools have counselors, nurses, coaches, and teachers who are willing to help. What else could you do?

Elicit responses and list other options—for example, doing research at the library or attending a sex education class.

Monitoring Knowledge and Comprehension

Ask the following questions and discuss.

1. Janie cooks dinner because her mother works late. She does not expect to be rewarded. Is Janie's love conditional or unconditional?

2. The teacher favors students only when they make A's and B's. Is the teacher's love conditional or unconditional?

3. Give a reply to the following: "Don't be such a baby. If you don't have sex with me, I'll find someone who will."

4. Don made an A in his sex education class. Still, he got a sexually transmitted disease during his first sexual experience. What do you think happened?

Guided Practice

Distribute copies of Figure 60 (Conditional or Unconditional?) and have students complete as instructed. Share responses.

Assessing Mastery

Distribute copies of Figure 61 (What's Wrong Here?) and have students complete as instructed.

RETEACHING

Independent Practice

Choose from the following activities.

1. Direct students to write three sentences reflecting conditional love and three sentences reflecting unconditional love. Check, discuss, and give feedback.

2. Have students research and write a brief essay on one of the following topics: "Sexual Development," "Consequences of Teen Sex," "The Sexual Revolution," "Teen Parenting."

Evaluation and Feedback

Distribute copies of Figure 62 (I'll Love You If . . .) and have students complete. Discuss answers in the larger group.

CLOSING

Summary

> In this lesson we learned about conditional and unconditional love. Unconditional love does not place restrictions on love, nor does it expect anything in return. Conditional love threatens to withdraw affection if certain conditions are not met. We also learned about relationships, social pressures, and assertive responses you can use in pressure situations. It is important to seek and use accurate information when you make decisions about sex.

Generalization

Unconditional love is giving of yourself with no expectations. Arrange to involve students in community activities by having them volunteer for such activities as Special Olympics, an Easter egg hunt for students with special needs, or Head Start. Elicit parents' help.

ENRICHMENT

Direct students to read a book reflecting the theme of unconditional love. Assign a short book report and discuss as a class. (The class may choose books listed for students in the bibliography or identify their own.)

Conditional or Unconditional?

Read the scenario and answer the following questions.

Gary had a crush on Sally and asked her to be his girlfriend. Sally agreed, but since she had a very jealous and possessive nature, she laid down a few conditions. Gary was not to speak with any other girl. He had to walk her home from school every day, and they always had to do homework together. He could only hang around with the guys during basketball practice. One day at school, Sally saw Gary talking to a cute new girl in the hall. After school, on the way to her house, Sally could not control her anger and said, "You two-timing slime, you were flirting with that pimple-faced girl. We're through."

1. Was Gary's love for Sally unconditional? Explain.

2. Was Sally's love for Gary unconditional? Explain.

3. Define Gary's and Sally's relationship.

What's Wrong Here?

Name: _____ Date:_____

Tell what is wrong with the following statements.

1. You can't get pregnant on your first sexual experience.

2. Everybody's doing it—being a virgin is not cool.

3. Only gays and druggies get AIDS.

4. You can't get pregnant at 13. Get real.

5. I can't get pregnant because it's the wrong time of the month.

6. Condoms take the fun out of sex.

7. Only dirty guys get sexually transmitted diseases. I shower every day.

8. You must have sex many times before you can get pregnant.

9. I love you. I won't let you get pregnant. I'll be careful.

10. Come on, let's do it—it's no big deal.

Figure 61

317

I'll Love You If...

Name: _____ Date:_____

Underline the condition in the following statements, then identify the underlying message. The first one has been answered as an example.

1. I'll kiss you <u>if you promise to take me out.</u>

   Message: *You better entertain me if you expect me to show you any signs of affection.*

2. If you mow the grass, I'll drive you to the movies.

   Message:

3. I will raise your allowance if you spend time with me.

   Message:

4. I promise to be yours only if we have sex.

   Message:

5. I am only happy when you buy me gifts and flowers.

   Message:

6. If you love me, you will not talk to Freddy.

   Message:

7. You can't join our group if you are still a virgin.

   Message:

ROLE-PLAY: LOVE & CARING

CHARACTERS

Chet, Paula, Paula's parents, Nadia, Mary, Sophia

SITUATION

Nadia, Mary, and Sophia are watching a movie on television entitled *Gone with the Feelings*. The movie is about a young man, Chet, who cares very much about a young woman named Paula. Chet is unaware that Paula's parents adopted her at birth. Paula's parents love her very much. They are from a different cultural background and look very different from Paula. Chet wants to have a sexual relationship with Paula, but she has asserted herself and told him that although she loves him very much, she is too young and not ready for sex. The couple has a platonic relationship in spite of Chet's persistence. They are very fond of each other, but Paula is afraid to introduce Chet to her family because he shows a lack of understanding of differences. At a ball game, Chet gets a glimpse of Paula talking to her parents from a distance. He wonders who they are and starts to approach them but loses them in the crowd. Later that evening Paula and Chet are having a conversation at the Pizza House.

Dialogue from the movie.

Chet: Who were those people you were talking to? Why were you talking to them?

Paula: What do you mean "those people"?

Chet: Well, they're not like us.

Paula: They're my parents. So what—they're people and they can love and have feelings. Being different doesn't mean that you are better or not as good.

Chet: Paula, I really like you, but they are not our kind.

Paula: Chet, you are dead wrong! They are my kind! I love them unconditionally. They have cared for me all of my life, no matter what.

Chet: Your parents! What about me? You know how I feel about those kind of people.

Paula: "Those kind of people" adopted me, and I love them very much. I love you, too.

Dialogue among the teenagers watching the movie.

Sophia: I'm adopted, and my parents are different, too. I know exactly how Paula feels.

Nadia: Yes, but you have to understand Chet's feelings.

Mary: Chet *is* a bigot, and his love for Paula is conditional, but I think Paula should have told him about her parents from the very beginning.

Sophia: Told him what? Paula wasn't trying to hide anything.

Nadia: Come off it, Sophia—the difference is so obvious, and Paula knew how Chet felt.

Sophia: The way I see it, their relationship should be strong enough to work it out.

EVALUATION AND FEEDBACK

1. How did Chet show his lack of tolerance?

2. Who else showed a lack of understanding of differences?

3. Why could Sophia empathize with Paula?

4. Why do think Nadia empathized with Chet?

5. Explain the different kinds of love Paula was experiencing.

6. Describe the relationship between Paula and Chet.

7. What do you think Paula meant when she said, "They have taken care of me all my life, no matter what."

8. What conditions did Chet place on his love for Paula?

TIME
MANAGEMENT &
ORGANIZATION

SKILL
AREA
8

WHAT TIME IS IT?

GOAL

- To be punctual

OBJECTIVES

- Becoming aware of the concept of time
- Defining time and recognizing the importance of being punctual
- Identifying reasons for lack of punctuality
- Recognizing skills needed to be punctual

MATERIALS

- Looking at Consequences (Figure 63)
- Tardy Tarfin (Figure 64)
- Chalkboard or easel pad

PROCEDURE

OPENING

Review

None needed.

Stating Objectives

In this lesson we will become aware of time and the importance of being punctual. When we put off or postpone doing tasks, we are procrastinating, or wasting time. We need to become good planners, to persist in being punctual, and to practice self-discipline in managing our time. We will learn some skills we need to be punctual and accomplish our tasks.

INSTRUCTION

Teaching and Guided Discussion

● ——— **Becoming aware of the concept of time**

(Personalize the following example.) The other day, my friend missed her flight to Los Angeles because she was late getting to the airport. She was late because she did not allow enough time for the drive to the airport, for parking her car and checking in, and for walking to the appropriate gate. She was very upset because her flight left without her. My friend was not aware of time. She left home an hour before flight time, but she was still late. She did not realize how much time she needed to get on that airplane. The airplane couldn't wait for her. Why not?

Elicit responses and discuss. Possible responses are as follows.

- The airline company would lose money.

- Other passengers would have to wait and might miss their connecting flights.

- Important mail or other cargo might not be delivered on time.

- The plane's late arrival at its destination might cause problems for other planes trying to land.

In school we also have schedules that need to be followed. What are some of your schedules?

Elicit responses and write individual students' class schedules on the chalkboard or easel pad. If students participate in after-school activities on a scheduled basis, include these in the discussion as well.

● ——— **Defining time and recognizing the importance of being punctual**

Being on time means being punctual. You've heard the expression "Time is money." What does that mean?

Elicit responses and discuss.

Were you ever responsible for a job—at home or outside the home—in which you were paid by the hour? What happened if you were late? *(Students respond.)* You lost money, so time is money. Some people are occasionally late, and other people are in the habit of being late.

Breaking bad habits and forming new ones isn't easy, but it is possible to learn from our bad habits. You must show a Thinking Me attitude and take charge of your time. The Thinking Steps can alert you to use your time wisely. STOP! Examine the cause of your tardiness. THINK! Consider the consequences. PLAN! Develop a plan to be punctual and implement it. CHECK! Check your plan—is it working? If it is, how do you feel?

● ——— **Identifying reasons for lack of punctuality**

Have you ever heard the word *procrastination?* What does it mean?

Elicit responses and discuss.

Procrastination means putting things off—in other words, wasting time. For instance, when you hear your alarm clock go off you might say, "I don't have to get up just now" and hit the snooze button. You put off getting up. Procrastination decreases your effectiveness. It also causes stress because it leads to last-minute rushes, poor work, missed deadlines, and the anger of others who have been kept waiting.

When you are late for school you miss out on information, instruction, and interaction. Your teachers are upset with you, and you are not happy with yourself. You feel hassled by everything. As a student, procrastination is your enemy. Putting off what needs to be done only hurts you. There is a sure cure for procrastination, and it's you!

Recognizing skills needed to be punctual

When you were younger, your parents helped you be punctual. Now that you are older you are expected to assume more responsibility in organizing your time. Suppose you have a friend who can't get to school on time. He wakes up early enough—about 6 o'clock in the morning, but instead of focusing on getting ready, he jumps from one task to another—brushing his teeth, watering the plants, coming back to brush his hair, answering the telephone, getting partially dressed and drinking some juice, then finishing getting dressed and eating the rest of his breakfast. By that time, the bus is outside, and he hasn't gathered the books and homework he needs for the day! What skills does your friend need to use to get to school on time? What could he say to himself?

Elicit responses and discuss. Stress the following skill areas.

- *Staying focused:* "I will finish getting dressed before doing anything else."

- *Prioritizing:* "I need to brush my teeth and hair, get dressed, and eat breakfast. Watering the plants and talking on the telephone are not as important."

- *Being self-disciplined:* "No, I will not water the plants now. They can wait until this afternoon."

- *Being assertive:* "Sorry, I can't talk to you on the phone right now. I'll call you back later."

- *Planning ahead:* "I need to get these books and homework papers together tonight so they will be ready to go in the morning. I'll also lay out the jeans and shirt I'll wear."

Managing time is a lifelong process. A Thinking Me attitude helps you plan your time wisely. You can STOP, THINK, PLAN, and CHECK your strategies for being on time and getting work done. You must be persistent, and that's hard work because it is easy to get bored or tired of schedules and routines. It's worth the work because wasted time is never recovered.

Monitoring Knowledge and Comprehension

Ask the following questions and discuss.

1. How can being unaware of time affect you and others?

2. Why is it important to be punctual?

3. Helen puts off doing her homework—she talks on the phone, watches TV, and bakes cookies. What is Helen's problem?

4. What are some skills that would help Helen?

Guided Practice

Distribute copies of Figure 63 (Looking at Consequences) and have students complete.

Assessing Mastery

Discuss students' answers. As a group, identify the skills needed to be punctual in the situations described.

RETEACHING

Independent Practice

Have students write an acrostic using the word punctual *or compose a poem on the theme of punctuality. A sample acrostic follows.*

> **P**romptness is a virtue.
> **U**nless you use time, you'll waste it.
> **N**ever underestimate its value.
> **C**onsider each minute carefully.
> **T**rack time and organize for work and fun.
> **U**se time wisely and don't procrastinate.
> **A**nalyze your time—you'll get more done.
> **L**earn and remember—you can never recapture time.

Evaluation and Feedback

Divide students into small groups. Distribute copies of Figure 64 (Tardy Tarfin) and have students answer the questions, then report their answers to the class. Evaluate for understanding of the need for punctuality.

CLOSING

Summary

In this lesson we became aware of time and the importance of being punctual. When we put off or postpone doing tasks, we are procrastinating, or wasting time. We need to become good planners, to persist in being punctual, and to practice self-discipline in managing our time. We learned some skills we need to be punctual and accomplish our tasks.

Generalization

Have students record how they spend their time for a 24-hour period. Encourage them to share their findings and analyze how they used their time. Ask the following questions and discuss.

1. Were you punctual?

2. Were you productive?

3. Did you procrastinate?

4. Did you allow time for rest and for fun?

ENRICHMENT

1. Discuss the following sayings, or have students create a thematic bulletin board including these and other mottos.

   To choose time is to save time.

   —Francis Bacon

   The use of time must be the tool of man, not his limitation.

   —John Rogers

   He who gains time, gains everything.

   —Cicero

   Nothing is ours except time.

   —Seneca

   You may delay, but time will not.

   —Benjamin Franklin

2. Divide students into small groups and direct each group to work cooperatively to write a script based on one of the following ideas. Role-play or discuss the scripts.

   A man or woman who procrastinates does not value life.

   Do you love life? Then do not squander time, for that's the stuff life is made of.

   Time is money.

   The past is spent. The present is cash in your pocket. The future is an investment.

   No one can stop the passage of time; therefore, spend it wisely and enjoy.

   Time is a healer. Use time to mend relationships.

Looking at Consequences

Name: _____ Date: _____

Describe the consequences that would be likely to occur in the following situations.

Situation

1. You are 30 minutes late for a religious service.

2. You overslept and are 2 hours late for school.

3. You have a job (baby-sitting, mowing lawns, or other). You are 45 minutes late for work.

4. You have a 3 o'clock dental appointment, and you get there at 5 o'clock.

Consequences

1. _____
   _____
   _____

2. _____
   _____
   _____

3. _____
   _____
   _____

4. _____
   _____
   _____

Figure 63

Tardy Tarfin

Read the scenario and answer the following questions.

Tardy Tarfin was always late, ever since his mother stopped reminding him and urging him to hurry up. She was tired of the hassle every morning and told him that being on time was his responsibility. One night, Tarfin sets his alarm for 7 o'clock in the morning, knowing that the school bus will arrive at 8 o'clock. He thinks 1 hour is plenty of time to get ready. In the morning the alarm rings. Tarfin turns it off, rolls over, and goes back to sleep. Forty-five minutes later, he wakes up and tries to get ready in 15 minutes. He rushes to the bus stop, just in time to see the bus pulling away from the curb. He runs all the way to school but is 40 minutes late. He starts his day in the assistant principal's office.

1. How did Tarfin procrastinate?

2. What are some of Tarfin's bad habits?

3. How did Tarfin lack self-discipline?

4. Should the bus have waited? Take a stand.

5. What are the results of Tarfin's allowing time to slip away?

6. What are some suggestions you would make for Tarfin?

Figure 64

TIME FLIES

GOAL

- To develop a system of time management

OBJECTIVES

- Recognizing that time must be valued
- Identifying time robbers
- Developing strategies to manage time
- Allowing for "cushion time" when developing plans

MATERIALS

- Taminika's Time Management (Figure 65)
- Paper and pencils

PROCEDURE

OPENING

Review

In the last lesson we became aware of time and the importance of being punctual. When we put off or postpone doing tasks, we are procrastinating, or wasting time. We need to become good planners, to persist in being punctual, and to practice self-discipline in managing our time. We learned some skills we need to be punctual and accomplish our tasks.

Follow up on any generalization activities assigned during the last lesson.

Stating Objectives

In this lesson we will learn that time must be valued and that certain activities rob us of time. We will learn how to avoid time robbers and consider strategies that will help us manage our time better. Finally, we will learn the importance of building in "cushion time," or extra time, in our plans.

INSTRUCTION

Teaching and Guided Discussion

●———— **Recognizing that time must be valued**

"To keep time," "To lose track of time," "Time heals all wounds," "Beware the ravages of time": These are all interesting sayings. What role does time play in your life?

Elicit responses and discuss.

One little second doesn't mean much, but those little seconds add up to hours, months, and years. Do you remember what was happening to you 5 years ago? Does 5 years seem like a long time or a short time?

Allow students to respond. Answers will vary.

Time is a valuable and limited commodity. The word *commodity* means an article of trade. You can trade or use a commodity for many things that you do. People often say, "Man, I have so much to do and so little time to do it." What are some ways that you trade, or use, time?

Elicit responses and discuss.

You might watch TV, play outside, do homework, participate in sports, or just hang out. When you trade your time for one of these activities, do you find that you need more time for your next activity? Do you miss a show you want to watch on TV? Do you come home so tired that you need time to relax or don't have time to complete some other important activity?

Elicit responses and discuss.

If you have such experiences, your activities are controlling you instead of you controlling your activities. A way of controlling your activities is to develop a system of time management.

●———— **Identifying time robbers**

Good time management involves doing what you need to do and controlling "time robbers." *(Personalize the following example.)* For example, I planned to work for 1 hour on a lesson after school. I went to the faculty lounge to get a soft drink and met some other teachers. I talked about the fire drill and how the students reacted. We all conversed about the upcoming election and discussed the ballot in detail. I returned to my classroom and watered the plants, went through the mail, and looked at some old student pictures I found in my desk. Before I knew it, it was time to go home. What time robbers invaded my schedule?

Elicit responses and discuss. Answers might include dealing with unimportant tasks or lack of organization.

●———— **Developing strategies to manage time**

How can you manage time to accomplish what needs to be done and still have time for activities you want to do?

Elicit responses and discuss.

Making a written daily schedule is one method professionals use to manage their time. You need to STOP, THINK, PLAN, and CHECK. STOP what you are doing. THINK of a plan to prioritize activities and to be finished within a certain block of time (for example, a day or a week). Write a list. Use self-talk: Ask yourself whether you are being realistic or whether you have listed too many activities. Next make a PLAN. Identify and group similar activities. Try to finish one activity before beginning the next one. Watch out for time robbers, especially impulsive interruptions. Finally, CHECK your plan to organize your time.

Allowing for "cushion time" when developing plans

You may become frustrated and stressed out whenever you schedule your time too tightly. Stress may cause you to develop an Impulsive Me attitude and prevent you from thinking reflectively. You need to plan a period of "cushion time" for unexpected events. Using cushion time means limiting yourself to a fewer number of activities and reserving some free time for emergencies or for rethinking your plan. Good use of cushion time prevents stress and failure.

In school when you are allowed time to change from one class to another, this is cushion time. Some businesses allow cushion time, and some do not. For example, let's suppose the policy of Pizza Castle is to deliver pizza 30 minutes from the time the order is placed. The pizza is free if it is not delivered on time. Is that a good policy? Why or why not?

Elicit responses and discuss. Point out that the consequences of such a tight schedule may include accidents.

Cushion time allows you to use a Thinking Me attitude and to slow down your Impulsive Me attitude. It allows you to analyze and make changes in your schedule when something unexpected happens.

Monitoring Knowledge and Comprehension

Ask the following questions and discuss.

1. Why must time be valued?

2. How do time robbers keep you from getting things done?

3. Name some strategies for good time management.

4. When is cushion time especially important in developing a schedule?
   (when you are under stress, don't feel well, or have much to accomplish)

Guided Practice

Ask students to develop a written list and identify personal time robbers that prevent them from completing activities. Have them write a specific plan to control these time robbers. Provide assistance and feedback as needed.

RETEACHING

Independent Practice

Choose from the following activities.

1. Have students pair up with a buddy to discuss various ways of managing time.

2. Direct students to write a short paragraph explaining one of the following sayings: "If time were a thing that money could buy, the rich would live and the poor would die" or "Life must be measured by thought and action, not by time alone."

Evaluation and Feedback

Distribute copies of Figure 65 (Taminika's Time Management) and have students complete as directed. Evaluate for understanding of the need for time management.

CLOSING

Summary

In this lesson we learned that time must be valued and that time robbers are things we do that keep us from using our time wisely. We learned how to avoid time robbers and considered strategies to help us manage our time better. Finally, we learned the importance of building in "cushion time" in our plans.

Generalization

Direct students to keep a detailed journal of how they spend their time during a specified 2-day period. Help them analyze their entries. Focus on identifying time robbers and encourage students to prioritize activities and include cushion time. Direct students to repeat the exercise for another 2 days, then compare the first period of time with the second. Did they show improvements in organizing their time?

ENRICHMENT

1. Have students write a schedule for school days. To help them get started, ask the following questions. Students can also make up schedules for a week, a month, or an at-home weekend.

   How many hours in a day?

   How many hours a day do you go to school?

   How many hours do you sleep at night?

   How many hours do you have left for study and other activities?

2. Discuss the following poem.

Take Time

Take time to play—it is the secret of youth.
Take time to read—it is the foundation of knowledge.
Take time to work—it is the price of success.
Take time to think—it is the source of power.
Take time to dream—it hitches the soul to the stars.
Take time to laugh—it is the singing that helps life's load.
Take time to love—it is the one sacrament of life.
Take time to enjoy friends—it is the source of happiness.

—*Anonymous*

Taminika's Time Management

Name: _____ Date: _____

Read about Taminika and answer the questions about her use of time management.

At School

Taminika is on her way to class. She sees her friend Clark, and they begin to talk. When the bell rings, Taminika rushes to class, dropping her homework assignment along the way. She gets to class, and the first task is to check homework. She realizes that her homework is missing.

1. What are the time robber(s)?

2. What difficulties does Taminika face as a result of her lack of time management?

3. What would have happened if she had allowed cushion time?

At Home

At home, Taminika has many chores. It is her responsibility to bring in the mail, tidy her room, put away her clothes, and do her homework assignments. She decides she has plenty of time, so she gets a snack and calls her friend on the phone. When she hangs up, she decides to watch only one of her favorite TV shows. Three TV shows later, Taminika hears her mother returning from work.

1. What are the time robber(s)?

2. What difficulties does Taminika face as a result of her lack of time management?

3. What would have happened if she had allowed cushion time?

Figure 65

TIME TO RELAX

GOAL

- To develop strategies to relax and reduce stress

OBJECTIVES

- Differentiating between stress and distress
- Identifying the effects of stress on emotional well being
- Identifying the effects of stress on physical well being
- Identifying ways to cope with stress

MATERIALS

Relaxation Exercise (Figure 66)

Stress Awareness (Figure 67)

Personal Stress Inventory (Figure 68)

Chalkboard or easel pad

PROCEDURE

OPENING

Review

In our last lesson we learned that time management is important for completing tasks. Good time management means doing what you need to do and avoiding time robbers, which keep us from accomplishing our goals. We learned some time management strategies and talked about how building in cushion time helps us allow for the unexpected.

Follow up on any generalization activities assigned during the last lesson.

Stating Objectives

In this lesson we will learn that stress is part of life. We all experience stress, but too much stress is harmful and turns into distress. We will examine different causes of stress and the effects of stress on physical and emotional fitness. We will also examine different ways to cope with stress.

INSTRUCTION

Teaching and Guided Discussion

●———— **Differentiating between stress and distress**

What is stress, and how does it affect your health and happiness?

Elicit responses and discuss.

Stress is the "wear and tear" of life. It is pressure from the outside that leads us to be tense on the inside. A certain amount of stress is helpful because it can keep you on your toes. Life would be dull without a little stress, and a reasonable amount can help us be productive and accomplish the things we need to do. However, too much stress becomes distress, and that can make us miserable, sad, or ill. Stress is a fact of life, but when we give ourselves negative self-talk, we become distressed.

You can also feel distress or stressed out when something is bothering you and weighs heavy on your mind. What are some examples of events that might be particularly stressful for you?

Brainstorm and list students' answers on the chalkboard or easel pad. In addition to the factors mentioned in the following discussion, answers may include exams, illness, failed love relationships, and quarrels with family members or friends.

Lack of time is a major stressor in many people's lives. Many people complain that there is not enough time to get everything done—too much work and not enough time. Another common cause of distress is change. Too many changes can cause tension. For example, a move to a different city causes stress because it takes time to move, learn new routines, and settle down. A change of school is also stressful because it takes time to get used to a new environment, new teachers, and new friends.

●———— **Identifying the effects of stress on emotional well being**

Can you tell me how you feel when you are stressed out?

Elicit responses. Answers may include tense, nervous, distracted, unhappy, tearful, moody, and so on.

Too much stress can make us experience many feelings, especially fear or anxiety. When people are very stressed out, they may also feel depressed. Depression is a feeling of unhappiness and gloominess that just does not go away. Sometimes depression leads to a feeling of hopelessness and a loss of self-control.

Some people try to get relief from stress by turning to drugs and alcohol. What do you think happens then?

Elicit responses and discuss.

We may fool ourselves into thinking that drugs and alcohol can cure stress. They may temporarily make us forget our problems or feel in control. But in the long run, they add stressors by creating dependency and damaging both our physical and emotional health.

• ———— Identifying the effects of stress on physical well being

Stress can build up until it causes physical as well as emotional problems. What are some physical symptoms that might suggest that you are under a lot of stress?

Elicit responses and discuss. Answers may include sleeping too much or too little, feeling tired, having headaches or stomachaches, and so forth.

Once physical symptoms appear, we must take care of ourselves by getting enough exercise, eating good food, and getting enough rest. We also must get to the bottom of what is causing us stress in the first place.

• ———— Identifying ways to cope with stress

There are many positive ways to take control of the stress in our lives. Everyone has his or her own way to relax and reduce stress. What works for me may not work for you. What are some ways you have tried to reduce stress?

Brainstorm and list ideas on the chalkboard or easel pad. Answers may include the following.

- Taking a walk

- Having a quiet moment to yourself

- Listening to music

- Exercising

- Talking to someone you trust

We can also use the Thinking Steps to help get stress under control. The first thing we need to do is STOP. If you have ever watched the Olympic Games on television you will notice that before an athlete jumps from the diving board or goes down the ski run, he or she will stop for a moment to take control, both mentally and physically. After you have been able to STOP and relax, you can go ahead and use the rest of the Thinking Steps: THINK about what is causing your stress, PLAN to do something about it, and CHECK your plan to see if it is working.

A good time management system can also reduce the stressors in your life. By allowing ourselves "cushion time," we can reduce anxiety and frustration.

Review from Lesson 2 as necessary.

Negative self-talk often leads to distress. Positive self-talk is another strategy we can use to help us decrease our stress. Talk to yourself out loud and listen to what you are saying. You may look in the mirror and even answer yourself. Self-talk can help you reflect on what is bothering you. If you are feeling self-pity or otherwise putting yourself down, think of your good qualities and of the last time you did something you thought was good. Clear, rational self-talk can help you control your stress level, shape your emotions, and direct your behavior.

Monitoring Knowledge and Comprehension

Ask the following questions and discuss.

1. When does stress turn into distress?

2. Yussef is always late. He develops a stomachache when he rushes. How is Yussef's tardiness affecting his health?

3. Joe has an important interview to determine whether he will get a job as a helper in a child care center. Joe is good with children but has a poor self-concept and feels stressed out. What emotions could Joe be feeling?

4. How could Joe cope with these feelings?

Guided Practice

Relaxing can help you become more in tune with yourself, reduce stress, and help you concentrate your thoughts and energy toward the day's activities. We are going to practice one way of relaxing. After you learn this technique, you can use it on your own to help you gain self-control before taking a test, tackling a difficult problem, asking for a date, and so on.

Lead students in the Relaxation Exercise (Figure 66). Students may giggle or make fun of the exercise. If so, reexplain the purpose of relaxation. If appropriate for your group, distribute copies of the exercise for students to use independently.

Assessing Mastery

Distribute copies of Figure 67 (Stress Awareness) and have students complete. Answers to Part I: 1–False, 2–False, 3–True, 4–False, 5–True, 6–True. Students' positive self-talk revisions on Part II will vary.

RETEACHING

Independent Practice

Distribute copies of Figure 68 (Personal Stress Inventory) and have students complete.

Evaluation and Feedback

Discuss students' reactions to the inventory and encourage them to evaluate their own levels of stress and particular stressors. If a student's responses indicate a very high stress level, consider the need for a referral to the school counselor or another helping professional.

CLOSING

Summary

We learned in this lesson that a certain amount of stress can help us accomplish our goals. Too much stress can have a negative effect, however. Feelings of fear, anxiety, and depression can result from too much stress, and we may even develop physical symptoms as a result. We can reduce distress by becoming aware of our own stressors, taking time to relax, and using our Thinking Steps.

Generalization

Direct students to ask a family member to complete the Personal Stress Inventory (Figure 68). Have them compare their own responses with those of their family member.

ENRICHMENT

1. Discuss the following quotations:

   I am more important than my problems.

   —José Ferrer

   Your brain may lie to you, but your body never does.

   —James Thurber

   If you keep your nose constantly to the grindstone, you'll wind up without a nose or a grindstone.

   —Phillip Stone

2. Direct students to write a poem based on the words *stressors, anxiety, depression,* or *tense*. Have them include positive self-talk.

3. Direct students to close their eyes, take a few deep breaths, and relax. Tell them to visualize a time when they were in a stressful situation. Next tell them to see themselves in control of this situation. Have them open their eyes and write a paragraph describing their plan to reduce stress and get control.

Relaxation Exercise

Breathing

You are going to take three slow, deep breaths. You will inhale for a count of three, then hold the breath for a moment longer. You will then let the breath out slowly on a count of four. After each complete breath, you will relax your entire body.

1. Inhale, 2, 3. Now hold.

2. Exhale, 2, 3, 4.

3. Notice yourself becoming more relaxed.

(Repeat three times.)

Legs

Now you will tighten and relax the muscles in your feet, toes, and legs.

1. Sit in a comfortable position, legs stretched out in front and slightly off the floor.

2. Tighten your toes, your feet, and your legs—very tight. Hold, 2, 3, 4, 5.

3. Now relax the muscles in your legs, your feet, and your toes, 2, 3, 4, 5.

4. Notice how the muscles feel when relaxed.

(Repeat three times.)

Figure 66

Arms

Now you will tighten and relax all the muscles in your arms.

1. First, stretch your arms out in front of your body.

2. Tighten your fists, your lower arm muscles, and your upper arm muscles—very tight. Hold, 2, 3, 4, 5.

3. Relax your arms and hands at your sides, 2, 3, 4, 5.

4. Notice how the muscles feel when relaxed.

(Repeat three times.)

Face

Now you are going to tighten and relax your face muscles. If you are wearing contact lenses, do not close your eyes too tightly.

1. Look straight ahead.

2. Close your eyes tightly. Tighten your face muscles, make a face, bite down and tighten your jaws, 2, 3, 4, 5.

3. Relax all the muscles in your face, 2, 3, 4, 5.

(Repeat three times.)

Breathing

Now you will breathe deeply again, as before. As you do, sense how relaxed you are in your legs, in your arms, and in your face.

(Repeat the breathing exercise.)

Figure 66 continued

Stress Awareness

Name: _____ Date:_____

Part I

Answer true (T) or false (F).

_____ 1. Stress always starts with pressure from within.

_____ 2. Stress is always bad.

_____ 3. A common reason for stress is change.

_____ 4. Using drugs and alcohol relieves stress.

_____ 5. Managing your time will help you reduce stress.

_____ 6. Negative self-talk will add stress to your life.

Part II

Rewrite the following sentences so they show positive self-talk instead of negative self-talk.

1. I really want the job helping out in the office, but what if I mess up filing or answering the phone?

2. I know I'll fail this test.

3. I've had it—what's the use?

4. I can't do this. I'm not good at it.

5. He always gets the breaks. I never do.

Personal Stress Inventory

Name: _____ Date: _____

Below is a list of statements. Check "Yes" if the statement is true about you. Check "No" if the statement is generally untrue.

0–5 yes = You are OK, but remember to take it easy and relax.

6–10 yes = You show definite signs of stress. Watch out.

11–20 yes = You are stressed out to the max. Get help right away.

	Yes	No
1. I do not schedule time for regular physical exercise.	☐	☐
2. I have poor eating habits and/or eat on the run (skip meals, eat too many fats, drink too many sodas).	☐	☐
3. I do not take time to participate in fun activities.	☐	☐
4. I do not take time to practice relaxation (relaxation exercises, positive self-talk, visual imagery).	☐	☐
5. I spend a lot of time in negative self-talk ("I'm so dumb," "I always get things wrong," and so on).	☐	☐
6. I cope with my problems by using short-term strategies that are harmful in the long run (drugs, alcohol, cigarettes, too much food, too little food).	☐	☐
7. I always try to satisfy the needs of others, but I neglect to take time to satisfy my own needs.	☐	☐
8. I ignore my problems and bury them inside, and I hope time will make them go away.	☐	☐
9. I lack purpose in my life. I have no or few goals (difficulty making decisions, no motivation, never finish projects).	☐	☐

Figure 68

345

	Yes	No
10. I spend almost all my time in one activity (sports, cheerleading, reading, and so forth). I can't seem to find time for anything else.	☐	☐
11. I procrastinate. I don't plan my time wisely.	☐	☐
12. I get depressed very easily. I wish I could get away from it all.	☐	☐
13. I spend a lot of time worrying about situations at home.	☐	☐
14. I feel left out. I don't seem to fit in.	☐	☐
15. I don't allow at least 8 hours a night for sleep.	☐	☐
16. I often lose control when I have too much to do and too little time.	☐	☐
17. I seldom talk about my problems.	☐	☐
18. I spend a lot of time worrying about situations in school or at home.	☐	☐
19. I seldom give or receive love.	☐	☐
20. I am experiencing one or more changes in my life (moving, parents divorcing, death of family member or friend, changing schools or jobs).	☐	☐

Figure 68 continued

AT YOUR BEST

GOAL

- To understand personal energy cycles

OBJECTIVES

- Identifying personal learning styles
- Identifying personal time preferences
- Recognizing and defining personal energy cycles
- Using awareness of one's own personal energy cycle to plan for success

MATERIALS

- Energy Interview (Figure 69)
- Learning Style Inventory (Figure 70)
- Energy Journal (Figure 71)

PROCEDURE

OPENING

Review

In our last lesson we learned that a certain amount of stress can help us accomplish our goals. Too much stress can have a negative effect. Lack of time often produces stress. Feelings of fear, anxiety, and depression can be the result of too much stress. We can reduce stress by becoming aware of our own stressors, taking time to relax, and using our Thinking Steps.

Follow up on any generalization activities assigned during the last lesson.

Stating Objectives

In this lesson we will learn to recognize our own learning styles, time preferences, and energy cycles. We will recognize that our ability to learn is influenced by our emotions, social group, and environment. We will consider what time of day we learn best. Knowing more about ourselves in this way will help us make adjustments to meet the demands of the day.

INSTRUCTION

Teaching and Guided Discussion

●———— **Identifying personal learning styles**

We learn in different ways. Some of us learn better by looking, others by listening, and still others by doing. Some of us prefer to learn alone, while some of us prefer to work with others. Our learning is also influenced by our emotions. For example, we learn best when we are interested in something and when we feel that what we are learning is useful to us personally. Our social group (peers, teachers, and parents) also affects how we learn. We are more likely to value learning when our peer group values learning. For example, Maurice was intelligent and capable of making top grades, but he was afraid his peers would call him a nerd, so he made C's instead. Parents can encourage their children to succeed in school; however, too much pressure from home can make learning more difficult. Finally, our environment plays a part in how we learn: Sounds, light, and temperature all affect our ability to concentrate and persist in tasks.

●———— **Identifying personal time preferences**

Time greatly influences our learning. Usually, the more time we spend on a task the better we learn it, whether the task is playing basketball or solving a math problem. We also all have a special time in the day during which we are best able to concentrate and sustain attention. Some of us are "early birds" and are more inclined to learn in the morning. Others are "night owls" and prefer the afternoon or evening for learning. Are you an "early bird" or a "night owl"?

Elicit responses and discuss.

Some tasks require greater attention than others. If we are able to work at the time of day we prefer, we are better able to pay attention and retain what we learn.

It is difficult for schools to meet the needs of night owls. Schools run on a daytime schedule and unfortunately cannot accommodate all students' time preferences. What if you are a night owl? What can you do to master a lesson you do not understand in school during the day?

Elicit responses and discuss.

You could spend some time at home in the afternoon studying the lesson. It might also help you learn if you pair up with an early bird friend after school.

●———— **Recognizing and defining personal energy cycles**

The pattern across a day of your ups and downs in concentration and alertness is your *energy cycle*. Ideally, your energy cycle matches the demands of your school or work day. In reality, however, the two are often "out of sync." Energy cycles differ, but most schools and work places will not allow you to work at the time and pace you choose. You must also interact with and respond to others who may have different energy cycles. To help you learn about your own energy cycle, you can keep notes on your productivity during various times during the day.

●————— **Using awareness of one's own personal energy cycle to plan for success**

It is important to be able to adjust your energy cycle to meet the demands of your environment. Suppose you are a night owl who needs to come to school an hour early for band practice. What could you do to make getting up and to school easier for yourself?

Elicit responses and discuss. Answers may include going to bed earlier and getting up earlier, eating a nutritious snack, engaging in physical exercise and relaxation techniques as energy restorers, planning and scheduling time, and including "cushion time."

Once you have identified your own energy cycle, you are ready to change your habits so you can meet the demands of your own day.

Monitoring Knowledge and Comprehension

Ask the following questions and discuss.

1. Think of a skill you learned and remembered in the past month. It could be a skill you learned at school, at home, or in the community. How did you learn it?

2. Are you an early bird or a night owl? What do you do to compensate for your time preference?

3. What is the pattern of ups and downs during the day called?

4. How can keeping track of your own energy cycle help you be more productive?

Guided Practice

Give each student a copy of Figure 69 (Energy Interview). Pair students and have them interview each other to collect the data.

Assessing Mastery

In the larger class, ask each student to describe his or her partner's energy cycle. Discuss differences and similarities. Evaluate for understanding of individual differences in energy cycles.

RETEACHING

Independent Practice

Direct students to complete the Learning Style Inventory (Figure 70).

Evaluation and Feedback

Have students discuss their responses to the inventory. Emphasize similarities and differences among individuals.

CLOSING

Summary

In this lesson we learned that we all have different ways of learning. We are influenced by our emotions, our social group, and our environment. We learned to recognize whether we learn best in the morning or later on in the day (early bird or night owl). We all have a personal energy cycle. Knowing when we work best can help us make adjustments to meet the demands of the day.

Generalization

Direct students to keep track of their energy cycles for a week. Distribute copies of Figure 71 (Energy Journal) as needed. At the end of the week ask, "What can each one of you change to help make your day more successful?" Discuss. Have students write their plans for improvement.

ENRICHMENT

1. Instruct students to graph their Energy Journal data, with time of day indicated along the horizontal axis and energy level indicated on the vertical axis.

2. Have students respond to the following hypothetical dilemma:

    Tony was good at math. Unfortunately, Tony was an early bird, and his math period was right after lunch. He felt sleepy and lacked energy to do his best. Solve Tony's dilemma and tell the rest of the story.

3. Divide students into small homogeneous groups according to their responses on the Learning Style Inventory (Figure 70). Direct each group to answer the following questions and then compare their responses with a group having a different learning style:

    How would you teach the lyrics of a song to a group of friends?

    How would you memorize a poem?

    How would you go about studying for an exam?

Energy Interview

Name: _____ Date:_____

Questions answered by: _____

Ask your partner the following questions. Use a check mark to indicate his or her answers.

1. When do you prefer to go to bed?

    ☐ a. before 11 o'clock

    ☐ b. after 11 o'clock

2. If you had a choice, when would you prefer to attend school?

    ☐ a. from 7 o'clock in the morning until 2 o'clock in the afternoon

    ☐ b. from 10 o'clock in the morning until 5 o'clock in the afternoon

3. When would you prefer your most difficult classes to be scheduled?

    ☐ a. in the morning

    ☐ b. in the afternoon

4. After school, when would you rather do your homework?

    ☐ a. shortly after I get home

    ☐ b. after dinner

5. When do you feel most energized?

    ☐ a. alone

    ☐ b. with people

6. In the evening after dinner, what do you prefer doing?

    ☐ a. relax and take it easy

    ☐ b. go out and party

Figure 69

Learning Style Inventory

Name: _____ Date: _____

Check the phrases that most accurately describe you.

1. I learn best by
   - ☐ a. listening to a lecture or an audiotape.
   - ☐ b. looking at a videotape or reading a book.
   - ☐ c. writing about the subject.
   - ☐ d. role-playing or doing what I'm supposed to be learning.

2. I prefer to study
   - ☐ a. by myself.
   - ☐ b. with a friend.
   - ☐ c. in a small group.
   - ☐ d. in a large group.

3. When I learn from a new book, I prefer to
   - ☐ a. get an idea of what the book is all about, then read the details.
   - ☐ b. read the details and then get an idea of the whole picture.
   - ☐ c. look at both the details and the whole picture.
   - ☐ d. I'm not sure how I learn.

4. I prefer to learn
   - ☐ a. in the morning.
   - ☐ b. in the afternoon.
   - ☐ c. in the evening.

5. I prefer to learn
   - ☐ a. in a cold room.
   - ☐ b. in a hot room.
   - ☐ c. in a comfortably warm room.

6. I can study best
   - ☐ a. when it's quiet.
   - ☐ b. with music or the television on.
   - ☐ c. with no interruptions.

Figure 70

7. I can concentrate better on my school work or homework when
   - ☐ a. I am eating something.
   - ☐ b. I am drinking something.
   - ☐ c. I am eating and drinking.
   - ☐ d. I don't need any food or drink to concentrate.

8. What motivates me to learn is
   - ☐ a. the way the subject is taught (for example, an interesting teacher).
   - ☐ b. the subject matter.
   - ☐ c. the way my friends react to the lesson.
   - ☐ d. my grades.

9. When I don't understand a lesson
   - ☐ a. I ask for help and try to understand.
   - ☐ b. I give up.
   - ☐ c. I try and try by myself until I get it.
   - ☐ d. It really doesn't matter. Maybe I'll learn it eventually, and maybe not.

10. I can remember facts better when I
    - ☐ a. create a visual picture of the information in my mind.
    - ☐ b. arrange and associate the information in a way that is easier for me to remember.
    - ☐ c. use the information in my daily life.
    - ☐ d. say and look at the information until I memorize it.
    - ☐ e. rhyme the information in a song or a verse.
    - ☐ f. pair the information with something else. For example, "The 49th state is Alaska. I'll ask ya (Alaska) 49 times: What is our 49th state?"
    - ☐ g. use an acrostic to remember information. For example, planets in our solar system: "My (Mercury) very (Venus) earthy (Earth) mother (Mars) just (Jupiter) served (Saturn) us (Uranus) nine (Neptune) pizzas (Pluto)."

Figure 70 continued

Energy Journal

Name: _____ Date:_____

For each time period, think of a one- or two-word description of what you are doing. Write this description in the box that shows your energy level. For example, for "Early morning" you might write "shower and breakfast" in the column marked "Low energy."

	Low energy	Medium energy	High energy
Early morning			
Midmorning			
Noon			
Midafternoon			
Evening			
Night time			

Figure 71

TIME FOR FUN

GOAL

- To choose appropriate leisure activities

OBJECTIVES

- Recognizing the importance of healthy leisure activities
- Identifying unhealthy leisure activities
- Recognizing the difference between inactive and interactive leisure activities
- Identifying leisure activities that correlate with interests, strengths, resources, and personality type

MATERIALS

- Interest Inventory (Figure 72)
- Leisure Time Review (Figure 73)
- Chalkboard or easel pad

PROCEDURE

OPENING

Review

In our last lesson we learned to recognize our individual learning styles. The way we learn is influenced by our emotions, our social group, and our environment. We learned to recognize the time of day when we learn best. We all have a personal energy cycle; knowing about this cycle can help us make adjustments to meet the demands of the day.

Follow up on any generalization activities assigned during the last lesson.

Stating Objectives

In this lesson we will learn that healthy leisure activities are necessary for a balanced life. We can engage in inactive and interactive categories of leisure activities. There are healthy leisure activities and unhealthy leisure activities. We need to consider our interests, personal strengths, and resources when choosing healthy leisure activities.

INSTRUCTION

Teaching and Guided Discussion

●————— Recognizing the importance of healthy leisure activities

Years ago, without modern conveniences, free time was limited. People spent most of their time working and had little time to play. Today leisure activities are an important part of everyone's life. Most everyone has free time to use for personal enjoyment.

Have you ever heard the saying "All work and no play makes Johnny a dull boy"? This means a person needs play to keep things in perspective and that, without play, a person would be very dull indeed. We all need time to work, but we also need time to play.

On the one hand, an Enthusiastic Me attitude leads us to too much play; on the other hand, a Bossy Me attitude can work us too hard. Many people are so involved in their work that they cannot chill out and have some fun. We have to take our work seriously, but we also need to use a Thinking Me attitude to balance time for work and play. What are some ways you like to spend your free time?

Help students brainstorm a number of healthy leisure activities. List on the chalkboard or easel pad.

- Team sports: baseball, football, basketball, track

- Individual sports: skating, jogging, walking, karate, hiking

- Hobbies: stamp or card collecting, photography, gardening, bird watching, drawing, auto mechanics, computers, cooking, playing a musical instrument, dancing

- Games: board games, computer games, card games

- Miscellaneous: going to the movies, watching television, reading, listening to music, attending concerts, going to museums

●————— Identifying unhealthy leisure activities

You choose leisure activities that are enjoyable. However, some choices of free time activities can lead to trouble. Drugs and alcohol might seem enjoyable in the short term but have undesirable long-term effects. What are some of these long-term effects?

Elicit responses and discuss. Responses may include dependency, physical and emotional illness, alienation from friends and family, and so on.

Irresponsible sexual behavior is also a poor choice. What might happen if you use your free time this way?

Elicit responses and discuss. Answers may concern pregnancy, sexually transmitted diseases, loss of self-respect and the respect of others, and so forth.

We need time to plan and manage our leisure time in a constructive way. Irresponsible use of leisure time is often destructive to ourselves and others. An Impulsive Me attitude almost always causes people to act irresponsibly. For example, some people spend their leisure time drinking and then driving. They allow their impulses and not their thinking to take charge.

● ━━━━ Recognizing the difference between inactive and interactive leisure activities

There are times when we want to enjoy leisure time with others, and there are times when we want to spend time alone. Many of us spend free time watching television. This is an *inactive* way of using leisure time. Can you give other examples of inactive uses of leisure time?

Elicit responses and discuss. Examples may include watching a movie, listening to music, or playing computer games.

Inactive uses of leisure time are OK as long as you do not limit yourself to this category. The *interactive* category of leisure time requires you to connect with other people. When you engage in a team sport or a board game, you have made the choice to be part of a group. What other leisure activities do you consider interactive?

Elicit responses and discuss. Examples include dancing, talking, and singing in a chorus.

● ━━━━ Identifying leisure activities that correlate with interests, strengths, resources, and personality type

Often young people complain, "I don't have anything to do." This is because their time management plans do not include an inventory of healthy leisure activities. Prior to choosing leisure activities, you need to determine your personal interests and your personal strengths. You also need to consider what resources are needed to participate in a certain leisure activity. Being realistic will help keep you from being disappointed. For example, you may want to participate in a sport but lack the physical ability to be successful and enjoy the activity. In this case you may want to choose a related activity, such as watching and becoming knowledgeable about the sport (for example, learning about player statistics or learning the history of the sport).

Your personality type will also lead you to choose your own preferred leisure activities. Some people are more reserved and shy, and may enjoy doing a puzzle or playing alone. People who are more outgoing will likely choose group activities.

If desired, review the material on personality types in Lesson 5 of Skill Area 6 (Cooperation and Collaboration).

Monitoring Knowledge and Comprehension

Ask the following questions and discuss.

1. Why do we need leisure time?

2. What is the difference between healthy and unhealthy uses of leisure time?

3. Name two inactive and two interactive uses of leisure time.

4. List two of your interests and two related activities you can engage in during your leisure time.

Guided Practice

Distribute copies of Figure 72 (Interest Inventory) and have students complete.

Assessing Mastery

Discuss the inventories. Direct students to assess their interests and determine whether they generally prefer individual or group activities.

RETEACHING

Independent Practice

Direct students to write a descriptive paragraph on one of the following topics: "My Favorite Leisure Activity," "My Least Favorite Leisure Activity," "My Secret Leisure Activity," or "My Strangest Leisure Activity."

Evaluation and Feedback

Distribute copies of Figure 73 (Leisure Time Review) and have students complete. Evaluate for understanding of the need for constructive leisure activities.

CLOSING

Summary

> In this lesson we learned that leisure activities are important. There are inactive and interactive leisure activities, healthy leisure activities and unhealthy leisure activities. Some activities that may be enjoyable in the short term can lead to trouble and should be avoided. We need to match our interests, personal strengths, resources, and personality types to our choice of leisure activities.

Generalization

Direct students to conduct a survey of leisure activities in school, at home, and in the community. Refer students to the school counselor, their parents, the telephone book yellow pages, and the local newspaper for information.

ENRICHMENT

1. Direct students to develop a thematic bulletin board or collage. They may use the following sayings or compose their own:

   An idle mind is the devil's workshop.

   Take time to smell the roses.

   Except for life-and-death moments, nothing is as important as it first seems.

   Don't worry—be happy.

2. Invite students to participate in one new leisure activity, keeping in mind the following questions:

Is it enjoyable?

Am I successful at it?

Would another activity suit me better?

Interest Inventory

Name: _____ Date: _____

Indicate whether the following statements are always, sometimes, or never true for you.

	Always	Sometimes	Never
1. I like to participate in individual activities.	☐	☐	☐
2. I like to participate in group activities.	☐	☐	☐
3. I like to participate in team sports.	☐	☐	☐
4. I like to participate in individual sports.	☐	☐	☐
5. I like to read.	☐	☐	☐
6. I like to watch TV and movies.	☐	☐	☐
7. I like to play games (for example, cards, darts, video games).	☐	☐	☐
8. I have a hobby (for example, rock collecting, photography, art).	☐	☐	☐
9. I like to listen to or play music.	☐	☐	☐
10. I like to create something with my hands.	☐	☐	☐

Figure 72

Leisure Time Review

Name: _____ Date: _____

Answer the following questions.

1. Name some passive and some active leisure activities.

2. What are some leisure activities found in the home, the school, and the community?

3. Why are some enjoyable leisure activities a poor choice and unacceptable?

4. Why do you need to determine your personal interests and strengths in choosing a leisure activity?

5. What does it mean to be realistic in your leisure activity choices?

Figure 73

Role-Play: Time Management & Organization

CHARACTERS

Sonya, Alma, Kenya, Harry, Monique, Mrs. Defoe

SITUATION

Sonya has arrived in a new town and is starting sixth grade. She is confused about the new schedule of the middle school. Sonya has always been a good student, but she is now failing. She is constantly tardy and is unable to manage her time. At home she complains about missing her friends. She has recently started drinking alcohol to get away from her problems. Sonya has always had difficulty getting up early, and this problem is becoming worse. In addition, she's made no friends and complains about having nothing to do. She is developing severe headaches. One day, while sitting alone at the lunch table, she notices a tall girl approaching.

Alma: You're new here. Come on over and sit with us.

Sonya: Naw, it's OK. *(Thinking it over)* Well, all right. *(She joins the group.)*

Alma: Sonya, this is Kenya, Harry, and Monique. We are part of the Kennedy Middle School hospitality group. We help new students get around. Mrs. Defoe is our counselor and sponsor, and she is just awesome. You'll really like her.

Kenya: Hi, Sonya. Welcome to our school. I really like your sweater. It's so cool.

Harry: Sonya, there are several activities in school. I'm on the school newspaper. I can teach you some neat layouts on the computer.

Monique: Not so fast, Harry. Sonya, the Healthy Environment Club is fun and educational. We go camping and hiking as well as working for our ecology.

After school, Alma introduces Sonya to Mrs. Defoe. The counselor befriends Sonya and tells her about daily sessions she can attend to help her adjust to her new environment. Sonya agrees to attend. Following 2 weeks of sessions, Sonya finally shares the following.

Sonya: Mrs. Defoe, there are so many changes in my life. My parents are getting a divorce, I'm in a new school, I'm in a new town, and it's so hard to make new friends. I'm so depressed I started drinking alcohol, and that just makes it worse. I'm always late for school. I just can't seem to get up in the morning or manage my time.

Mrs. Defoe: I hear you saying that you want to try something else besides alcohol—that's great. I'll help you develop a time management schedule to decrease your tardiness. But first let's discuss your energy cycle. We all have different energy cycles. I am a morning person and can't do much in the evening. It sounds like you're just the opposite. A plan will help you adjust your energy cycle.

Together Sonya and Mrs. Defoe work on a plan. The counselor teaches Sonya relaxation strategies and how to plan leisure time to reduce her stressors. Sonya chooses to join the hospitality group and spends her free time helping and socializing with newcomers to Kennedy Middle School. She is also co-editor of the paper with Harry. She continues her relaxation exercises and talks to Mrs. Defoe occasionally.

EVALUATION AND FEEDBACK

1. How did Sonya's tardiness increase her stress?

2. Make up a time schedule for Sonya.

3. How did Sonya's personal energy cycle add to her tardiness?

4. What do you think of Sonya's choice to use alcohol to reduce her stress?

5. Identify the three procedures Mrs. Defoe and Sonya chose to help her reduce her stress.

6. Was Sonya's original choice of a leisure time activity appropriate? Her choice after meeting with Mrs. Defoe?

APPENDIX

A

PARENT
NEWSLETTERS

INTRODUCING THE PROGRAM

Early adolescence is a time of challenges and conflicts for both children and their parents. Despite their maturing appearance and "know-it-all" attitude, many students in the middle grades need direction in learning how to act and how to develop their strengths. This newsletter introduces you to the *Connecting with Others* program. This program teaches specific behaviors to help young people develop self-discipline and positive relationships.

The program is organized according to eight units, or skill areas. Your child will be receiving instruction with other students in some or all of these skill areas:

- Awareness of Self and Others

- Communication

- Responsibility

- Self-Advocacy and Assertiveness

- Conflict Resolution

- Cooperation and Collaboration

- Love and Caring

- Time Management and Organization

Before we begin lessons in these areas, the group will learn some basic concepts:

- The Thinking Steps: STOP, THINK, PLAN, CHECK

- The different Me's: Enthusiastic Me, Impulsive Me, Caring Me, Bossy Me, Thinking Me

- The difference between assertive, aggressive, and nonassertive behavior

You will receive newsletters throughout the program to keep you informed of the skills your child is learning. We will also be suggesting some activities you can use to practice the skills at home and in the community.

Please join us and learn with us!

THE THINKING STEPS: STOP, THINK, PLAN, CHECK

Many young adolescents are dependent on adults to control their behaviors. Many are impulsive rather than reflective in reaching decisions, and as a result succumb to peer pressure rather than reach an independent decision. The Thinking Steps are a decision-making process that helps students learn to think independently and anticipate the consequences of their actions.

There are four Thinking Steps:

- **STOP:** Use a technique to keep yourself from acting impulsively—for example, taking a few deep breaths, counting to 10, or taking a walk around the block.

- **THINK:** Examine the situation and think about the consequences of certain behaviors. Ask, "What am I doing? What will happen if I continue?"

- **PLAN:** Think about possibilities, brainstorm alternatives, choose the best plan, and put it into effect.

- **CHECK:** After you have tried one plan, check to see if it is working. If so, give yourself credit. Enjoy a sense of satisfaction—you've earned it. If not, start over and use another plan.

TO DO AT HOME

Help your child use the Thinking Steps to resolve problem behaviors. Encourage a positive attitude. Some typical problem areas are as follows:

1. Improving a relationship with a brother, sister, or other family member

2. Developing a plan to complete homework efficiently

3. Improving a low or failing grade at school

4. Decreasing time talking on the telephone

TEACHER'S MESSAGE

THE ME'S

The idea that we have different aspects of our personalities helps us understand our own feelings and behavior, as well as the feelings and behavior of other people. Young adolescents can change their behavior by considering their attitudes in relation to time and place. In the *Connecting with Others* program, these attitudes are referred to as different "Me's."

- An Enthusiastic Me attitude shows energy and eagerness in work and play. This attitude is OK in the right situations and as long as it does not get out of hand.

- An Impulsive Me attitude doesn't stop to think before acting and often loses control. This attitude is usually thoughtless—and sometimes downright malicious.

- A Caring Me attitude is loving and concerned about oneself, others, and the natural world. This attitude is often reflected in acts of kindness and thoughtfulness.

- A Bossy Me attitude is authoritarian. It tries to command or control other people. Sometimes this Me sounds like a parent or teacher.

- A Thinking Me attitude is very important because it is necessary for rational thinking and for making choices and plans. This is the attitude that prevents impulsive decision making and inappropriate behavior.

Once we know which Me is appropriate to which situation, we choose from among these different ways of feeling and behaving. At a basketball game, we enjoy our Enthusiastic Me attitude. When we need to study, the Thinking Me tells us it's time to get down to work.

TO DO AT HOME

1. Ask your child to demonstrate the five "Me" attitudes to you.

2. Reverse roles and demonstrate these five attitudes to your child.

3. Catch yourself and point out to your child when you are using the different Me attitudes.

4. Praise your child for using a Thinking Me attitude.

TEACHER'S MESSAGE

AGGRESSIVE, NONASSERTIVE, & ASSERTIVE BEHAVIOR

Young adolescents are attempting to separate from adults and searching for a personal identity. Sometimes this search shows up as what adults view as rebelliousness and rudeness. Many young people do not know how to express their feelings, thoughts, and needs directly without getting into conflict. Assertion training can help adolescents express their independence without violating the rights of others.

There are three different kinds of behavior:

- Aggressive behavior: Being aggressive means acting in a way that will get you what you want but that does not consider the rights of others. Shouting, hitting, destroying property, and cursing are all aggressive behaviors.

- Nonassertive behavior: Behaving nonassertively means going along with what other people want without standing up for your own rights. Because you don't say what you think or feel, you don't get what you want, and you may become resentful. If resentment builds up, you may try to get what you want in a sneaky way, like telling a lie to get another person in trouble.

- Assertive behavior: Behaving assertively means being honest about your own feelings and wants while still respecting other people's rights. There are two basic types of assertion. *Direct assertion* is honest and direct: "No, thank you, I don't smoke." *Empathetic assertion* also includes a statement that shows you understand how the other person is feeling: "Mom, I know you want to help me, but I want to cook the spaghetti myself tonight."

TO DO AT HOME

Practice empathetic assertion with your child, and encourage your child to do the same. This means:

1. Consider the other person's feelings.

2. Verbalize those feelings.

3. Assert yourself politely.

For example: "I know the party is important and you'll have fun, but you must be home by 11 o'clock."

TEACHER'S MESSAGE

SKILL AREA 1

AWARENESS OF SELF & OTHERS

Many young adolescents need help learning that the people around them are important and deserve their consideration, care, and respect. They can also work to develop an "I-can" attitude to promote their own self-esteem. In this skill area, the group will be working to achieve the following specific goals:

- To develop personal awareness and understanding

- To recognize feelings

- To appreciate true friendships

- To show gratitude and accept appreciation

- To accept and give compliments

TO DO AT HOME

1. Compliment your child and look for the good things he or she does in the home and community.

2. Encourage responsibility in your child. Assign household chores and give positive reinforcement when the work is done.

3. Talk to your child when he or she misbehaves. It is OK to make mistakes—nobody is perfect. It is also OK to make reparation and to avoid repeating unacceptable behavior.

4. Explain to your child the value of friendship: People need people. Encourage positive associations among family members.

5. Ask your child to perform an act of kindness for someone else.

6. Tell your child how each member of your family is special.

7. Listen, listen, listen to your child's feelings. Look for situations in which you can discuss feelings.

As opportunities arise, review the basic *Connecting with Others* concepts:

- Encourage your child to apply the Thinking Steps: STOP, THINK, PLAN, CHECK.

- Discuss the different Me's: Enthusiastic Me, Impulsive Me, Caring Me, Bossy Me, Thinking Me.

- Help your child choose assertive rather than aggressive or nonassertive behavior.

TEACHER'S MESSAGE

COMMUNICATION

Communication means talking to others about our feelings and thoughts. It also means listening to theirs. Very often, students in the middle grades experience problems because of poor communication skills. In this skill area, the group will be working to achieve the following specific goals:

- To demonstrate effective listening

- To communicate positively with others

- To recognize the importance of nonverbal communication and cultural differences in nonverbal expression

- To recognize social aspects of communication

- To recognize language taboos and learn the importance of using more acceptable words and expressions

TO DO AT HOME

1. Talk to your child about yourself, your childhood, and your friends.

2. Listen to your child and allow your child to talk uninterrupted, without your being judgmental.

3. Practice active listening: Listen to feelings as well as words. What is your child really trying to tell you? Switch roles—ask your child to listen actively to you.

4. Watch television with your child and discuss the programs.

5. Participate in your child's interests and find something to talk about.

6. Discuss cursing and how this kind of language is not accepted in many situations and places—in the home, at school, or at work.

As opportunities arise, review the basic *Connecting with Others* concepts:

- Encourage your child to apply the Thinking Steps: STOP, THINK, PLAN, CHECK.

- Discuss the different Me's: Enthusiastic Me, Impulsive Me, Caring Me, Bossy Me, Thinking Me.

- Help your child choose assertive rather than aggressive or nonassertive behavior.

TEACHER'S MESSAGE

RESPONSIBILITY

Your child is preparing for adulthood and the many responsibilities that accompany it. In this skill area, the group will be working to achieve the following specific goals:

- To plan long-term and short-term goals

- To complete assigned tasks independently

- To follow and give directions

- To identify and apply self-management skills

- To assume responsibility for personal actions

TO DO AT HOME

1. Sit down with your child and make a list of your child's home responsibilities.

2. Discuss school responsibilities.

3. If your child has an outside job such as baby-sitting or delivering newspapers, list and discuss associated responsibilities.

4. Study your community. How can you and your child participate in a community project (for example, visiting a nursing home or hospital, helping a charitable organization, donating food or clothes to a homeless shelter)?

5. Talk to your child about your responsibilities and the responsibilities of other family members. Discuss what might happen if everyone in the family decided to be irresponsible.

6. Help your child to remember responsibilities by providing reminders and helping your child devise reminders of his or her own.

As opportunities arise, review the basic *Connecting with Others* concepts:

- Encourage your child to apply the Thinking Steps: STOP, THINK, PLAN, CHECK.

- Discuss the different Me's: Enthusiastic Me, Impulsive Me, Caring Me, Bossy Me, Thinking Me.

- Help your child choose assertive rather than aggressive or nonassertive behavior.

TEACHER'S MESSAGE

SELF-ADVOCACY & ASSERTIVENESS

Parents want their children to grow up to be self-sufficient, independent adults. To achieve this objective, young people must learn to speak up for themselves in an assertive way. In this skill area, the group will be working to achieve the following specific goals:

- To ask assertively for assistance

- To offer and give assistance

- To analyze and discuss fair and unfair rules and practices

- To respond positively and assertively to authority figures

- To respond logically to peer pressure

TO DO AT HOME

1. Arrange situations in which your child can demonstrate assertiveness (for example, returning purchases to a store or helping organize a party).

2. Model empathetic assertiveness by combining awareness of another's feelings with a directly assertive statement. For example: "I know you would like to stay out later, but . . ."

3. Discuss the effects of aggression as they relate to a current news story.

4. If your child is shy, help him or her practice assertive responses in typical situations your child might experience.

As opportunities arise, review the basic *Connecting with Others* concepts:

- Encourage your child to apply the Thinking Steps: STOP, THINK, PLAN, CHECK.

- Discuss the different Me's: Enthusiastic Me, Impulsive Me, Caring Me, Bossy Me, Thinking Me.

- Help your child choose assertive rather than aggressive or nonassertive behavior.

TEACHER'S MESSAGE

CONFLICT RESOLUTION

Young teenagers frequently do not know how to resolve conflicts peacefully. In this skill area, the group will be working to achieve the following specific goals:

- To practice self-control

- To find alternative solutions in conflict situations

- To demonstrate understanding of the processes of negotiation, mediation, and compromise

- To respond appropriately to teasing

- To accept and give constructive feedback

TO DO AT HOME

1. Model self-control. Children often imitate adults, and parents and teachers are their primary models.

2. Teach children to solve problems using logic, not aggression. The Thinking Steps are important here.

3. Be willing to act as a mediator and help your child negotiate solutions with family members. Please remember not to take sides and to let both people talk it out.

4. If you disagree with your child, reach a solution through compromise that is fair and acceptable to both of you.

As opportunities arise, review the basic *Connecting with Others* concepts:

- Encourage your child to apply the Thinking Steps: STOP, THINK, PLAN, CHECK.

- Discuss the different Me's: Enthusiastic Me, Impulsive Me, Caring Me, Bossy Me, Thinking Me.

- Help your child choose assertive rather than aggressive or nonassertive behavior.

TEACHER'S MESSAGE

COOPERATION & COLLABORATION

Many people believe that children must be taught to be competitive to succeed in society. Yet more and more, the world of work and school requires students to work collaboratively in groups. In this skill area, the group will be working to achieve the following specific goals:

- To develop the concept of cooperative teamwork

- To learn to delay gratification and practice patience

- To learn how to interact successfully with others

- To become aware of the importance of equality

- To understand how one's own and other people's personality types influence group interactions

TO DO AT HOME

1. Plan a family project where all members can work cooperatively (for example, gardening, cleaning, painting).

2. Organize a family meeting to outline home chores. Assign chores where family members pair up to complete the job—for example, washing the car (one washes, one rinses) or mowing the yard (one mows, one edges).

3. Plan a special seasonal party and involve all family members in the planning.

4. Reinforce any cooperative behaviors you observe (setting the table, washing the dishes, and so forth). Say, "I think it's great that you are working together. It makes the job a lot easier, doesn't it?"

5. Talk to your children about how you cooperated on a project when you were a teenager or how you cooperate now in your work.

As opportunities arise, review the basic *Connecting with Others* concepts:

- Encourage your child to apply the Thinking Steps: STOP, THINK, PLAN, CHECK.

- Discuss the different Me's: Enthusiastic Me, Impulsive Me, Caring Me, Bossy Me, Thinking Me.

- Help your child choose assertive rather than aggressive or nonassertive behavior.

TEACHER'S MESSAGE

LOVE & CARING

Young children eagerly receive affection from their parents, but as adolescence approaches, young people sometimes experience confusion about the many forms of love and their expression. In this skill area, the group will be working to achieve the following specific goals:

- To show tolerance, respect, and understanding for differences

- To show empathy

- To recognize that love can be felt and expressed in many ways

- To identify behaviors and responsibilities associated with intimate relationships

- To distinguish between expressions of unconditional versus conditional love

TO DO AT HOME

1. Show your child affection every day.

2. Talk to your child about the responsibilities associated with intimate love, marriage, and family.

3. Provide comfort when your child has a problem. Teach him or her to do likewise for a brother, sister, or pet.

4. Respond lovingly when your child is caring and thoughtful.

5. Ask your child to be responsible for feeding a pet or caring for a brother, sister, or grandparent. Consider your child's maturity level when assigning this chore.

As opportunities arise, review the basic *Connecting with Others* concepts:

- Encourage your child to apply the Thinking Steps: STOP, THINK, PLAN, CHECK.

- Discuss the different Me's: Enthusiastic Me, Impulsive Me, Caring Me, Bossy Me, Thinking Me.

- Help your child choose assertive rather than aggressive or nonassertive behavior.

TEACHER'S MESSAGE

TIME MANAGEMENT & ORGANIZATION

As an adult identity begins to emerge in the adolescent years, teenagers begin to develop interests that may lead to future careers. The ability to manage time, organize tasks, and control stress is critical to both school and work. In this skill area, the group will be working to achieve the following specific goals:

- To be punctual

- To develop a system of time management

- To develop strategies to relax and reduce stress

- To understand personal energy cycles

- To choose appropriate leisure activities

TO DO AT HOME

1. Spend special time with your child.

2. Teach your child to record special events and appointments (doctor, dentist, meetings) on a monthly calendar.

3. Expect your child to be responsible for setting the alarm clock and getting up on time in the morning.

4. If your child has difficulty being punctual, make a plan together and guide your child to use it.

5. Talk to your child about the importance of time and completion of tasks.

6. Take time to relax, have fun, and enjoy your family.

As opportunities arise, review the basic *Connecting with Others* concepts:

- Encourage your child to apply the Thinking Steps: STOP, THINK, PLAN, CHECK.

- Discuss the different Me's: Enthusiastic Me, Impulsive Me, Caring Me, Bossy Me, Thinking Me.

- Help your child choose assertive rather than aggressive or nonassertive behavior.

TEACHER'S MESSAGE

BIBLIOGRAPHY

BIBLIOGRAPHY

SKILL AREA 1: AWARENESS OF SELF AND OTHERS

For Professionals

Canfield, J., & Wells, H. (1976). *One hundred ways to enhance self-concept in the classroom.* Englewood Cliffs, NJ: Prentice Hall.

Cartledge, G., & Milburn, J.F. (1980). *Teaching social skills to children.* New York: Pergamon.

Clark, A., Clemens, H., & Bean, R. (1980). *How to raise teenagers' self-esteem.* Los Angeles: ENRICH.

Dinkmeyer, D., & Dinkmeyer, D., Jr. (1982). *Developing understanding of self and others* (rev. ed.). Circle Pines, MN: American Guidance Service.

Fox, C.L. (1990). *Unlocking doors to self-esteem.* Rolling Hills Estates, CA: Jalmar.

Frey, D., & Carlock, C. (1984). *Enhancing self-esteem.* Muncie, IN: Accelerated Development.

Gardner, H. (1993). *Multiple intelligences: The theory in practice.* New York: Basic.

Glasser, W. (1976). *Positive addiction.* New York: Harper and Row.

Gray, W., & Gerrard, B. (1981). *Understanding yourself and others.* New York: Harper and Row.

Jackson, J.F., Jackson, D.A., & Monroe, C. (1983). *Getting along with others: Teaching social effectiveness to children.* Champaign, IL: Research Press.

Kehayan, A.V. (1990). *Self-awareness growth experiences.* Rolling Hills Estates, CA: Jalmar.

McGinnis, A. (1979). *The friendship factor.* Minneapolis: Augsburg.

Pottenbaum, G., Brooks, R., & Ward, J. (1991). *Seeds of self-esteem.* Circle Pines, MN: American Guidance Service.

Rubin, Z. (1980). *Children's friendships.* Cambridge, MA: Harvard University Press.

For Students

Clements, B. (1993). *Coming about.* Alpharetta, GA: Ariel.

Ferris, J. (1986). *The stainless steel rule.* New York: Farrar, Strauss & Giroux.

Feuer, E. (1987). *One friend to another.* New York: Farrar, Strauss & Giroux.

French, M. (1987). *Us against them.* New York: Bantam.

Garden, N. (1986). *Peace o river.* New York: Farrar, Strauss & Giroux.

Greenberg, J. (1985). *Bye, bye, Miss American Pie.* New York: Farrar, Strauss & Giroux.

Greene, B. (1974). *Summer of my German soldier.* New York: Bantam.

Hermes, P. (1984). *Friends are like that.* New York: Scholastic.

Herzig, A.C. (1985). *Shadows on the pond.* Boston: Little, Brown.

Johnson, J. (1991). *Celebrate you: Building your self-esteem.* Minneapolis: Lerner.

Johnson, J. (1992). *Making friends, finding love: A book about teen relationships.* Minneapolis: Lerner.

LeShan, E. (1990). *When kids drive kids crazy: How to get along with your friends and enemies.* New York: Dial.

Malecka, J. (1992). *Valuing yourself: 22 ways to develop self-esteem.* Portland, ME: J. Weston Walsh.

Mazer, N.F. (1987). *My name is Bunny.* New York: Scholastic.

Mazzio, J. (1992). *The one who came back.* New York: Houghton Mifflin.

McDonnell, C. (1991). *Lucky charms and birthday wishes.* New York: Houghton Mifflin.

Newman, M., & Berkowitz, B. (1980). *How to be your own best friend.* New York: Random House.

Palmer, P., & Froehner, M. (1992). *Teen esteem: A self-direction for young adults.* San Luis Obispo, CA: Impact.

Pfeffer, S.B. (1982). *Starting with Melodie.* New York: Scholastic.

Pincus, D. (1990). *Feeling good about yourself.* Carthage, IL: Good Apple.

Powell, R. (1992). *Is kissing a girl who smokes like licking an ashtray?* New York: Farrar, Strauss & Giroux.

Rochman, H. (Ed.). (1993). *Who do you think you are? Stories of friends and enemies.* Fountain Valley, CA: Joy Publishing.

Sachs, M. (1965). *Laura's luck.* New York: Doubleday.

Sheperd, S. (1990). *What do you think of you? And other thoughts on self-esteem.* Minneapolis: CompCare.

Varenhorst, B. (1983). *Real friends: Becoming the friend you'd like to have.* New York: HarperCollins.

Zindell, P. (1977). *Pardon me, you're stepping on my eyeball.* New York: Bantam.

SKILL AREA 2: COMMUNICATION

For Professionals

Burgoon, J.K., Buller, D.B., & Woodall, W.G. (1989). *Nonverbal communication: The unspoken dialogue*. New York: Harper and Row.

Condon, J.C., & Yousef, F. (1975). *An introduction to intercultural communication*. Indianapolis: Bobbs-Merrill.

DeVito, J.A. (1991). *Human communication: The basic course*. New York: HarperCollins.

Faber, A., & Mazlish, E. (1980). *How to talk so kids will listen, and listen so kids will talk*. New York: Avon.

Gudykunst, W.B. (Ed.). (1983). *Intercultural communication theory: Current perspectives*. Newbury Park, CA: Sage.

Knapp, M.L. (1984). *Interpersonal communication and human relationships*. Boston: Allyn & Bacon.

Mayo, P., & Waldo, P. (1986). *Scripting: Social communication for adolescents*. Eau Claire, WI: Thinking Publications.

Rogers, C., & Farson, R. (1981). Active listening. In J.A. DeVito (Ed.), *Communication: Concepts and processes* (3rd ed.). Englewood Cliffs, NJ: Prentice Hall.

For Students

Ailes, E.G. (1988). *You are the message*. New York: Doubleday.

Barad, D.S. (1984). *Talk it up*. Tucson: Communication Skill Builder.

Cross, D.W. (1983). *Mediaspeak: How television makes up your mind*. New York: New American Library.

DeVito, J.A. (1989). *The nonverbal communication workbook*. Prospect Heights, IL: Waveland.

Floyd, J.J. (1985). *Listening: A practical approach*. Glenview, IL: Scott, Foresman.

Gilbert, S. (1991). *You can speak up in class*. New York: Beech Tree Books.

Hamlin, S. (1988). *How to talk so people will listen*. New York: Harper and Row.

Infante, D.A. (1988). *Arguing constructively*. Prospect Heights, IL: Waveland.

Irwin, H. (1990). *Can't hear you listening*. New York: McElderry.

Re, J., & Schneider, M. (1991). *Social savvy: A teenager's guide to feeling confident in any social situation*. New York: Summit.

Stern, Z., & Stern, E. (1993). *Questions kids wish they could ask their parents*. Berkeley, CA: Celestial Arts.

Weinrich, B.D., Glaser, A.J., & Johnson, E.B. (1986). *A sourcebook of adolescent pragmatic activities*. Tucson: Communication Skill Builder.

SKILL AREA 3: RESPONSIBILITY

For Professionals

Farris, D. (1990). *Type tales*. Palo Alto, CA: Consulting Psychologists Press.

Glasser, W. (1975). *Schools without failure*. New York: Harper and Row.

Glasser, W. (1976). *Positive addiction*. New York: Harper and Row.

Glenn, H.S., & Nelsen, J. (1989). *Raising self-reliant children in a self-indulgent world*. Rocklin, CA: Prima.

Goleman, D. (1995). *Emotional intelligence: Why it can matter more than IQ*. New York: Bantam.

Jones, V., & Jones, L. (1981). *Responsible classroom discipline*. Newton, MA: Allyn & Bacon.

Johnson, A. (1978). *The value of responsibility*. La Jolla, CA: Values Communication.

Keirsey, D., & Bates, M. (1978). *Please understand me*. Del Mar, CA: Prometheus Nemesis Books.

Lawrence, G. (1979). *People types and tiger stripes: A practical guide to learning styles*. Gainesville, FL: Center for Applications of Psychological Type.

Lipsitz, J. (1984). *Successful schools for young adolescents*. New Brunswick, NJ: Transaction.

Maple, F. (1977). *Shared decision making*. Beverly Hills, CA: Sage.

Murphy, E., & Meisgeier, C. (1989). *Murphy-Meisgeier type indicator for children*. Palo Alto, CA: Consulting Psychologists Press.

Myers, I.B. (1995). *Gifts differing: Understanding personality types*. Palo Alto, CA: Davies-Black.

Purkey, W.W., & Novals, J.M. (1984). *Inviting school success* (2nd ed.). Belmont, CA: Wadsworth.

Rychlak, J.F. (1979). *Discovering free will and personal responsibility*. New York: Oxford.

For Students

Bautista, V. (1990). *Improve your grades: A practical guide to academic excellence*. Miami: Bookhaus.

Collier, J. (1986). *When the stars begin to fall*. New York: Delacorte.

Cooney, C.B. (1992). *Flight #116 is down*. New York: Scholastic.

Duncan, L. (1978). *Killing Mr. Griffin*. New York: Dell.

Dyer, W. (1977). Pulling your own strings. New York: Avon.

Geoffrion, S. (1993). *Get smart fast: A handbook for academic success*. Saratoga, CA: R & E Publishers.

Haas, J. (1992). *Skipping school*. New York: Greenwillow.

Harmon, E., & Jamin, M. (1988). *Taking charge of my life: Choices, changes and me*. Bossier, LA: Barksdale Foundation.

Hughes, D. (1989). *Family picture*. New York: Atheneum.

Jensen, E. (1989). *Student success secrets*. Hauppauge, NY: Barron's.

Lang, D. (1990). *But everyone else looks so sure of themselves: A guide to surviving the teen years*. White Hall, VA: Shoe Tree Press.

Lukes, B. (1986). *How to be a reasonably thin teenage girl without starving, losing your friends or running away from home*. New York: Atheneum.

Maloney, M., & Kranz, R. (1991). *Straight talk about eating disorders: High school help line*. New York: Dell.

McCutcheon, R. (1985). *Get off my brain: A survival guide for lazy students*. New York: Free Press.

Owen, L. (1991). *What's wrong with me? Breaking the chain of adolescent codependency*. New York: Deaconess.

Parsley, B. (1992). *The choice is yours: A teenager's guide to self-discovery, relationships, values, and spiritual growth*. New York: Fireside.

Phipson, J. (1985). *Hit and run*. New York: Macmillan.

Sachs, M. (1984). *The fat girl*. New York: Dutton.

Thompson, M., & Strange, J. (1992). *Discover skills for life*. San Diego: Educational Assessment.

SKILL AREA 4: SELF-ADVOCACY AND ASSERTIVENESS

For Professionals

Ehly, S.W., & Larsen, S.C. (1980). *Peer tutoring for individualized instruction*. Austin, TX: PRO-ED.

Gardner, A., Kohler, M., & Reissman, F. (1971). *Children teach children*. New York: Harper and Row.

Gardner, S. (1990). *Teenage suicide*. Englewood Cliffs, NJ: Julian Messner.

Goldstein, A.P., & McGinnis, E. (1997). *Skillstreaming the adolescent: New strategies and perspectives for teaching prosocial skills* (rev. ed.). Champaign, IL: Research Press.

Jakubowski, P., & Lange, A.J. (1978). *The assertive option: Your rights and responsibilities.* Champaign, IL: Research Press.

Pierce, M.M., Stalhbrand, K., & Armstrong, S.B. (1984). *Increasing student productivity through peer tutoring programs.* Austin, TX: PRO-ED.

Robinson, S.E. (1989). *Why say no: Substance abuse among teenagers.* In D. Capuzzi & D.R. Gross (Eds.), *Youth at risk.* Alexandria, VA: American Association for Child Development.

Strain, P.S. (1981). *The utilization of classroom peers as behavior change agents.* New York: Plenum.

Waksman, S.A., & Messmer, C.L. (1985). *Assertive behavior: A program for teaching social skills to children and adolescents.* Portland, OR: Enrichment Press.

For Students

Cohen, S., & Cohen, D. (1988). *What can you believe about drugs? An honest and unhysterical guide for teens.* New York: Evans.

Cormier, R. (1991). *We all fall down.* New York: Delacorte.

Durrant, L., Frey, D., & Newbury, K. (1991). *Discover skills for life.* San Diego: Educational Assessment Publishing.

Ehrlich, A. (1991). *The dark card.* New York: Viking.

Fernsterheim, H., & Baer, J. (1975). *Don't say yes when you want to say no.* New York: David McKay.

Hall, L., & Cohn, L. (1988). *Dear kids of alcoholics.* New York: Gurze.

Irwin, H. (1990). *Can't hear you listening.* New York: McElderry.

Kaufman, G., & Raphael, L. (1991). *Stick up for yourself.* St. Petersburg, FL: Trend.

Knudson, R.R. (1972). *Zanballer.* New York: Dell.

Leite, E., & Espeland, P. (1987). *Different like me: A book for teens who worry about their parents' use of alcohol.* Minneapolis: Johnson Institute.

Marek, M. (1988). *Matt's crusade.* New York: Knopf.

Miklowitz, G. (1989). *Anything to win.* New York: Delacorte.

Pevsner, S. (1981). *And you give me a pain, Elaine.* New York: Pocket Books.

Pfeffer, S.B. (1982). *A matter of principle.* New York: Dell.

Rostkowski, M.I. (1993). *After the dancing days.* New York: HarperTrophy.

Ryan, E. (1989). *Straight talk about drugs and alcohol.* New York: Dell.

Smith, M.J. (1975). *When I say no, I feel guilty.* New York: Dial.

Vedral, J. (1987). *I can't take it anymore: How to get up when you're really low.* New York: Ballantine.

Wesson, C. (1988). *Teen troubles: How to keep them from becoming tragedies.* New York: Walker.

Willis-Brandon, C. (1990). *Learning to say no: Establishing healthy boundaries.* Deerfield Beach, FL: Health Communication.

SKILL AREA 5: CONFLICT RESOLUTION

For Professionals

Bodine, R.J., Crawford, D.K., & Schrumpf, F. (1994). *Creating the peaceable school: A comprehensive program for teaching conflict resolution.* Champaign, IL: Research Press.

Cartledge, G. (1996). *Cultural diversity and social skills instruction: Understanding ethnic and gender differences.* Champaign, IL: Research Press.

Gibbs, J.C., Potter, G.B., & Goldstein, A.P. (1995). *The EQUIP Program: Teaching youth to think and act responsibly through a peer-helping approach.* Champaign, IL: Research Press.

Goldstein, A.P. (1990). *The refusal skills video: Preventing drug use in adolescents.* Champaign, IL: Research Press.

Goldstein, A.P., & Huff, C.R. (Eds.). (1992). *The gang intervention handbook.* Champaign, IL: Research Press.

Guerra, N.G., Moore, A., & Slaby, R.G. (1995). *Viewpoints: A guide to conflict resolution and decision making for adolescents.* Champaign, IL: Research Press.

Hammond, W.R. (1993). *Dealing with anger: A violence prevention program for African American youth* (Video). Champaign, IL: Research Press.

Kreidler, W. (1990). *Teaching concepts of peace and conflict.* Cambridge, MA: Educators for Social Responsibility.

Luft, J. (1969). *Of human interaction.* Palo Alto, CA: National Press Books.

Mattox, B.A. (1975). *Getting it together: Dilemmas for the classroom.* San Diego: Pennant.

Morganett, R.S. (1992). *Skills for living: Group counseling activities for young adolescents.* Champaign, IL: Research Press.

Schrumpf, F., & Crawford, D.K. (1992). *The peer mediation video: Conflict resolution in schools.* Champaign, IL: Research Press.

Schrumpf, F., Crawford, D.K., & Bodine, R.J. (1996). *Peer mediation: Conflict resolution in schools* (rev. ed.). Champaign, IL: Research Press.

Shure, M.B. (1992). ICPS: *I Can Problem Solve—An interpersonal cognitive problem-solving program for children.* Champaign, IL: Research Press.

Stolberg, A.L., Zacharias, M., & Canplair, C.W. (1991). *Children of divorce.* Circle Pines, MN: American Guidance Service.

Vernon, A. (1989). *Thinking, feeling, behaving: An emotional education curriculum for children and adolescents* (Vols. 1 & 2). Champaign, IL: Research Press.

For Students

Arrick, F. (1986). *Nice girl from good home.* New York: Dell.

Bennett, J. (1986). *To be a killer.* New York: Scholastic.

Fugitt, E. (1983). *He hit me back first.* Rolling Hills Estates, CA: Jalmar.

Hayes, E.K., & Lazzarino, A. (1978). *Broken promises.* New York: Fawcett.

Heyman, A. (1983). *Final grades.* New York: Dodd, Mead.

Hughey, R. (1984). *The question box.* New York: Delacorte.

Kerr, M.E. (1978). *Gentlehands.* New York: Harper and Row.

Lowry, L. (1990). *Find a stranger, say goodbye.* New York: Dell.

Mazer, N. (1981). *Taking Terri Mueller.* New York: Avon.

Paterson, K. (1979). *The great Gilly Hookins.* New York: Avon.

Shreve, S. (1981). *The masquerade.* New York: Dell.

Shusterman, N. (1991). *What Daddy did.* Boston: Little, Brown.

Slepian, J. (1987). *Something beyond paradise.* New York: Philomel.

Wolitzer, H. (1980). *Toby lived here.* New York: Bantam.

Wolverton, L. (1987). *Running before the wind.* New York: Houghton Mifflin.

SKILL AREA 6: COOPERATION AND COLLABORATION

For Professionals

Allen, V. (Ed.). (1976). *Children as teachers: Theory and research in tutoring.* New York: Academic.

Bouton, C., & Garth, R. (Eds.). (1983). *Learning in groups.* San Francisco: Jossey-Bass.

Bridges, S.E. (1989). *Notes for another life.* New York: Knopf.

Chasnoff, R. (Ed.). (1979). *Structuring cooperative learning experiences in the classroom.* Minneapolis: Cooperative Network Publication.

Hirsh, S., & Kummerow, J. (1989). *Life types: Understand yourself and make the most of who you are.* New York: Warner.

Johnson, D.W., & Johnson, F.P. (1975). *Joining together.* Englewood Cliffs, NJ: Prentice Hall.

Johnson, D.W., & Johnson, R.T. (1975). *Learning together and alone: Cooperation, competition and individualization*. Englewood Cliffs, NJ: Prentice Hall.

Johnson, D.W., Johnson, R.T., & Holubeck, E.J. (1994). *The new circles of learning: Cooperation in the classroom and school*. Alexandria, VA: Association for Supervision and Curriculum Development.

Karns, M. (1994). *How to create positive relationships with students: A handbook of group activities and teaching strategies*. Champaign, IL: Research Press.

Keirsey, D., & Bates, M. (1978). *Please understand me*. Del Mar, CA: Prometheus Nemesis Books.

Lyons, V. (1980). *Structuring cooperative learning: The 1980 handbook*. Minneapolis: Cooperative Network Publication.

Myers, I.B. (1995). *Gifts differing: Understanding personality types*. Palo Alto, CA: Davies-Black.

Pepitone, E.A. (Ed.). (1980). *Children in cooperation and competition*. Lexington, MA: Lexington Books.

For Students

Alcock, V. (1990). *The trials of Anna*. New York: Delacorte.

Cormier, R. (1985). *Beyond the chocolate wars*. New York: Knopf.

Hamilton, V. (1982). *Sweet whispers, brother Rush*. New York: Philomel.

Kent, D. (1989). *One step at a time*. New York: Scholastic.

Levitin, S. (1986). *A season for unicorns*. New York: Atheneum.

Meyer, D. (1985). *How to live with a brother or sister with special needs: A book for sibs*. Seattle: University of Washington Press.

Peck, R. (1987). *Princess Ashley*. New York: Delacorte.

Rogers, T. (1980). *At the shores*. New York: Simon & Schuster.

Stevens, J. (1982). *Take back the moment*. New York: New American Library.

Wirths, C.G., & Bowman-Kruhm, M. (1992). *Are you my type? Or why aren't you more like me?* Palo Alto, CA: Davies-Black.

SKILL AREA 7: LOVE AND CARING

For Professionals

Bradshaw, J. (1992). *Creating love*. New York: Bantam.

Buscaglia, L. (1986). *Loving each other: The challenge of human relationships*. New York: Fawcett Columbine.

Buscaglia, L., & Kimber, D. (1992). *Born for love: Reflections on loving*. Thorofare, NJ: C.B. Slack.

Buscaglia, L., & Short, S. (1983). *Living, loving and learning*. Thorofare, NJ: C.B. Slack.

Duberman, M. (1994). *Lives of notable gay men and lesbians*. New York: Chelsea House.

Elliott, J. (1992). The eye of the storm. In P. Jennings (Ed.), *Answering children's questions on prejudice*. New York: ABC Special Production.

Foreman, M. (1994). *Homophobia*. New York: Chelsea House.

Fromm, E. (1989). *The art of loving*. New York: HarperCollins.

Gabor, D. (1989). *How to talk to the people you love*. New York: Simon & Schuster.

Minkowitz, D. (1993). *Issues in gay and lesbian life*. New York: Chelsea House.

Minkowitz, D. (Ed.). (1994). *AIDS and other health issues*. New York: Chelsea House.

Purves, A. (1990). *How porcupines make love: Teaching a response centered literature curriculum*. Reading, MA: Addison Wesley–Longman.

Rubin, Z. (1973). *Liking and loving: An introduction to social psychology*. New York: Holt.

For Students

Arrick, F. (1978). *Steffie can't come out to play*. Scarsdale, NY: Bradbury.

Arthur, S. (1991). *Surviving teen pregnancy: Your choices, dreams, and decisions*. Buena Park, CA: Morning Glory Press.

Beck, A.T. (1988). *Love is never enough*. New York: Harper and Row.

Bell, R. (1987). *Changing bodies, changing lives: A book for teens on sex and relationships*. New York: Vintage.

Blume, J. (1975). *Forever*. Scarsdale, NY: Bradbury.

Borich, M. (1985). *A different kind of love*. New York: Holt.

Brown, D. (1972). *Bury my heart at wounded knee: An Indian history of the American West*. New York: Holt, Rinehart and Winston.

Cohen, S., & Cohen, D. (1989). *When someone you know is gay*. New York: Dell.

Colman, H. (1984). *Happily ever after*. New York: Scholastic.

Crutcher, C. (1989). *Chinese handcuffs*. New York: Greenwillow.

DeVault, C. (1989). *Don't let it get around*. Santa Cruz, CA: Network.

DeVault, C. (1989). *Too soon for sex?* Santa Cruz, CA: Network.

Dizenso, P. (1976). *Who me? The story of Jenny*. New York: Avon.

Ferris, J. (1988). *Looking for home*. New York: Farrar, Strauss & Giroux.

Frank, A. (1952). *Anne Frank: The diary of a young girl*. New York: Dell.

Garden, N. (1991). *Lark in the morning*. New York: Farrar, Strauss & Giroux.

Gardner-Loulan, J. (1991). *Period: Revised and updated with a parent's guide*. Volcano, CA: Volcano Press.

Kerr, M.E. (1986). *Night kites*. New York: HarperCollins.

Klein, N. (1979). *Love is one of the choices*. New York: Dial.

Koertge, R. (1988). *Where the kissing never stops*. New York: Dell.

Kuklin, S. (1991). *What do I do now? Talking about teenage pregnancy*. New York: Putnam.

Lindsay, J. (1995). *Teenage couples: How to build a relationship*. Buena Park, CA: Morning Glory Press.

Lowry, L. (1988). *Rabble Starkey*. New York: Dell.

Luger, H. (1981). *Lauren*. New York: Dell.

Mathes, P.G., & Irby, B.J. *Teen pregnancy and parenting handbook*. Champaign, IL: Research Press.

Mazer, N.F. (1989). *Silver*. New York: Avon.

Parks, R. (1992). *Rosa Parks: My story*. New York: Dial.

Rench, J. (1990). *Understanding sexual identity: A book for gay and lesbian teens and their friends*. Minneapolis: Lerner.

Rylant, C. (1990). *A kindness*. New York: Dell.

Silverstein, H. (1989). *Teenage and pregnant: What you can do*. Englewood Cliffs, NJ: Julian Messner.

Spock, B. (1971). *A teenager's guide to life and love*. New York: Pocket Books.

Steinbeck, J. (1939). *The grapes of wrath*. New York: Viking.

Strasser, T. (1985). *A very touchy subject*. New York: Delacorte.

Strauss, S. (1991). *Sexual harassment and teens*. Circle Pines, MN: American Guidance Service.

Voight, C. (1983). *A solitary blue*. New York: Atheneum.

SKILL AREA 8: TIME MANAGEMENT AND ORGANIZATION

For Professionals

Bernstein, D.A., & Borkovec, T.D. (1973). *Progressive relaxation training*. Champaign, IL: Research Press.

Blanchard, K.H. (1982). *The one-minute manager*. New York: William Morrow.

Cautela, J., & Groden, J. (1978). *Relaxation: A comprehensive manual for adults, children, and children with special needs*. Champaign, IL: Research Press.

Cohen, D., & Cohen, S. (1984). *Teenage stress*. New York: Dell.

Cooper, J.D. (1971). *How to get more done in less time*. Garden City, NY: Doubleday.

Lender, S. (1970). *The harried leisure class*. New York: Columbia University Press.

Loen, R.O. (1971). *Manage more by doing less*. New York: McGraw-Hill.

Love, S. (1978). *Mastery management of time*. Englewood Cliffs, NJ: Prentice Hall.

Mamchak, P. (1993). *Teacher's time management survival kit: Ready to use techniques and materials*. Englewood Cliffs, NJ: Prentice Hall.

Weber, R.A. (1972). *Time and management*. New York: Van Nostrand Reinhold.

For Students

Baker, R. (1982). *He got there*. New York: The New York Times Company.

Blanchard, K.H. (1989). *The one-minute manager meets the monkey*. New York: William Morrow.

Dulaney, S. (1992). *Stop! look! listen! for healthier, happier teenagers*. (Available from Stop! Look! Listen! P.O. Box 270986, Corpus Christi, TX, 78427-0986)

Fitzwater, I. (1979). *Finding time for success and happiness*. San Antonio: Mendell.

Fleming, A. (1992). *What, me worry? How to hang when your problems stress you out*. New York: Scribner.

Hipp, E. (1985). *Fighting invisible tigers: A stress management guide for teens*. Minneapolis, MN: Free Spirit.

Hipp, E. (1991). *Feed your head: Some excellent stuff on being yourself*. Center City, MN: Hazelden.

Maloney, M., & Kranz, R. (1991). *Straight talk about anxiety and depression: High school help line*. New York: Dell.

Newman, S. (1991). *Don't be S.A.D.: A teenage guide to handling stress, anxiety, and depression*. Englewood Cliffs, NJ: Julian Messner.

Oncken, W. (1984). *Managing time: Who's got the time?* New York: William Morrow.

Youngs, B. (1991). *Management guide for young people*. Rolling Hills Estates, CA: Jalmar.

ABOUT THE AUTHOR

Dr. Rita Coombs Richardson is presently an associate professor of special education at Southeastern Louisiana University in Hammond, Louisiana, where she developed this volume of the *Connecting with Others* program. She taught previously at Prairie View A & M University, the University of Texas at Brownsville, and the University of Southwestern Louisiana. Dr. Richardson received her Ph.D. from the University of New Orleans. She has taught at the elementary and secondary levels, in special and general education in both public and parochial schools.

Dr. Elizabeth T. Evans is a professor in the Department of Special Education at Southeastern Louisiana University in Hammond, Louisiana. She received her doctorate in special education from the University of Alabama. She has extensive experience as an educator in elementary and special education settings. In addition, she has designed a program for gifted learners in public schools as well as developed and implemented distance learning courses in the state of Louisiana.